MEMORY'S VOICE

MEMORY'S VOICE

DECIPHERING THE BRAIN-MIND CODE

DANIEL L. ALKON, M.D.

HarperCollins*Publishers*

The views expressed in this book do not necessarily represent those of the United States government.

HarperCollins books may be purchased for educational, business, or sales promotional use. For information please write: Special Markets Department, HarperCollins Publishers, Inc., 10 East 53rd Street, New York, NY 10022.

FIRST EDITION

Designed by George J. McKeon

Library of Congress Cataloging-in-Publication Data

Alkon, Daniel L.
  Memory's voice: deciphering the brain-mind code / Daniel L.
Alkon.—1st ed.
    p.   cm.
  Includes index.
  ISBN 0-06-018300-4
  1. Memory. I. Title.
QP406.A627 1992
612.8′2—dc20   92-52573

92 93 94 95 96 ❖/HC 10 9 8 7 6 5 4 3 2 1

For Michelle

Canst thou not minister to a mind diseased,
Pluck from the memory a rooted sorrow,
Raze out the written troubles of the brain,
And with some sweet oblivious antidote
Cleanse the stuffed bosom of that perilous stuff
Which weighs upon the heart?

William Shakespeare, "Macbeth"
Act. V. Sc. III

CONTENTS

ACKNOWLEDGMENTS

I am deeply grateful to John Pfeiffer for his guidance, friendship, and confidence in me. I cannot thank my wife, Betty, enough for her patience, clearheadedness, and wisdom, and for being there. Without René Etcheberrigaray's help in all aspects of this effort, it would not have reached fruition.

INTRODUCTION

In the laboratory, I ask questions about neurons, how they communicate, and how they change. But, like most people, I also periodically question my own unconscious habits, my style, my purposes. It is an internal laboratory that, on occasion, yields its own discoveries. Here, I experiment with the relationships of my present feelings to events in the past. Memories long forgotten are the data, quiet introspection is the method. The language that describes neuron function is quantitative, often mathematical; that for self-analysis is subjective, metaphorical, sometimes nonverbal. The questions, though in different languages, are often the same. I am still curious about who and what I am, whether the questions are about my own behavior or that of an animal, about neurons or computer models of brain functions.

The joy of discovery in either laboratory is unforgettable. A mixture of excitement, pleasure, and relief surges through my body. Everything around me seems brighter, lighter. I feel more secure, friendlier. My thoughts race to savor and then encompass the new insight—to offer it power and authority, to reconcile it with my past misconceptions. My thoughts take flight as I try on the implications for unsolved mysteries.

Over the years, I peel back one layer after another, gaining a little better perspective each time. Aha, that's me again—my style assertive, overactive. I draw energy from frustration and anger to mobilize, make plans, execute strategies. I don't leave time for a sense of helplessness or sadness. My penchant for measuring, probing, observing is in my father's tradition. My willingness, even eagerness, to take charge, be responsible, is in answer to my mother's expectations. More slowly, I have begun to recognize the limitations of my insight—even the illusions of understanding who I am and what drives me. The awesome power of human intelligence to predict events in the world inevitably creates an illusion of control. So I can forgive myself for so easily falling under its influence and taking comfort in a deceptive sense of certainty. Only in retrospect have I begun to understand that my most calculated experimental protocols and research strategies had a totally unscientific source. My so-called objective, quantitative science was born in the midst of my grief and anger.

No science, even the most quantitative, is independent of the scientist. Observations once validated, however, can take on a life of their own. Observations about intractable mysteries sometimes benefit from subjective as well as objective frames of reference. Gustave Flaubert, Nathaniel Hawthorne, George Sand, and Marcel Proust had their ways of understanding and analyzing human behavior, just as Sigmund Freud and Ivan Pavlov had theirs. Borrowing from such different traditions, I will try to describe in this book my exploration of learning and memory and their impact on human psychology.

I began with a sea snail's brain that had simple wiring but stored real memories. The snail's memory molecules and the signals that control them turned out to be remarkably similar to those my colleagues and I found in much more complex brains. From studies of neuron signals, molecules, and computer models of large clusters of neurons, I have constructed my own "picture" of how the brain creates memories. That picture, though necessarily out of focus, offers a perspective on how we become what we are as conscious and unconscious beings. I cannot convey this perspective without talking about real people with real problems. And the picture loses meaning without the context provided by the pictures of my intellectual ancestors. So here I will include the personal and historical, the figurative and literal, the impressionistic and measurable, all in the hope of involving you, my reader, in the search I have found so fascinating for so long.

Only twenty years after I began my scientific odyssey did I begin to comprehend what galvanized my efforts, what forged my intense commitment to understand memory storage in the brain. As a medical student, I was aware that genetic defects and organic changes could contribute to mental illness. But I was more intrigued by how mental disease could arise out of human interaction. I did not begin with a scientific conclusion or even hypothesis. I had not carefully formulated a thesis to be tested with observations according to an experimental protocol. But I had noticed certain things. Among all the variables—socioeconomic status, birth order, physical endowment, intelligence, ethnic background, family lineage—there seemed to be a factor that was comparatively constant. My observation, anecdotal and certainly not original, was that trauma can produce long-lasting changes in behavior.

There is no doubt, for example, that a victim of rape is traumatized. Though physically intact, a woman may be left mentally scarred for years to come. She may have recurrent nightmares, waking fears, a sense of shame and worthlessness, a loss of confidence. Her relationships with men become painfully anxious. She relives her trauma countless times when a familiar context triggers its memory. How a woman reacts depends on who she was before—her personality, her self-image, her natural endowments, the strengths and weakness of her relationships. Some women are badly shaken; others recover more quickly. But all women suffer from the violation, all have changed expectations of the future. This is not a case of genetic traits, although they have their influence. Nor must trauma, to be destructive, occur in early childhood when a woman's personality and physiology are still developing. Mature women learn in a single trial from their experience, and what they learn hurts them, often for many years.

For the past generation, we have been dealing with the traumas of the Vietnam War. Many soldiers returned unscathed physically but emotionally devastated. Again, a constellation of factors, genetic and experiential, conspire to choose a victim. One man witnesses the maiming of a close friend. Another is commanded in the course of the war to commit atrocities. One of violent disposition takes to killing as second nature. Another is plagued by conscience. There is, for instance, the story of a university professor whom I shall call Frank. Frank is a big man, muscular and fit even long after middle age. Frank is assertive, some might say aggressive, and totally forthright. He readily and responsibly assumes command. As an officer during the Second World War, he was often in the thick of battles. Leading his men, he was severely wounded and had to be carried off the battlefield. Fully conscious, he was unable to move himself. Medics eased his large frame onto a stretcher which was then loaded onto a jeep. He was tightly strapped to the stretcher, which in turn was secured to the jeep. As the jeep rushed Frank to a field hospital, an artillery barrage began to rain down murderously on the road. Incoming shells surrounded the jeep, offering no way out. Terrified, the driver leapt out of his vehicle, abandoning his wounded charge. Wounded, weak, and strapped to the stretcher, Frank was utterly helpless and an easy target for the enemy gunners. Seized with terror, he was certain he was about to die, abandoned by a fellow soldier.

Frank is the stoic, macho type with little tolerance for sentiment and weakness. He is all mission. Yet every few years, totally by surprise, in a situation of helplessness, Frank is transported back to the jeep in Germany. He might have lost his passport, been unable to find his way in a strange town, or be bedridden with an illness. The helplessness and uncertainty trigger the memory of his trauma, which he then relives with such vividness that he feels it is actually happening again. I am not at all sure that the rest of his life is untouched by this recurring nightmare. Perhaps his wartime ordeal resonates with childhood feelings of abandonment to create recurrent flashbacks. Maybe Frank inherited traits that predispose him to walling off trauma so that it periodically bursts forth from his unconscious. Maybe. I don't have to question, however, the lasting traumatic imprint made on Frank. I am convinced he would be a different man today had he not been deserted among the exploding shells.

Adults can undergo profound psychological change or impairment because of what they experience. And if this is true of adults, why shouldn't it also be true of children, who are far more impressionable? How can a young girl who is forced to have sexual relations with her father from age five on not be profoundly and immutably affected by the psychological trauma of those experiences? However courageous and accomplished she may be in overcoming her memories, she will never be what she might have been.

I was drawn to the psychological effects of trauma partly because of my own early experience. Not a victim myself, I was, however, indirectly victimized. As a child, I witnessed repeated trauma to a young girl I will call Michelle. Michelle, whose story unfolds in the course of the book, was beaten frequently from the age of eight or nine until she was thirteen or fourteen. The provocation for the beatings, administered by her father, might have been minor disobedience, a negative comment, or a disapproving glance. In his rage, which was accompanied by his terrifying screams, he struck her many times with a belt across the body and even across her face. Perhaps most frightening was his total lack of control. A murderous force would seize his body, which seemed as if propelled by an irresistible convulsion as he pummeled his daughter. The uncontrollability of this man threatened much worse. Michelle, too, became uncontrollable. Terrorized, screaming, she would become hysterical—to no avail.

I remember my feeling of helplessness. I cried for her, with her, but there was also a part of me that could not help being relieved that she, not I, was the target. I knew that Michelle's father had drawn no blood, had broken no bones. He had not come close to murdering her. I feared even then, however, that he had murdered her future. I did not base my conviction on any systematic study. I had no large population to analyze with the necessary controls. But what I experienced vicariously transformed me forever. I could comfort Michelle, as I tried to for many years. I could try to help her forget what she could not forget. My efforts painfully futile, I fantasized about doing something more. But I sensed that the real battle was with forces of nature, which had branded her, me, and probably her father, forever. Yet strangely, all of my resolve soon became submerged in the activity of my everyday life, my plans. The fantasy went underground.

The experiences and dreams of my youth faded from consciousness long before I understood them and their impact on my future. The helpless rage and aimless mobilization seemed to abate. They were not gone, they were just not visible. In retrospect, it was as if a powerful river of feeling within my brain was forever seeking and making new channels through which to flow. A channel might find expression in my hunting through the pages of classic novels for insights about human psychology. I developed an intense interest in people-watching, learning about their histories and looking for patterns in their behavior.

As a medical student, I had the opportunity to conduct psychiatric interviews and to study case histories. I learned the formal classifications of syndromes, typical symptoms, and therapeutic alternatives. At the same time, my quantitative, measuring side found outlets in laboratory research on physical chemistry, protein synthesis and chemical messengers in the brain. For many years my different interests seemed unrelated, sometimes even at odds with each other, until an unconscious need finally joined them into the single, focused pursuit of a biological basis for human memory. I didn't consciously decide to channel my helpless rage into brain research. My thoughts and plans, instead, were carried along by a subconscious emotional current. I had no way of stopping what was happening to Michelle—or to the patients I later came to know. I didn't understand enough about them or how they thought even to begin to reach them. Listening to their stories, I wanted to offer advice. Why don't you escape from such a relationship? Leave your home, don't submit! Seek out others, expect more for yourself, I wanted to say. But I came to realize that they could not really hear me. They heard my words, perhaps even agreed with my recommendations. They had brain compartments to which new information, my suggestions for example, had easy access. But habits, learned emotional responses, and remembered expectations were buried deep in their brains that dictated the course of their lives. These patients, like victims of encephalitis, could not be awakened.

Only twenty years later did I begin to awaken myself and to discover how various elements of my own experience fit together—why I study memory, the brain, and behavior. It is as if during childhood, a shower of thoughts, experiences, and feelings were mixed together, with no apparent order or sense. Like falling snowflakes that obscure a miniature landscape under glass, the memories take time to settle down before the scene within slowly becomes visible.

MEMORY'S DOMAIN

As a medical student, I was fascinated by how memory's permanence maintains trauma's grip on our behavior. So I tried to identify for myself those features that defined the essence of human memory, in humans and in other creatures. The psychiatric clinic of Cornell University Medical College provided opportunities to observe memory at work in human experience.

One of my professors, Dr. Edward Liang, taught me to conduct psychiatric interviews. An interview was more than a carefully constructed list of questions, although there was certainly a structure to follow. An interview involved being invited into a patient's world, not invading it. Dr. Liang taught me to respect that world, however maladaptive it might be. The world was not revealed all at once. Nor was it revealed directly. It emerged from the totality of a patient's history, feelings, plans, and dreams, from the patient's reactions to me and my reactions to the patient. It was present in voices, facial expressions, postures and movements. More than what was said, how it was said conveyed the individual's personal chemistry. Dr. Liang taught me to be a better observer of human behavior, including my own. Through his kind, respectful treatment of me as well as his patients, he taught more by example than by instruction. He also readily accepted our differences. He knew I had interests in quantitative sciences and encouraged me to follow my penchant for measuring. From thousands of records that he and others made available, I constructed a multivariable survey to study the relationship between diagnostic categories and the traumatic loss of a parent in early childhood. Certain patient groups showed a higher incidence of early parental loss than the non-patient population. So while he was a model for my clinical identity, he also encouraged my scientific aspirations.

Smooth, unwrinkled, Dr. Liang's face betrayed few hints of emotion. He talked in the crisp monotone of a radio announcer delivering the news. The news, however, was frequently punctuated with a slight crack in his voice, somehow signalling his feelings of bafflement, sadness, and resignation. Peering out of his mask, his eyes, too, told the tale of his inner being. They communicated his intense interest, his caring and his warmth. He was clinically precise in his description of a patient's psychiatric history, disciplined in his analysis of the symptoms, and specific in his plan of treatment.

Susan was an attractive, intelligent and seductive woman in her mid-twenties. Between relationships, she spent her days as a single parent supporting a daughter. Her pattern was to look for salvation in sexual liaisons. She had all the needs of a neglected, abused child looking for a parent to love and protect her. Inevitably, the men she found would exploit her, become overwhelmed by her dependence, and soon after, leave her. When she found someone who treated her kindly and offered the possibility of commitment, her interest waned quickly. Most men like this were not sufficiently masculine or assertive for her. She was drawn inexorably only to those men who would bring her the pain she had known since childhood. In other words, she was a neurotic woman who was rigidly conditioned to repeat self-destructive behavior. Dr. Liang had little hope of making her recognize this behavior and perhaps change it. Instead, he provided support in times of crises, practical planning to meet everyday necessities, and intermittent antianxiety medication.

Curtis, a thin, handsome-featured patient in his thirties, projected a strange lack of vitality. His sunken eyes appeared always in shadow. He spoke softly, carefully, seeming at first to make sense. Somewhere in the conversation, the sealed-off nature of his artificial world emerged. He had no frank delusions or hallucinations, but he attributed elaborate motives to the people he met during his daily routine, and the motives, though not overtly hostile, were never friendly. It was not surprising, given his consistent expectation of rejection, that he kept his contacts with people at a minimum. He filled his days maintaining his parents' estate. Living alone, he kept the house in the same perfect condition that his mother had demanded throughout their life together. As long as she was alive, the intact, pure cleanliness of her house could never be compromised by playful activity of her son. Her love of her furnishings displaced her love for her son. He remained enslaved to these objects, his daily loneliness interrupted only by obsessive fantasies of old movie stars, particularly Greta Garbo. For this severely ill, some might say schizophrenic patient, Dr. Liang's compassion was of less value. Major tranquilizers were somewhat helpful, and counseling helped Curtis to cope with everyday responsibilities.

For both Susan and Curtis, a life-pattern seemed to have been established early and rigidly adhered to thereafter. Susan's behavior, although compulsive, did not always dominate her life. She had many periods filled with hope, during which she was not actively self-destructive, whereas Curtis's gloom, paralysis, and isolation were unrelenting. In both cases, however, expectations of punishment permeated their conscious moments. Memories of trauma-filled childhood years dictated their present and future experience.

The monolithic, inaccessible quality of these and many other patients' memories humbled Dr. Liang in his effort to offer treatment. I understood his frustration but could not accept his resignation. There were patients who *could* be reached. While painful memories could not be exorcised, their grip on behavior and feelings could be loosened. Some patients could acquire new expectations, even new behavior. Such patients were rare, but I found it fascinating that learning new life-patterns might be possible at all.

My attention was riveted on the psychological imperative that governed these patients' lives. They followed a fairly simple but rigid sequence of behaviors. Their repeated, almost stereotypical responses to loneliness reminded me of the imprinting learned by Konrad Lorenz's geese. Shortly after hatching, a gosling learns to recognize the image of the first moving object it sees with any frequency. That object, usually its mother, can also be a human, such as Lorenz, or even a wooden decoy. From the time of its early learning the gosling thereafter follows the imprinted image wherever it goes. People, too, form an image, albeit much more complex, which forevermore represents the love and sustenance they seek. It does not matter that the image might include dreadful deprivation and pain. If this is the image that has been imprinted, it remains with them for the rest of their lives. Susan learned from her father that "love" was accompanied by the harsh treatment of a man, while Curtis learned that "love" was associated with an extremely repressive mother. Once learned, these images of love were the only ones these patients could recognize. It was not possible for them to even consider the possibility that love could assume a different form. What they had learned actually prevented new information from being perceived by their nervous systems, in effect filtering it out of their consciousness.

The essence of such powerful learning seemed to be the association or "coming together" of love with something else—a harsh, abusive father; a suffocating, controlling mother. This "coming together" of love with a recognizable human image seemed to be a critical clue, clearly reminiscent of the training experienced by Pavlov's dog. During training, the sound of a bell repeatedly came together with the smell of meat. The dog learned to respond to the bell as if it were also the smell of meat. For the dog, these two events were no longer separate but had become connected in its memory and therefore in its expectations of the future. Could a human be similarly trained? Were there universal cellular and molecular mechanisms common to the most sophisticated and fundamental of learned behaviors? If so, might not the particular molecules that cause memory storage become targets for clinical intervention? With memory-specific drugs, perhaps the cycle of eternally reenacting learned self-destructive behavior might be broken.[1] These questions captured my imagination when I was a medical student.

Undoubtedly, many different areas of the brain are enlisted to generate diverse memories. Yet it seemed possible that there were universal principles of memory function just as there were universal physical laws. Perhaps there is a general law dictating that memory is formed for all events humans sense occurring together or close together in time. This law might apply to remembered events as uncomplicated as the flash of lightning, the sound of thunder, the sting of a bee, or the smell of a rose or as multifaceted as the first day at school, the embrace of a loved one, a religious vision, or solving a mystery. A universal law of memory might even teach us how we formulate other physical laws about the universe. Memories are shaped by events in our lives, but memories in turn determine the physical laws we derive from those events.

For example, when a doctor obtains a blood sample by pressing a small needle into a child's finger, the child observes the sequence: the doctor's appearance, pressure on a needle, a finger prick, bleeding, and crying. If the events in the sequence are repeatedly linked in time, they become linked in the child's mind. Each mental link of one event to another is also an association—a "coming together." At a later stage, the child notices that a ball thrown with sufficient speed produces a stinging sensation when it lands in his mitt. With a few repetitions, the child has learned a new sequence. These events, too, are first linked in time and then become linked in the child's mind. The pressure of the ball is linked to the stinging sensation. The pressure of the doctor's needle was also linked to a sting, albeit much more painful and much more localized. There is sufficient similarity between the two types of painful sensations, however, that the speeding baseball recalls the memory of a stinging finger and therefore the pressure of the doctor's needle. With a sufficient number of additional linkages, the child begins to form an entire collection, or category, of events, all of which link pressure with pain. This collection of events in turn may come to be linked in the child's mind to his experience of pushing on a door to open it, smacking the surface of a pool to produce a splash, or pressing on pedals to propel his bicycle. A primitive idea of a physical law about equal and opposite forces begins to emerge.

As an intelligence-gathering device, the brain is performing a specific function when it senses and records how events are related in time. Memories are the records of those relationships within the brain. The brain is measuring and recording the likelihood, or probability, of events occurring together. The more times the brain encounters two events occurring together, the greater is the probability it assigns to their occurring together in the future. Repetition beyond a critical minimum number of times causes the brain to assign a 100% probability. The brain has determined that the events occur together with virtual certainty. Of all members of earth's animal kingdom, humans have by far the most sophisticated capacity to assign probabilities among events, make predictions based on these probabilities, and from these predictions arrive at choices. This is the essence of adaptive behavior. The vast majority of events when first sensed by the brain have uncertain value. That value can change drastically in different contexts. The sound of a siren toward noon in a factory setting may signal that lunch is being served in the cafeteria. That same siren in wartime England signaled the imminent onset of falling bombs. In one case, the appropriate behavior is to stop work and prepare for a meal. In the other, it is to run for shelter. The sound of the siren occurs in memory repeatedly accompanied by other sounds, sights, and movements. The learned relationships among these stimuli allow us to predict what is about to happen and, based on the prediction, to decide what to do.

Early in life, context for our memories is powerfully determined by those on whom we depend. The opinions and wishes of parents, role models, and authority figures receive great weight among the links we remember from an experience. Within the family circle, a child's brain is engraved with the values of its parents. Within larger community circles, societal values also provide context for memories. The collective memory of a nation can influence the course of history. A people steeped in the same cultural traditions, accepted practices, and prejudices shares experiences remembered over the course of centuries. Context is taught by one generation to the next, within and outside the family, by authorities and by peers. The learned records serve as an embodiment of national identity. Individual memories guide and enable the expression of a society's will.

Thirteenth-century Spanish religious and secular rulers, for example, ordered that Jews no longer be allowed to practice their religion, already thousands of years old. The price of disobedience, exacted by the Inquisition, was ghastly torture as well as execution. Many Jews who were baptized and converted to Catholicism undertook to follow their original religion and traditions in secret. Candle lighting, songs, and prayer continued only under cover of darkness and behind locked doors. By day they were Catholics, by night they listened to their memories. Even after a royal banishment in 1492 scattered the Jews from Spain and all of its colonies to points around the globe, many of the *marranos* (a Spanish name for secret Jews[2]) maintained their religious dichotomy. Some of their descendants, often speaking in a unique dialect, seem unaware today of why they follow centuries-old customs that are no longer necessary. It is as if memories of horrific persecution, transmitted from one generation to another, entered into a collective unconscious. The original trauma still shapes the group's behavior. They seem not to know that they no longer need to seek forgiveness in the hallowed Kol Nidre[3] prayer for breaking religious vows in thirteenth-century Spain. Perhaps in some hidden corners of their minds lurk musty records of the original fear and guilt with which they struck their life-and-death compromise.

We all have a compelling need not to violate our expectations of the future. If a principal function of memory is to assess and predict the probabilities with which events occur, this also serves to minimize uncertainty in our lives. Having a library of probabilities appears to reduce the number of situations whose consequences we cannot predict. These basic probabilities, when borne out, allow us to achieve an equilibrium. Daily needs arise, and they are satisfied in specific, familiar ways. Our expectations are fulfilled.

When learned expectations are not fulfilled, confusion and anxiety follow. Attempts to reestablish the equilibrium of certainty by finding familiar contexts can temporarily yield to seeking and trying out new contexts. An immigrant submits to months, even years of uneasiness, confusion, and often loneliness as a strange language, customs, and values compete with those of his past. Old expectations are not fulfilled, context is inconsistent, certainty is rare, and anxiety a constant companion.

Dr. Liang never neglected the social and cultural context of a patient's feelings and expectations. A Chinese-American himself, he made me keenly aware of how sociocultural traditions are linked to personal judgments of self-worth and acceptability. One example of such linkage stands out. The day he recounted the story, the usually somber-appearing paneled rooms and corridors of the Payne Whitney Psychiatric Clinic assumed a darker, more hopeless, even sinister aspect. The silence of the place, with its scarcely visible doctors and patients, conveyed a sense of isolation rather than nurture and support. He told me about a young student from Taiwan who had attended a fine New York undergraduate school. In her third year, perhaps because of language difficulties, she failed one of her major subjects. Her failure precipitated a depression that neither she nor antidepressant drugs could dispel. In addition to the academic and social circumstances that contributed to her problems, she was seeing an American therapist who emphasized the need for more independence from her parents. To someone in a strange land, already separated by half the globe from her family, the emphasis on autonomy had little meaning. With entirely different conceptions of filial devotion and loyalty, she felt that she owed her parents evidence of her success in return for the unusual freedom she had already been granted. In her mind, the love and respect of her parents was tightly linked to her academic performance. Although physically separated from them and in some ways emotionally independent, she still viewed herself as a spoke in the family wheel. Her success was her family's success. Her dishonor was her family's dishonor. In her mind, failure was linked not only to a loss of acceptance but to an overwhelming sense of shame, which could be expiated by taking her own life. In many other societies, suicide itself might be closely linked to shame and so be ruled out, but for this unfortunate student, self-destruction was associated with regaining acceptance. The primordial records of these childhood associations were buried so deeply that they permitted little access to new ways and certainly not to new ways of a foreign culture. Such unconscious behavioral patterns resemble reflexes. Their execution neither requires nor allows the acceptance of information from present circumstances. Failure was linked to shame, which in turn was linked in the young woman's mind to an unopposable command for self-destruction.

To defy that command, she would have had to question her role and position in her family unit and the foundation on which her relationships with her parents was predicated. She would thereby be threatening her parents, whose own equilibrium derived from the collective expectations of their family and culture. The young Chinese student simply could not hear her doctor's urging that academic failure need not lead inevitably to isolation and hopeless shame. His friendly reassurances were only foreign whispers drowned out by the chorus of parental authority. She heard only the voice of her memories. Those who would be heard by such a patient in the future must learn to speak with that long-buried voice.

TWIST AND SHOUT

My experience with psychiatric patients and my interest in memories of trauma began long before medical school, at a time when interests chose me as much as vice versa. I didn't choose to become aware of Michelle and her unfolding story. My growing awareness was complicated by all the feelings of any prolonged adolescent friendship. Mine was not an analytical perspective but one of curiosity mixed with love, hope, mutual dependence, sometimes anger and frustration, and all too often sorrow. I didn't decide to treat or study Michelle. I cannot pretend to any semblance of detachment or objectivity. In spite of my involvement, however, and perhaps because of it, I learned from her.

In those early days, when I first met Michelle, she was striving for perfection. She hadn't fully matured, but her form already suggested its later classic beauty. Her face, unblemished, rosy-cheeked, seemed to draw all attention to her innocent, tentative, crystal-blue eyes. They beckoned and distanced at the same time, concealing a sorrow she could never entirely admit to. She talked quickly, intensely, intelligently. She was an outstanding student and a talented dancer. She drove herself mercilessly. Her uneasy manner suggested an inner conviction that no effort would be sufficient, that her ultimate failure, her intrinsic unacceptability, had already been decided. The terrible irony was that such a beautiful creature would never know her own beauty.

Such a perceptive, expressive soul could never appreciate her own gentle spirit. If my father was harsh her father was cruel. If my father was punitive, hers was abusive. If my father disapproved, hers abandoned.

Her desperate battle for acceptance ended with adulthood. With physical maturity, she entered another world. All of the energy she had devoted to winning approval was given over to extracting approval. She struggled with her father rather than try any longer to meet his demands. She fought him directly. Her tentativeness was replaced by bravado. Now, she rejected him before he rejected her. To show that she didn't need his love, she flaunted her independence to antagonize him as much as to convince herself. It wasn't that she was free of his destructive grip. It just took a different form. She told me of the savage beatings. In her early teens she began what became part of her lifestyle—massive retaliation. She literally drove him off. Screams, curses, and blows formed the dialogue between them. She won her independence and lost it forever at the same time. She won it by totally disowning her father, by denying her own need to satisfy his wishes and expectations, her need even to accept his abuse. She survived by walling off the side of herself that said she deserved such treatment. Distracting herself with music, she spent hours dancing, alone or with friends, abandoning herself to the beat. She could not hear other sounds through the driving beat of "Twist and Shout" or "Blueberry Hill." Moving rhythmically with her eyes closed, she could not see her own face and figure, which, beautiful as they were, only reminded her of her feeling of abject undesirability. Too much of her daily life involved exposure to pain for her to forget, however. She could not think other thoughts; there was too much to remind her at every turn of excruciating memories. For Michelle, learning new links, new associations to divert her attention, was not possible. Michelle had to stop thinking, period. She had to blunt the source of the painful memories—her senses. She clouded her senses at first by filling them with music, not for the pleasure of music but so that she could not sense anything else. Later she drowned them in alcohol.

There was a progression in Michelle's responses to what life meted out. This was a wonderfully endowed child who depended for her survival on a parent who inflicted intolerable pain. The pain and her dependence could not coexist. She had to make a choice. As a child, she was too young to live without parents. Her dependence had to come first. How then was she to live with the pain? Her early childhood responses were to seek to reduce the pain by being "good"—by being perfect. She would behave in such a way as to win her father over. She would remove any cause for him to abuse her. Her behavioral pattern during this period, before her adolescence, was adaptive in the sense that behavior throughout the animal kingdom is adaptive. A bee increases the smell of the nectar by reflexively flying to the flower. A child reduces the burning heat of a flame by reflexively withdrawing her hand. Michelle initially responded to abusive treatment by behaving in ways she thought would reduce the abuse. She accumulated a library of her father's dislikes and linked to them behaviors that might remove the source of his displeasure and therefore the pain she would have to endure. As she entered adolescence, the links between avoiding the pain and any response she might make became more and more tenuous. She was also accumulating a library of failed links. More and more of her father's dislikes could not be avoided by any response. She learned to link her desire for his love to unavoidable suffering. Her preadolescent efforts to please were gradually replaced in her teens by efforts to coerce. Then, since most responses of any kind were useless, the futility of responding at all also became linked to her father. A figure of overwhelming importance throughout her childhood became linked with her feeling of hopelessness and paralysis. I know of no more likely recipe for depression, which began to haunt Michelle as she entered adolescence. The need for love was linked to unavoidable suffering, which was linked to the futility of responding. The depression brought its own pain and suffering, to be avoided at almost any cost.

As she adopted strategies to cope, Michelle followed an anatomical path to torment. An assault on her senses was integrated and processed within her brain, determining behavioral outcomes. Working backwards along this path from behavior to sensing, she began by desperately casting about for a behavior that worked. Failing, she resorted to manipulating her own integrative processes. And with no choice left, she altered her sensing capacity itself. There are in each of these strategies the hallmarks of distinct syndromes of mental illness spanning the scale of severity from neurosis to psychosis.

Prisoners sometimes fill their days by remembering past experience. They temporarily forget their unavoidable confinement by focusing their attention on memories. Remembered time substitutes for real time. When Michelle had exhausted her response options, those of behavior, she began to use her thought options, integrating memories with fantasies. She began to substitute remembered time for real time. Whenever she thought of her father and felt depressed, she focused her attention on other thoughts and soon focused obsessively on an idealized boyfriend. She shifted her energy from attempts to please her father to serving her fantasy of a boyfriend-knight in shining armor. She walled off the memories linked to her father with a new collection of memories linked to an imagined savior.

Her fantasies were synthesized from real memories of actual relationships. She dated many young men with whom she had varying degrees of intimacy. She knew well their strengths and weaknesses, their stages of maturity, their aspirations, their origins, their identifications. She also understood their total unpreparedness for commitment and the assumption of responsibility. Yet she fantasized, dreaming that one would choose such obligations. In the beginning of this postadolescent phase of Michelle's life, she could distinguish between her dreams and reality. Later, she could not. Inevitably, the reality of her boyfriend would fail to measure up to her expectations. The fantasies that distracted her attention from her suffering broke down. Between boyfriends, she felt the pain and became depressed. This cycle continued throughout her teens. She achieved a marginal equilibrium by trying to substitute thoughts of a fantasized boyfriend for the impossibility of her home environment. When the fantasy failed, the horror and grief returned.

The steps in this progression did not take place in isolation from each other. Michelle never discontinued all of her efforts to please her father. She just made progressively fewer attempts. Nor did her reliance on fantasy and obsessive thinking begin in adolescence. This began earlier but increased as she grew older. Nor did she alter her sensing capacity only after the first two major steps—mobilized efforts to please and then fantasies—had failed. Her long hours listening and dancing to music were, I believe, the beginning of her attempts to control what she sensed. The din and beat of the music blotted out other sensations, which might remind her of the misery she wished to forget. Selective attention allowed the sensations of the music through, but not many others. This was only a hint of the self-destruction that was to follow. It was the first significant compromise Michelle had made in the balance of life and death. To avoid unbearable sorrow, which meant death, she diminished her life by restricting her sensory experience.

When the fantasies failed, she entered a new phase, of increasingly frequent failed relationships interspersed with depression and sometimes thoughts of suicide. Gradually she grew to rely more and more on alcohol to blunt her pain. Her progress down the slippery slope of a life-and-death compromise began to accelerate. There were periods of normalcy. Even when she had become dependent on alcohol, there were still gratifying moments in her life. She managed to finish college and find occasional employment. Marriage and two lovely children followed. Her relationships with her employers, husband, siblings, parents and children were always stormy however. The slightest hint of disagreement, criticism, or rejection caused her unbearable pain. Her characteristic response was retaliation. Shouting abuse, she constructed elaborate rationales to shift all blame from herself to others, although inside she was certain that the opposite was true. The same tooth-and-nail fighting she was driven to with her father occurred regularly in each of her relationships. She became so fragile that she felt criticized even in the absence of criticism, rejected when acceptance was still possible.

Earlier in her life, she learned to link her father with abuse. This link was so strong, so causal, and so important that it spilled over into her expectations of other relationships. She generalized her experience with her father to her relationships with all other men and eventually women too. The strength of this link had caused an early filtering of sensory experience at an integrative level. She was still sensing what was happening, but her interpretation of what she sensed, her perceptions, were distorted. She perceived events in her life as fulfilling the expectations she had learned. So rigid was her perception, and so taut was her sensitivity, that she reflexively classified real time events only in terms of her own ghastly remembered time, leaving her little capacity for learning new possibilities. This was Michelle's chain of self-fulfilling experience, linking every new personal interaction with all those that preceded. This is the inherent conservatism of human learning and memory gone destructively awry.

Later Michelle's remembered chain of experiences had a more ominous feature. Childhood trauma had distorted her perception of events, fostered a reliance on fantasies, and restricted her attention to limited portions of her sensory experience. Eventually, I believe, the trauma cut off the sensory experience itself.

In the absence of sensory experience, memories assume control and begin to be transformed into fantasies by fear and desire. When Michelle fantasized during her teens about the perfect boyfriend, she knew the difference between fantasy and reality. She still retained the capacity to sense her immediate present. Though her actions were undoubtedly influenced by fantasies and obsessive thoughts, they were still reality-based. As she entered her early twenties, however, the alcoholic assault on her senses gained strength. And as her senses became less important, her fantasies blossomed until, in her thirties, the distinction between real-time sensory experience and fantasy became blurred. Memories, and their reincarnations as fantasies, filled the vacuum left by sensory deprivation. Here, too, in this more advanced stage of her decline were elements of behavior suggested earlier. Michelle may have fantasized about ideal boyfriends, but those she found were unable to live up to her expectations. They often exploited her. The gap between reality and her fantasy was a hint of worse yet to come, when the gap would widen into a chasm.

Her further decline seemed inevitable, but the steps in her descent remain obscure. Perhaps as Michelle filtered out her sensations she created a state of chronic sensory deprivation. In the absence of a rich sensory experience, memories that previously occurred only during dreams began to occur during periods of wakefulness. Normally subconscious fears and fantasies began to be interspersed with sensory-based thoughts and memories. Bizarre, dreamlike juxtapositions, fantasies gone wild, started to characterize her perception. As she approached early middle age, she quit drinking when her life was threatened by alcoholic hepatitis. Not long after withdrawal, however, her fantasies began to assume a new reality. These were not the hallucinations that sometimes transiently plague alcoholics, such as visions of snakes. These were elaborate constructs with actual characters, voices, scenes, and plots. During her first thirty-five years, she never experienced a trace of such crazy thinking. Hints were there earlier, but a true break with reality had never occurred. This was the stuff of psychosis. During the last several years of her life, before she ended it, the breaks became ever more frequent and more florid. The fantasy of a romantic savior now became an entire belief system. Before, she might have dwelt on a wished-for relationship that would lead to marriage, children, and acceptance. Earlier, such a reverie was easily interrupted. In her final years, she lived her dream. Divorced, no longer in custody of her children, she lived imaginary weddings. She bought a dress, made plans, talked to a fiancé who was not there. She would not be distracted. Now the realm of fantastic images within her brain took precedence over the sensory realm. Whole chains of images derived from old memories absorbed her attention. Remembered time replaced real time. Michelle had become disconnected from her senses. She could no longer distinguish what she wished to be happening from what was actually happening. Nor could she tell the difference between what she dreaded most might happen and what was actually happening. Her most fervent wish was a transforming wedding with her handsome prince. Her waking nightmare was her father transformed into Satan. Satan appeared more frequently, issuing commands of self destruction which she was powerless to resist. For Michelle, now cut off from the outside world, her Satan-father was real. Because she no longer experienced sensations as we know them, I believe she no longer felt pain the way we do and the way she once had. She felt pain, but largely remembered pain, in certain ways far more horrible. She did not feel the throbbing when Satan ordered that she bang her head against the wall. There were still many interludes of lucidity when she was totally connected. During those periods, she knew of her other world's existence. But, as with dreams of sleep, I suspect she remembered few details of her mad dreamscapes.

Was it Satan's final command that sent her flying from the ledge? Did she know then the consequences of this last self-destructive act? What would I have wished for Michelle? To have made a purposeful decision to free herself from her life's misery or to have followed in mad obedience the order of her nightmare? If she made a purposeful decision, it must have taken great courage, but then she would have had to be aware, senses functional, feeling the rush of the wind and perhaps the penultimate sadness of her end. If she heard only Satan's voice, entranced, she may have been numbed to her impending death, but stricken with the kind of shock only nightmares instill.

WHY SEARCH

It might strike some as strange that I should find beauty in neural networks or pleasure in deciphering their codes. I found murder mysteries boring, but puzzles, especially those in logic and mathematics, captured my attention. Certainly, part of it is what you're good at. Math and science were second nature to me. Even in high school, I brought an uninhibited intensity to experiments, while writing often brought anxiety and self-consciousness. I also had little awareness of the risks that could be involved in doing science.

My high-school chemistry teacher, Harold Blum, offered only encouragement. Dr. Blum was short, bushy-browed and talkative. He spoke rapidly, conveying his wide-eyed excitement about chemistry in action. (Only later did I realize he had a glass eye, the result of an injury from a chemical explosion.) A friend and I decided we would recreate on a small scale an industrial process for making nitric acid. This process, a series of chemical reactions, required a complicated maze of glass tubing and flasks. After many days of assembling our after-school project, we put the starting ingredients in one of the flasks. The heat of a Bunsen burner under the flask produced a vapor that slowly progressed down the chain of glass tubing. Fluid, presumably nitric acid, began to condense and accumulate in the last flask. It was working. Excited, I increased the heat from the flame by placing the tip of its blue cone right at the flask surface. Seconds later, the room was filled with a shattering explosion. White mist enveloped the room, obscuring everything. In fact, I could see nothing. Dr. Blum led me out of the room. For many minutes, I thought I had lost my sight forever and was seized by panic. Ever so gradually, my burning eyes discerned faint, blurred images. When sight finally returned, we went back to the room to survey the damage. To our surprise, there were no glass fragments to be found. Our best guess was that the explosion had been so powerful that it had disintegrated the glass into tiny particles not forceful enough to penetrate my safety glasses. Ammonia, one of the products of the chemical reactions, probably caused my temporary blindness. It surprised no one that after-school experiments were banned from that day on. It had, nevertheless, been fun, and if I hadn't been so careless, I might have relished my first minor success.

Four years later I found new encouragement from a college professor. Philip George, a jolly Britisher, had glasses so thick that his magnified eyes seemed to reach over his forehead toward his hairline. His huge-appearing eyes together with thick salt-and-pepper hair parted in the center gave him a distinctly owl-like appearance. As my undergraduate research supervisor, Philip served as a guide to the world of science. He drew a complex sequence of biochemical reactions on the blackboard in his office and, circling one of the steps, said, "This is your reaction." Recommending a protocol that sounded anything but elementary, he asked that I try to measure the energies of the bonds that held together the atoms of complex sugar molecules. He then brought me to an old, empty room filled with huge benches sorely in need of paint. He informed me, quite seriously, that this was my laboratory. I would have to justify every piece of equipment, every chemical, every bottle I thought necessary for my thesis research. For the next several months, as I built the laboratory and developed a research strategy, each day began with a knot in the pit of my stomach and a weak-in-the-knees anxiety. But Philip was true to his word. He approved every realistic proposal I made, if it was carefully and economically formulated.

In fact, he approved much more. I remember the thrill of unwrapping a new set of quartz crystal cuvettes, made with precisely ground optical surfaces. Chemical solutions within the cuvette could be assayed by their absorbance of a light beam. Like polished gems, the cuvettes had their own physical beauty. Eager to use my new acquisitions, I prepared a set of test solutions. In my enthusiasm, I rushed to the bench with the cuvettes to measure the light absorbed by the solutions. The cuvette container, slightly wet, slipped from my grip and crashed to the floor, scattering the gleaming shards in all directions. Embarrassed to the point of humiliation, I reported the details to Philip who immediately understood that no warnings or instructions were necessary. He quietly authorized the purchase of new cuvettes without a hint of reprimand. In the delicate balance he struck in those days, Philip asked that I reach for the greatest independence of which I was capable, yet he was always available to provide the support I sometimes needed. He never obscured the difficulty of doing research, yet he communicated clearly that it could be done, and done with pleasure.

With the laboratory functional and all the necessary equipment in hand, I entered a second phase of my experimental initiation. I had to implement my plan by making a complex set of biochemical reactions occur in a test tube. Over the next several months, I was teased by an elusive success. The reactions worked sometimes, sometimes not. I could not identify the crucial uncontrolled factor. I began a kind of hunt. At the end of each day, successful or not, I would sit in solitude, eyes closed, and recreate every step of the experiment. After many such reviews, one step in the protocol seemed, on different occasions, to take different amounts of time. Depending on my dexterity, one of the reaction mixtures sat for a variable period before being added to the final test tube. On those days when I was particularly clumsy, taking the longest time, the final reactions proceeded well. It soon became clear that this chemical step required more time than had been described in the literature. This was the devil in the works. From that point on, I feverishly conducted one successful protocol after another. I was so stimulated by my daily experience in the laboratory, I decided to spend an additional year as an undergraduate to complete my project. Toward the end of that year, I decided I loved this work enough to do it for the rest of my life. I have never forgotten my parents' unambivalent delight at this news.

My parents had tried to provide an environment without material want, in which we lived by moral and intellectual values. Nevertheless, equality was not one of those values. In our home, might made right, mostly my father's might. He was brilliant, erudite, tormented, and tyrannical. I did not have to go out of my home to be challenged.

Demanding perfection, he was constantly critical. Terrified that we might fail, he was ever ready to punish his children's missteps.

His approval was always out of reach, yet I never stopped reaching. It was not until I left my home forever that I could separate what he wanted from what I wanted and decisively disavow his impossible expectations. I did so with a vengeance. When I began work in the laboratory, it was as if a switch were thrown inside my brain. Never again could I apply my energies intensely, without reservation, unless it was in a direction I alone had chosen. A hint of an assignment, an external command, soured my taste. I thrived in situations, such as those provided by Philip George, that allowed me total independence. Many years of striving in vain had left me with little hope of winning my father's approval. Whatever approval I sought in the future would, for long periods, have to be primarily my own.

When does a rat, shocked every time it eats, stop eating? Part of its strategy has to involve delay. The rat avoids the pain of the shock by delaying satisfaction for food. The hunger is suppressed temporarily, but inevitably returns. Children, as well as adults, need approval as they need food. My strategy was to suppress my need for approval until I thought the shock had diminished or perhaps disappeared. Therefore I had to wait for relationships that sustained and reinforced my energies. Somehow I learned to substitute a Harold Blum or a Philip George for a harsh father. Slowly I was able to work around the link in my mind between a father's love and his unrelenting disapproval. It was not that I forgot the original link. I just managed to learn new links that occupied more and more of my attention. I could never erase the learned expectation that seeking my father's approval would occur together with his harsh rejection. I could only hope that for me approval might be attainable elsewhere, creating new probabilities different from those I had learned as a child.

Experiments were not just my interest, they became my life-style. I continually tried on new thoughts, new responses, and adventures such as hitchhiking to Florida, roofing in Denver, or farming in Oregon. I worked on biochemical thermodynamics with Philip George, molecular biology in Philadelphia, epidemiologic surveys in New York, and electrophysiology in Washington. I never once began one of these new and strange exposures without a feeling of silliness. Of course this feeling was not just my own, but my father's as well. How silly it was for me to try to write a composition or a poem, with my ignorance of word usage, the awkwardness of my sentence structure, the clumsiness of my rhythm. If only I could be like my brother, younger, yet able to express himself so beautifully. How could I possibly go to medical school? I would never have the self-discipline, convey the aura of respect and care for patients, the insight, the sense of responsibility that would lead others to trust me with their lives. It was laughable. But although I laughed and was filled with fear and trembling, I wasn't paralyzed. Ever so slowly, I learned that that feeling of silliness would usually be linked to a new adventure that would allow me to transcend these restrictive ways of thinking and behaving.

Did I really want to know how a memory is stored, how a neural network records information? Could I accept the total fallibility of my hypotheses? Would I be willing to try on new and sometimes strange perspectives and to be wrong over and over again? Isn't it silly to think that a snail can learn an association that has similarities to those of humans? Why should a human or rabbit brain learn with mechanisms similar to those of a snail? Even if such diverse species do learn a single simple association with common mechanisms, would we ever be able to find the critical memory sites among the billions of neurons in a mammal's brain? Is it possible that thousands of neurons store this single association? As I say, such possibilities seemed at times laughable. But through tears of laughter I was resolved to look.

During my childhood, I slowly built my strength. Although we were financially comfortable, I struggled to accumulate my own means of support. I knew there would be times when I would need every resource to resist my father's domination. For many years I not only resisted, I also incorporated some of his ways and a few of his values. Most of all I admired his uncompromising honesty and—his most endearing feature—a keen, almost driven curiosity. Most of all I hated his brutal, sometimes even sadistic coerciveness. As I came of age, I incorporated less and resisted more. I really had no choice. I could either succumb to his domination and accept the prospect of utter failure, or fight it and learn to function on my own, even when engulfed by fear.

At twenty, confused, rebellious, and often unwisely disdainful of risk, I set out between semesters to see the country. Roaming from Iowa to Washington State to Denver, I took any work available, meeting friends I had made in college as I went along. We picked rye, harvested potatoes, gathered apples, and shingled roofs. One sunny afternoon a friend and I decided to climb a mountain not far from Colorado Springs. The climb was more than I had anticipated. Straining, but determined to keep up with my friend, I was more tired than usual, my muscles somewhat aching and tremulous, my footing less sure. Nevertheless, the worst seemed over as I scampered down the mountainside. But as I turned a corner of high rocks and boulders, the path suddenly dropped off 5 or 6 feet. Without interrupting my pace, I jumped onto the narrow ledge below. I landed solidly, but because of fine gravel covering the ledge's surface, the force of my jump translated into a rapid slide, which began carrying me off the mountainside. Instinctively, I fell onto my stomach and dug my hands and arms into the treacherous surface. Pure will possessed my body at that moment. I didn't have time to think about what could happen. I only knew that part of me had become welded to that ledge, and that part pulled the other part back from the precipice. The thoughts of a lifetime poured into a single unbreakable resolve to hang on.

The strength of my will more than my muscles stopped my near-fatal slide. Resuming my descent, I felt uplifted, lighter, more secure, as I do upon making a scientific discovery. Toward the bottom, other climbers described how far out I had been, sharing their relief that I had made it. Only then did I become conscious of the full danger. Only then did I notice the involuntary shaking movements that had seized my body as the intensity of my effort to survive relinquished its demand on every last quantum of my energy. Only then did the pain in my fingers draw my attention to their tips where there was no longer flesh, only the white of bones peering through dark pools of blood.

When I was younger, I chose heroes for their willingness to endure great hardships to follow their ideals, their dreams. I admired their tenacity in the face of overwhelming odds. The odds might be set by a natural disaster. They might lie in the unfathomable reaches of the universe and its origins or in the unopposable will of a mob incited by prejudice and hatred. My heroes were people who hung on in spite of the pain of ostracism and isolation while searching out eternally elusive answers to difficult questions. My heroes were people who, by their wits as well as their endurance, solved mysteries and boldly hypothesized about apparent insolubles. I rarely thought of great pioneers in brain science such as Helmholtz, Freud, Mach, Pavlov, Sherrington, and Hartline as people. It never occurred to me that Pavlov could speak and think of Sherrington with complete contempt and arrogance, or that Sherrington could greet Pavlov with disdain; that Volta could hound Galvani to his end, or that Newton could despise rather than revere Leibnitz. Politics seemed unnecessary if the science was original and rigorous.

But in spite of my childish naïveté, I was also prepared by life for its worst. It was as if I grew up in two different emotional worlds—one positive and expecting the best in people, the other hard, armed and aggressive. One nurtured, the other tested; one I knew in the grace of my mother, the other in the harshness of my father.

One purpose served by such a childhood, then, can be to develop a willingness to marshal all one's resources, hold nothing back, and struggle wholeheartedly. With this willingness to commit all of my energies came also a willingness to challenge authority, and even society, to defend what I believed.

If I were to distill the essence of what I loved in my father, the pleasure I shared with him, it would be the thrill of being surprised by the unanticipated. It might be our unexpected glimpse of a red fox, a beaver at dusk, a red-winged blackbird, a doe and her fawn. We also shared discoveries in our reading—in diaries describing the horrors of the Inquisition or in the journal of Ponce de León exploring a new continent, in the arctic wastes of Jack London's *Call of the Wild* or the chaos of revolution in Dickens's *Tale of Two Cities.* Those were the only times my father was free from his own primordial voices—the remembered life-patterns that darkened his life as well as ours. There was a bittersweet irony in the contrast between his enslaved, enslaving moments and those times when he relished the unexpected. He sought in his intellectual pursuits a freedom that was absent from the rest of his life.

Tension between curiosity and a need for the familiar is minimal early in life. Animals will make great efforts to receive sensory stimulation for its own sake, even in the absence of any other reward. Children enjoy exploring the richness of their environment because of the varied and abundant stimulation their senses receive, with little competition from the remembered past. As they develop, their nervous systems require a steady diet of such stimulation. Some retain an appetite for new experience into adulthood. Nevertheless, even the curious observer strives to make order out of disorder, predictability out of chaos. In science, as in the rest of our lives, experience builds a library of probabilities and expectations based on them. Remaining curious over a lifetime involves confronting a paradox not easily resolved. How do you learn from the abundant observations made in the past by others and still remain open to entirely new observations of your own? How do you understand the grand collections of events already linked together in time by predecessors but also generate new and original collections, new syntheses? New observations come from loyalty to one's own primitive curiosity. New syntheses come from remaining free of unquestioning loyalty to the syntheses of others, particularly those in authority who may adhere to already established ways of thinking. Just as any of us may resist counsel to change familiar expectations, values, and behavioral patterns, so will scientists often not lightly concede accepted theory and practice. I was to learn over the years that winning the right to pursue my own search strategy would require all of my resolve to rebel against authority.

It would not be enough to possess the curiosity I shared with my father. It would not be enough to be compulsively honest and open-minded about what I observed. It would not be enough to apply myself untiringly and to accept the discipline of years of concerted effort. I would also need the will to resist, which my painful struggle with my father had developed. There would be times when mentors and colleagues would try to dominate and interfere with my efforts. I would have to look to myself to prevent that. And I would have to tolerate the necessary periods of loneliness.

To overcome my own natural desire to accept conventional wisdom required more than curiosity and a thirst for adventure. Desperation also played a role. People don't change unless they have to. They don't readily accept new ideas or seek new methods unless there are few alternatives. The Jews, the Huguenots, the Quakers, the Puritans, if given the opportunity to pursue their religious beliefs, would never have fled countries that had been their homelands for centuries. Intolerance and, often, persecution provided the impetus for radical change in their lives, for a willingness to risk awesome uncertainty in setting out for distant lands. Early experiences left me with the kind of desperation that made me willing to take chances. Later, the desperation would subside, but my habit of striking out on my own had by then become familiar and more comfortable. In fact, these solitary voyages of discovery, limited though they might have been, became an intellectual home. However troubled the rest of my life, I could always find refuge in my scientific adventures. In perspective, within a different context, I now realize that this was also my father's pattern. Amazing, these life-patterns. As memories, they seem to be transplanted from one generation to another—learned, not genetically programmed, yet inherited nevertheless.

THE SEARCH STRATEGY

In medical school, the predictability with which people seek out the familiar fascinated me. Patterns of human behavior, even if traumatic, recur again and again. It begins perhaps when a child cannot imagine a future different from the past. The present appears as if it will last forever. Resigned, the child prepares for the inevitable and becomes uneasy, disbelieving, when it doesn't happen. Rather than live with the anxiety of not knowing when the trauma will recur, the child makes it happen, recreating the present in the image of the remembered past.

I wanted to learn more about this hold traumatic memory has on human behavior. Perhaps the secrets of memory's power would be revealed in the physics and chemistry that make it possible. First, I had to develop a strategy to get at its basic mechanisms. I needed quiet moments far removed from the noise, regimentation, and obligations of medical school. I was bored and felt hamstrung by the monotonous telephone books of details to be swallowed whole. For me, asking exciting questions was part of rebelling and I could never imagine a more exciting intellectual adventure than exploring how memory works. In medical school, during the week, I often studied the curriculum late at night and early in the morning, leaving many hours during the day for doing experiments in biochemistry. On weekends, which began on Saturday afternoon, I might visit my fiancée's home. Here, I felt accepted into another world. The peaceful rhythm of long walks, dinner with her family, and a trip to the movies restored a sense of balance to my life and renewed a feeling of control over my choices. I had the free time to think about networks of neurons that store memory rather than how many different types of bacteria can cause pneumonia. I spent many pleasant hours thinking, warmed by the sun and surrounded by trees and shrubs in the privacy of her backyard. There, in her garden, I formulated my game plan.

I began by reflecting on my own conscious experience. It was not difficult to distinguish between sensation and perception. Perceptions emerge from the seamless interweaving of present sensations with past memories. It is, for example, one thing to see a squash ball as a small black sphere. It is quite another to perceive that this sphere is struck with a particular type of racket toward a low red line on the forward wooden wall of a squash court. I see a large light-blue rectangular container mounted on wheels. In steps, I perceive it as a car, a four-door sedan, and specifically the 1967 model which belongs to my fiancée's parents. The actual physical appearance of the squash ball and the car is first sensed and then immediately imbedded in a complex matrix of memories. Sensations derive meaning from the memories they trigger, and together with this meaning, constitute perceptions.

A number of armchair observations followed. No matter how hard I tried, I could never remember an isolated event, object, sound, or emotion. The most discrete memory was always linked in time to many other memories. A face was linked to the full appearance of a person, the person's personality, relationships, and behavior. The sound of a bell was linked to the image of a steeple, a hedge surrounding a church, a quiet street, the end of a workday, six o'clock, and time for dinner. I became convinced that human memories are not stored as sensations themselves. Rather, as suggested in the preceding chapters, memory seemed to be stored as the relationships among those sensations in time. Memory of the relationships reactivates the sensations. These initial observations led to the hypothesis that all human memory is relational or associative. This hypothesis could not easily be proved, but it seemed reasonable.

Another observation, familiar to anyone who has used mnemonic devices, generated further hypothesis. I could decide to associate *any* sensation with *any* other. For example, I could, associate the letter *B* with the squash ball or the letter *C* with the church bell. Simply because I so decided, such associations could be made, and they could be made almost instantaneously. Some review or practice of the association might be necessary for it to be remembered permanently. But one brief willed juxtaposition of the letter and the visual image was enough to preserve the association even hours later. The speed with which an association could be formed, and the apparently unlimited number of sensations that could be associated, suggested a fascinating feature of the brain.

Somewhere within the brain there must be a point, a physical locus, where signals from one image (the letter B) encounter and mix with signals from the other image (the ball). Furthermore, to form the association so quickly, the point where signals mix must already exist within the wiring of the brain. What an unbelievable number of wired intersections must be necessary for such a variety of associations to be possible!

I then asked myself what wiring designs could make such pluripotential signal mixing and linking possible. First, there would have to be both "hard-wired" and "soft-wired" pathways. Hard-wired circuits in the spinal cord, for example, allow us to sense a painful stimulus and jerk back our limbs within a fraction of a second. These reflex pathways are present in every normal individual member of a species, be it a rabbit, a dog, or a human. Because they vary little from individual to individual, the pathways must conform to genetically specified designs. A genetic blueprint programs the nervous system in a reproducible manner so that every normal adult has essentially the same reflexive pathways. This is what is meant by the term *hard-wired*.

Hard-wired reflexive pathways mediate responses that have an unequivocal value for an animal's survival. It is virtually always adaptive for an animal to withdraw its limb from a burning hot surface. In the course of evolution, the certainty of this value for a species' survival is translated, in effect recorded, by the selection of DNA, which programs the adaptive response into the nervous system. Similarly, a substantial portion of the sophisticated sensory circuits underlying vision, hearing, touch, and smell are hard-wired. The ensembles of neurons that control fine motor movements are also hard-wired, since there is always a need to move precisely. So a substantial portion of any nervous system has wiring that has been specified during evolution of a species. But what of stimulus patterns that have no universal adaptive value?

For ambiguous stimulus patterns, the wiring is most adaptively determined during the lifetimes of individual animals. The bee's taste for nectar is hard-wired. The yellow color of a flower, however, is neutral for the bee until it learns to associate this color with the hard-wired smell and taste of the flower's nectar. The circuit that allows the yellow-elicited signals to mix with the smell-elicited signals is soft-wired. This wiring has a variable strength because there is no intrinsically positive value for yellow. Another bee might learn to associate the color red with the smell of nectar. Since there is no consistently adaptive association of color and smell for all adult members of the bee species, there is no means of selecting a hard-wired circuit for the entire species.

So in my hypothetical designs of neural circuits I would have to include both hard-wired and soft-wired connections. The hard-wired connections would underlie clearly valued responses; the soft-wired connections would handle those responses of undetermined value. But were soft-wired circuits already present in some form before they were constructed, or did they have to grow? The observation that any stimulus pattern can be arbitrarily associated with any other told me that *de novo* creation or growth of the soft connections was not possible. To some degree, the soft-wired connections had to be already present. In that sense, they too were genetically specified. But the strengths of these connections could not be genetically specified. They would have to be specified by experience.

When I toyed mentally with circuit designs to incorporate hard and soft wiring, the designs always involved the activity and function of neurons and their synaptic connections. I was not thinking of radio transistors, circuit boards, or microchips. Instead, I thought of the essential characteristics of neurons. A neuron fires its large electrical signals, called impulses, when excited beyond a threshold level. Some neurons continually generate impulses, spontaneously, without excitation. The output of a neuron is determined by the many incoming signals it receives on its different branches. The neuron's output takes the form of chemical messages released by the impulses onto target neurons. It was in these terms that I came upon an intuitive belief. It was not a belief that I could justify by a logical argument. Rather, it emerged from the totality of what I knew about human memory and animal nervous systems. As I have discovered over the years, this belief also emerged from what I knew at that time but did not know that I knew.

My intuition was that an arrangement of connections among a small number of neurons could achieve the learning of a discrete association. This arrangement would provide for a soft-wired pathway to change into a connected hard-wired path when the hard-wired and soft-wired signals repeatedly occurred close together in time.

Such a network of neurons would probably have seemed reasonable to many students of the brain at that time. My further intuition that these elementary associative networks existed throughout the brain required a greater leap of faith, however. Higher cognitive functions of humans would be constructed from simple associations, such as that underlying a Pavlovian conditioned response. Multiplication into vast arrays of the simple associative networks underlying Pavlovian conditioning would generate a capacity to recognize patterns. From these intuitions, I put together a plan to test their reality.

If complex memory systems are composed of elementary memory systems, then perhaps the elementary memory systems emerged early in the course of evolution. As animals evolved, their memory systems might have acquired increased numbers of elementary associative networks, with some of these networks becoming joined together in a kind of matrix. Then my experimental approach should be to look among lower animals for the elementary associative network. Once found, the network would then have to show the anticipated features for learning an association. If those features were present and actually enabled the animal to learn an association, I would then undertake a much more painstaking molecular analysis. The specific molecular mechanisms of memory identified in the lower animal's network could then be sought in more complex mammalian brains. In this way, I might directly test the generality of memory mechanisms. On the basis of that accumulated evidence, it might then become possible to create a mathematical model of how complex systems might be built from the simple associative networks found in lower animals. If the model showed unusual pattern recognition capabilities, I might make inferences about how advanced brains memorize and recognize patterns. This would be my strategy.

To begin, I had to ask if it was possible to find in nature the hypothetical network I imagined should be able to learn an association. If I found the network, would that network learn an association? Would I find the memory site for the association? Would the mechanisms generalize to mammalian brains? I would have to answer these and many other questions to validate the strategy. I knew that at any point along the hypothesized route I could meet a fatal discrepancy, which would mean starting over, looking for another preparation, a new strategy, or a new hypothesis. But as long as my small steps were confirmed, I would be encouraged to continue. I expected that somewhere, sometime, my strategy would fail, but the thrill of the notion that my hypothesis might be correct was too seductive for me to resist.

ROOTS

MEMORY, EXPERIENCE, PRACTICE ARE ALSO FACTS, THE LAWS OF
WHICH CAN BE INVESTIGATED, AND WHICH CANNOT BE DECREED
AWAY, EVEN IF THEY ARE NOT TO BE SMOOTHLY AND SIMPLY
REFERRED TO THE KNOWN LAWS OF EXCITATION AND CONDUCTIVITY
IN NERVE FIBERS. . . .

—Hermann von Helmholtz

I didn't begin my search in a vacuum. Although my dual interests in psychology and biology reflect my own development, they also continue a tradition of inquiry rooted in the thoughts and observations of previous generations. From the time of Aristotle, the strange dichotomy of mind and body, form and substance, has piqued human curiosity. It wasn't until Descartes, however, that the puzzle began to assume a more modern guise.

Somewhat indulged even as a schoolboy, Descartes enjoyed a gentleman's leisure, often spending hours lying in bed contemplating the universe. His view of the body and the soul as "substances," one "extended" and the other "unextended," suggests his empirical, analytic approach to abstract philosophical issues. Although he was a brilliant mathematician (he invented analytic geometry while serving as a military officer), he was also deeply religious and concerned that his adventuresome thoughts not lead him into heresy. Recorded almost

29

four centuries ago, his thoughts show precocious insight into nervous system physiology. He was intuitively beginning to understand how the brain interacts with the body through the electrical signaling of all the elements of the peripheral nervous system—the sensory and motor nerves and neurons in our limbs and spinal cord, the nerves that control digestion, heart rate, and blood pressure. He wrote, for example,

It is to be observed that the machine of our bodies is so constructed that all the changes which occur in the motion of the spirits may cause them to open certain pores of the brain rather than others, and reciprocally, that when any one of these pores is opened in the least degree more or less than is usual by the action of the nerves which serves the senses, this changes somewhat the motion of the spirits, and causes them to be conducted into the muscles which serve to move the body in the way in which it is commonly moved on occasion of such action. . . .

Descartes (1596–1650) never resolved the problem of how an observable machinelike body communicates with an unobservable soul. Observing his own thoughts through introspection, however, did seem to make his spiritual world more accessible. Despite being constrained by religious beliefs, his was one of the first clear suggestions that an organ like the brain can contribute to the "soul" and to conscious experience.

Descartes's dual interests in philosophy and empirical science continued in the work of Leibnitz (1646–1716). Like Descartes, Leibnitz was a brilliant mathematician. He shares credit with Newton for developing calculus, in response to the need for a precise description of the movement and interaction of natural bodies such as the planets. But while Newton chose to focus on physics, Leibnitz, like Descartes, was captivated by the relation of the observer to the observed. He, more than anyone of his time, directed philosophy into the realm of psychology. He brought a physicist's outlook to psychological questions and a new degree of analysis to the thinking process itself.

In the early eighteenth century, Leibnitz's careful introspective observations led him to an awareness of associative memory. He conceived of associative memory events as being constituted of physical entities, which he called monads. Monads could associate during perception just as substances combine to form compounds. He also attempted with surprising success to distinguish between memories, perception, and feelings. In *Monadology* (1714), he wrote, for example "since feeling is something more than a simple perception, I agree that the general name of monads or entelechies is enough for simple substances which have only perception and that only those should be called souls in which perception is more distinct and accompanied by memory." Leibnitz's foreshadowing of experimental psychologists in the late nineteenth and early twentieth centuries is nothing less than startling. He already understood the essential nature of Pavlovian conditioning. He knew Pavlov's dog before Pavlov. He wrote, for example,

Memory provides a kind of consecutiveness to souls which simulates reason, but which must be distinguished from it. True, we see that, when animals have a perception of something which strikes them and of which they had a similar perception previously, they are led by the representation of their memory to expect whatever was connected with it in this earlier perception and so come to have feelings like those which they had before. When one shows a stick to dogs, for example, they remember the pain it has caused them and whine or run away.

Or in Pavlov's terms, the stick is at first a neutral stimulus, which the dog learns to associate with a clearly valued stimulus, namely the blow. The dog learns to react to the stick as if it were the blow itself. The dog whines at the mere sight of the stick. Leibnitz goes on to describe classical phenomena of learning psychology. Learning improves with practice, and if sufficiently strong stimuli are used, learning can occur in one trial: "The strong imagination which strikes and moves them [animals] comes either from the magnitude or from the number of the perceptions which preceded it. For often one single strong impression produces at once the effect of a long-formed habit or of many frequently repeated ordinary perceptions."

Leibnitz, and to a lesser extent Descartes, was moving toward a unified natural framework for both mind and body. They were, in effect, reducing the differences between body and soul, seeing that each was composed of similar basic material. This conceptual movement to include the mind in a natural framework, to include psychology within biology, was the forerunner of a related controversy between those who did and did not believe that life forms must derive from materials that are entirely absent from nonliving substances. Helmholtz (1821–1894) was the most famous and effective spokesman for the school which held that all entities in nature, live or inanimate, are composed of elements that obey the same universal chemical and physical rules. According to Helmholtz, there was no unique "vital force" required for nature to construct living beings. This intellectual position was an important step in the evolution of human thought and inquiry. Mind and body would eventually be conceived as governed by the same natural principles, some of which could be described by physical equations. In Helmholtz's work, there was a transformation of philosophy into psychology, psychology into biology, and, in a preliminary way, biology into physics and mathematics.

No one individual personally influenced these transformations as much as Hermann von Helmholtz. Over the span of a phenomenally productive career, this one individual measured the velocity of electrical signals in nerves, invented the ophthalmoscope (the instrument we still use to visualize the human retina in the clinic), formulated fundamental principles of physics and chemistry, and inspired the beginning of physiological psychology. It is fitting that his thesis, his first published work, demonstrated that fibers extending from a leech ganglion were in fact extensions of nerve cells within the ganglion. These fibers, now called axons, allow electrical signals to travel great distances through an organism from one neuron to another. Helmholtz later found that the speed with which the signal was conducted along a fiber, about 30 meters per second, was surprisingly slow. To make these measurements, he had to refine the accepted notions about electricity.

At this time, in keeping with his formal training as a physician, Helmholtz developed a keen interest in vision. His interest in the origin of colors, the path of light into the eye, and visual perception were embodied in his classic volumes on physiological optics. Also during this period, he formulated the physical principle of conservation of energy. This principle was Helmholtz's mathematical description of an insight first arrived at by Robert Mayer and later experimentally confirmed by Joule. The principle—which states that a quantity of energy is constant, independent of the form it assumes, whether in objects or in life forms—was Helmholtz's major success in laying to rest the controversy about "vital forces." Living organisms do not possess energy or "vital force" distinct from that of inanimate objects.

A common thread running through all of Helmholtz's work is its reference to perception. He was, it seems, always assessing the physical basis of human perception, whether he was studying nerve conduction, electrical currents that stimulate and flow along nerve fibers, energy forms that stimulate the senses (particularly those of vision and hearing), or the physiological basis of illusions. He vigorously advocated the view that optical illusions derive from learned experience and not just from the intrinsic properties of the human brain. He wrote, for example, that "The explanation of the possibility of illusions lies in the fact that we transfer the notions of external objects, which would be correct under normal conditions, to cases in which unusual circumstances have altered the retinal pictures. . . . We always believe that we see such objects as would, under conditions of normal vision, produce the retinal image of which we are actually conscious." He wrote further, "These illusions obviously depend upon mental processes which may be described as false inductions. But there are, no doubt, judgements which do not depend upon our consciously thinking over former observations of the same kind, and examining whether they justify the conclusion which we form." Here again, who can help but be impressed by his powerful juxtaposition of introspective conjectures with biological and physical observations. He was always working toward an integrated view (i.e., mind as a part of body), but he never hesitated to analyze mind function at the macroscopic level, in his own and others' thoughts, as well as at the microscopic, in terms of molecules and energy. He was keenly aware of how these different levels interact (i.e., how physics can determine psychology but also how our brain functions shape our notions of physical phenomena):

All that we apprehend of the external world is brought to our consciousness by means of certain changes which are produced in our organs of sense by external impressions, and transmitted to the brain by the nerves. It is in the brain that these impressions first become conscious sensations, and are combined so as to produce our conceptions of surrounding objects. If the nerves which convey these impressions of the brain are cut through, the sensation, and the perception of the impression, immediately cease. In the case of the eye, the proof that visual perception is not produced directly in each retina, but only in the brain itself by means of the impressions transmitted to it from both eyes, lies in the fact (which I shall afterwards more fully explain) that the visual impression of any solid object of three dimensions is only produced by the combination of the impressions derived from both eyes.

Helmholtz's style of science was to measure as precisely as possible the quantifiable features of natural phenomena, but his measurements were always in the context of more global questions. He never measured for the sake of measuring. He was curious about nerve conduction of electrical signals, for instance, because of its implications for human mental functions. Nor did he develop techniques because he was a tinkerer. For him, the challenge was not to make a better mouse-trap. He wanted to see inside the mouse. He invented the ophthalmo-scope to see into the eye and, indirectly, into the brain. The questions he had about human perception motivated the design of his experiments and the nature of his measurements. His interpretation of his experimental results took on meaning from these questions. Even his contributions to physics grew out of his passionate curiosity about how mind is explainable by the concrete natural phenomena that make up and interact with the body.

I believe that creative temperament is the product of such a complex interaction of experience with natural endowments that it is not now possible to teach our students to become scientists like Helmholtz. I also believe, however, that an intellectual environment can significantly affect a student's development. During the nineteenth century, global questions were of common concern. The Age of Enlightenment was still working its way into human views of nature and the place of humans in nature. Science, the infant daughter of philosophy, hadn't yet broken the umbilical cord. It was appropriate for scientists to think philosophically and vice versa. During the twentieth century, we, the recipients of so many pathfinding discoveries and revolutionary insights, suffer from an embarrassment of technological riches. Our techniques for measuring are so powerful and so abundant that it is easy to become enamored of the techniques in the absence of any burning questions. There is an entire lore to be learned in each technology, whether it be astronomy, nuclear physics, electrophysiology or molecular biology. Of course, we need our inventors and technology-oriented investigators, but in our current intellectual environment, the need for highly specialized knowledge as well as a sense of the mastery of science can encourage a loss of perspective and perhaps even curiosity. Discouragement can also come from too great an emphasis on the mathematical description of natural phenomena. When we can describe a natural principle mathematically, we have achieved the highest level of understanding it. We can then begin to use it to predict real events, and engineers can begin to make applications that can change the lives of everyone. Still there are many natural phenomena that we don't understand well enough to describe mathematically. They should not be considered less important or of lower value. Pecking orders sometimes seem to be created on the basis of how mathematical is the language used by scientists. The "hard" scientists look down on the "soft" scientists who make all those speculations. Psychologists, to this day, suffer from this attitude, although often their experimental designs and sophisticated analyses of data are as rigorous or even more rigorous than those of other disciplines. The nature of their subject matter, however, often does not yet lend itself to concise descriptions in which every variable can be accounted for and written into an equation.

Helmholtz grappled with the same difficulties during his career. He drew inspiration from psychology yet was always ambivalent toward it. And he was no stranger to controversy, even in his physics. His principle of the conservation of energy required persistent and vigorous defense, not only among his peers but with his own father, who although not a scientist held strong opinions and never hesitated to prosecute them with his son. Helmholtz had long grown accustomed to resisting his father and going in his own chosen directions. While at his father's request he learned several languages and steeped himself in classical literature, he had no great interest in any of it. While his father wanted him to write poetry, Helmholtz toyed with ideas about optics and vision. He developed confidence, not only in his own interests but in his own efforts. He needed that confidence to resist the initial suppression of his principle of the conservation of energy. Many of the senior physicists of the day dismissed it as simply borrowing from past work in the field and not sufficiently empirical. They did not appreciate that Helmholtz had been able to formulate the principle so precisely as to give it mathematical expression. Incredibly, Helmholtz did not succeed in publishing his paper in an accepted scientific journal. He was forced to publish it as a private monograph.

His difficulties in psychology were much greater. There were many more differences of opinion in this arena. Opinions about human perception could not be definitively confirmed or disproven. Helmholtz could never realize in questions about brain function the satisfying resolutions that he enjoyed in physics. He felt misunderstood and sometimes misinterpreted among the psychology-oriented thinkers of the day. He would therefore never have wanted to be considered the founder of experimental psychology, which in fact he was. He left this mission to his student, Wilhelm Wundt, who created the first laboratory exclusively devoted to psychology in the latter part of the nineteenth century. Yet Helmholtz never hesitated to hypothesize about, to push back the frontiers of our understanding of the mind.

He had no illusions that these were more than initial conjectures, and he could not understand that others could not easily make the same distinction between observations and working hypotheses. When he proposed his theory about "unconscious inference," he was making a formulation in a language different from the mathematics he used for laws of chemistry and physics. He was integrating all that he knew from introspection and natural observation into a gestalt that attempted to explain how learned experience determines perception. In that gestalt, memory of accumulated visual experience provides a context for sensations in the present to produce perception. Helmholtz was not addressing emotional experience in perception, but the principles could be the same. He was not describing the unconscious, yet the kind of brain processing involved in such perception was correctly thought of as unconscious. These same ideas fascinated me during my own ruminations. What we sense in the present takes on meaning and becomes perception from the vast stores of memories triggered by our sensations. A visual image that becomes a perception does not just trigger visual memories; it triggers memories acquired from other senses (e.g., hearing, smell, touch), as well as memories of the emotional milieus with which the sensed images have been associated. A Corot landscape may elicit a mood of tranquility; an El Greco scene of stormy clouds and lightning might make us fearful. Our feelings are part of the perception, although they do not directly contribute to recognition of the image or to distortions due to optical illusions. In this context, Helmholtz, with his roots in physics and chemistry, was not intellectually unrelated to successors with clinical and behavioral orientations such as Sigmund Freud and Ivan Pavlov. They were just focusing on different illusions—Helmholtz on visual illusions, Freud and Pavlov on emotional illusions.

I became familiar with Helmholtz, his life, his perspective, and his contributions, only after I had pursued my own research strategy for many years. Yet I came to feel as if I had always known him. I knew his tendency toward illness as a boy, encouraging his adventures in an inner landscape. For me, it was asthma so severe for about ten years of my childhood that for at least six weeks of each year I could not be exposed to ragweed pollen. As those annual days of isolation approached, I was seized by pangs of loss and separation. But then I prepared a set of choices for myself within the severe limits imposed upon me. I chose what I would read and what intellectual problems I would wrestle with. It was as if I planned my own minicurriculum and gedanken experiments. These games would substitute for those I played with friends in the fresh but for me temporarily poisonous air. Not surprisingly, when the hay fever season ended, I went through another period of separation and loss, only this time it was for the solitary but still exciting universe that I explored in a never-ending journey.

I knew Helmholtz's relationship with his father. His father, like mine, was well educated, fluent in many languages, excited by the philosophical and political issues of the day. His, like mine, had clear ambitions for his son and, as long as he had the power, disciplined and guided the study of his charge. Helmholtz, like me, had to come to grips with his own strong differences with his father. He learned to prepare rigorously and defend his own views, to discover his own true interests and passions. It was Helmholtz's interests, his Weltanschauung, however, with which I was most familiar. I have never identified intellectually with anyone as I have with Helmholtz. Here was someone who wanted to know how the mind works in terms of physical laws, and who was not willing to compromise. He never studied physics in total isolation from his study of the mind or vice versa. That Helmholtz was a Mozart and I a minor composer does not impair my identification with him. I don't know what kind of person he was, what his morals were, how he behaved toward others, although in his writings he never seems arrogant. I do know that as a thinker and a scientist for me he is a heroic figure.

Descartes's hint of the mind as a substance[1] took on a new meaning with electrical recording from nerve tissues, begun by Galvani[2] and continued by Helmholtz, Du Bois-Reymond, Bernstein, Adrian, and their twentieth-century successors. According to their observations, *substance* meant electrical signals. But it acquired another more concrete meaning over the course of the nineteenth century. Substance of mind also means tissue aggregates, or centers, in the brain. Fluorens, an Italian physician, showed that by destroying specific areas of an animal's brain he could eliminate specific mental capacities such as vision, smell, or hearing. In spite of his pioneering work relating brain damage to behavioral deficits, Fluorens did not believe in the localization of brain function. In his view, functions were spread throughout the brain, and therefore the loss of many distinct regions could affect the same function. This view was in direct conflict with that of his predecessor Franz Josef Gall who, without the benefit of discrete brain lesions, conceived of the brain as having regions whose functions were localized according to a precise map. In support of Gall's approach,

Paul Broca demonstrated a pathological brain lesion at autopsy of a patient who had lost the power of speech. Broca had had the opportunity to examine the patient a few days before and thereby establish that the patient's muscles and their nervous control for making speech sounds were intact, as was his ability to hear. This was the first convincing evidence that a localized brain region was responsible for control of a higher mental function. Later it would become clear that mental functions such as speech could often be impaired or eliminated by lesions in a number of regions. The principle of localization was still confirmed, however, albeit in somewhat greater complexity than originally assumed.[3]

It remained for Camilo Golgi in Italy and Ramon y Cajal in Spain to make the next giant step, to further reveal the "extensions" of what Descartes had called the "unextended substance" of mind. Golgi had discovered a wondrous technique for staining the entire structure of individual nerve cells or neurons. There were other stains that colored brain tissue, but the stained cells were so densely packed that it was not possible to tell where one cell ended and another began. The Golgi technique, for reasons not entirely understood even today, picked out single neurons among a host of others in the immediate vicinity. It was as if by chance the stain, often appearing like black ink, found an opening through which it poured in to fill up every remote corner of the neuron's structure. This allowed Golgi, as well as his contemporaries, to reveal the complete structure of individual neurons. Even the often complex, delicate branches conducting signals to and from the main trunks of the neuronal tree could be defined. Although Golgi used his technique to explore many neuronal tissues, his efforts paled by comparison to those of his soon-to-be arch rival, Ramon y Cajal.

Cajal was, from childhood, a tough fighter who prided himself on his physical prowess. There was always a wild side to Cajal, a side that refused to submit to authority, whether about how he should behave, what he should study, or in what he should be interested. Like Helmholtz, he had a father who had strong and rigid ideas about how his son should be molded. Cajal's love of art, particularly painting, did not fit into his father's ideas. As in many struggles between Cajal and his father, Cajal never conceded his true interests but made important gestures of compliance. Later in his career he was grateful for the disciplines that had been imposed, which he could use toward goals he himself had chosen.

Trained as a physician, Cajal specialized in pathology, which focused his attention on the structures of cells and tissues. In his now classic anatomical studies of nervous systems, he could use his analytical and scientific abilities and his artistic flair. His pictures of stained neurons and neuronal networks are scientific and artistic marvels. Even to the nonscientist, who cannot see the function implicit in the structure, the intricate details of each neuron's anatomy have an intrinsic beauty. Cajal combined stains of many individual neurons into collections, or networks, which he painted as they would occur naturally. They might occur in the retina, which processes visual patterns sensed by the eye, or in the cerebellum, a central brain region important for coordinating movement. He also sketched collections of neurons outside the brain, as in ganglia of the sympathetic nervous system, responsible for our involuntary functions such as heart rate, blood pressure, and digestion. Not only are the sketches exquisite, but as integrations of thousands of individually stained neurons in separate tissue slices, they represent a conceptual synthesis, suggesting testable hypotheses about how the brain works.

Using Golgi's technique, Cajal revolutionized our concept of what the brain and, by implication, the mind is. The brain is a seemingly infinite collection of precisely ordered networks of cells communicating with each other in the language of electrical signals. The activity, or processing, of these networks allows us to sense, remember, feel, plan, decide, and act. The biological and physical basis for mind had at last been seen.

A particularly interesting implication arose from Cajal's stains and sketches that would be fiercely contested by Golgi and many other contemporaries. Cajal found that the branches of one neuron ended in very discrete terminals on the branches of other stained neurons. Using the idiosyncratic property of the Golgi technique to stain one neuron at a time in isolation from its neighbors, Cajal reasoned that the terminal endings of one neuron were sending signals to the next neuron at their discrete points of contact. These points of contact, which would come to be known as synapses, assumed a role of paramount importance in Cajal's mind. This was where information collected and integrated by one neuron was transferred to the next. From his studies of brain tissue at different stages of development, he further inferred that the points of contact multiplied as the networks developed postnatally. Presumably this was how networks could change not only during development but also with aging and perhaps even with experience.

Golgi championed an almost opposite point of view. He claimed that these points of contact were merely sites where one neuron received nourishing ingredients from the other. In Golgi's view, the nourishment did not constitute signaling, which he thought was accomplished by dense tangles of neuronal fibers coming together in the form of tracts, which course from one brain region to another.

The controversy that raged between Cajal and Golgi was not entirely resolved in their own time, although the majority opinion leaned in Cajal's favor. Cajal's view had gained wide acceptance by the end of the nineteenth century, and during the next ninety years, many breathtaking experiments using high-powered microscopy and electrophysiology would confirm and extend Cajal's inferences about the synaptic junctions that convey signals between neurons. Yet Golgi also deserves and receives an enormous amount of credit. He not only discovered the technique that made Cajal's observations possible, his own observations, like Cajal's, pointed toward an anatomical basis for the brain—networks of neurons. In spite of Golgi's mistaken notions of how the neurons communicated with each other, he did deduce that there must be an important traffic of signaling among the neurons, which is the essence of the neuronal network. Golgi's general inference about large groups of neurons, then, was not unlike Cajal's. This idea would come to dominate the efforts of twentieth-century neurobiologists, and even mathematicians, who attempted to model higher brain functions.

In the perspective of history, the rivalry between these two men seems to have stemmed not so much from intellectual differences as from their emotional needs and responses. It is said that their rivalry was so intense that throughout their long careers they spoke to each other only once, when they exchanged a few words at the time they shared the Nobel Prize.

There were, then, two strong currents of investigation rushing nineteenth-century thought toward the incorporation of mind into body. One arose from physicists' studies of the electrical properties of the nervous system. The other gave structural definition to the brain, which ultimately came to be known as a dense concentration of neuronal networks. However, a third empirical thrust was needed to transform philosophical inquiries about the mind into neuroscience. The mind and the behavior it controls had to be assessed by quantitative empirical methods, not just introspection. Although Helmholtz contributed, a few scientists developed an entire methodology now called psychophysics. Their objective was to directly measure perception as experienced by humans. A contemporary of Helmholtz, Gustav Fechner, played the leading role.

Like Helmholtz, Cajal, and Descartes, Fechner was trained as a physician. Like them, he was also passionately interested in both quantitative empirical phenomena, things one could touch and see, and intangible phenomena such as mind and perception. For the first part of his scientific career (he never did practice medicine), he was chiefly concerned with physics. In the course of this work, he began to analyze perceived images left after looking into bright lights, such as the sun. Perhaps as a result of damage to his eyes from these studies, Fechner experienced several years of painful illness. Among other symptoms, his eyes were hypersensitive to light and could only be used for brief intervals. Fechner, like Descartes and Helmholtz during their childhood illnesses, withdrew to an inner world of thought. Here he began new investigative adventures, now focused on human sensations and their relationship to stimuli in the external world.

Another contemporary, Ernst Weber, provided a foundation on which Fechner could build his conceptual framework. Weber had brilliantly demonstrated that two pins touching a person's skin will only be perceived as two stimuli if they are a minimum distance apart. This distance will vary with the part of the body's surface stimulated: the tip of a finger can distinguish two pins at a much smaller distance than the back of a hand. Weber concluded that the noticeability of the difference between stimuli must be related to the strength of the stimulus. Weber was claiming something hard to believe in his day: the perception of a stimulus had quantifiable features. In other words, principles beginning to be accepted for electrical signals in nerve fibers might also be applied to mental functions.

Fechner first described in a mathematical equation what Weber had observed and postulated. He then wrote an equation that described how the magnitude of sensation that first becomes noticeable depends upon the stimulus intensity. This equation was the first mathematical expression for what Fechner had intuitively believed all along. *Mind is made up of bodily parts and functions.* Mind, in this case sensation, has a measurable relationship to stimuli with physical properties. Here was Fechner's attempt to wed mind and physics—still considered today as the founding of psychophysics. Radical concepts and discoveries are seldom accepted easily, and Fechner's Law was no exception. It stirred controversy that was both international in scope and long-lasting. Still, he received considerable recognition in his lifetime, and his law is still valid today for a limited range of stimulus strengths.

In historical perspective, Fechner, with Weber's brilliant assistance, was responsible for a major breakthrough in ending the assault on mind-body dualism.[4] But there were two other revolutionaries whose contributions to this conceptual breakthrough cannot be overlooked—Sigmund Freud and Ivan Pavlov. They analyzed sensory and remembered experience and concluded that minds did not just function for their own sake or for some higher other-worldly purposes; minds worked in the service of basic physical needs and drives. In their view, the human organism was more predictable, even more machinelike than ever before imagined.

In scientific style, Sigmund Freud and Ivan Pavlov could not have been more different. Pavlov conducted careful quantitative experiments with animals. He measured the amount and properties of dogs' gastric secretions released into a surgically created pouch, which allowed continuous monitoring. Freud, for most of his career, worked as a clinician. His observations were not carefully controlled. They were largely anecdotal, anything but quantitative, and certainly not reliably reproducible. Listening to and watching his patients, Freud made inferences about the nature of their thought processes, their motivations, and the interaction of thought and motivation. These two men, with very different styles and points of view, eventually concentrated their efforts on similar mysteries. One of these was associative memory.

Freud became aware of how his patients, following the "talking-cure" developed by his mentor, Josef Breuer, began to make connections, or notice links, in their memories. They talked to Freud of one memory after another, linked together as if in a chain of past experiences. Often the sense of the links was not immediately apparent. Events that occurred at approximately the same time or place might be associated. Or, less easily deduced, events might be linked to the same emotion. Freud found that patients encouraged to associate freely, without an immediate or directed goal, would sometimes remember events long forgotten that had powerful emotional significance. He eventually developed this technique of "free association" into an entire therapeutic approach, which became known to the world as psychoanalysis.

Pavlov, on the other hand, found that dogs learned to salivate at the sound of a bell that repeatedly occurred just before the smell of meat.

Soon his interest shifted from the control of gastric secretion to the organic basis for the dog's learned salivation behavior. The dog, like Freud's patients, could also learn associations that involved satisfaction of primary drives. Whenever the dog heard the sound of the bell, it learned to expect the presentation of meat and to salivate based on this expectation. A bell's sound and the smell of meat are not the same as the name or face of a parent recalled by a patient. But the process of association, of the linkage between such simple and complex sensed events, seemed to Pavlov to be potentially quite similar. This was Pavlov's brilliant contribution. He understood that the association learned by a dog might serve as a model for far more complex associations, not only for the dog but also for humans. The associations Freud studied in all of their complexity in the clinic, Pavlov abstracted and analyzed in the laboratory. The exalted status of homo sapiens, already questioned by Darwin, now was further challenged by the observations of Freud and Pavlov, but this challenge raised the hope of approaching heretofore inaccessible illnesses of the mind.

Implicit in both men's questions was the belief that there was an apparatus to account for human behavior and thought, an apparatus whose malfunctions might be repaired. By the end of the nineteenth century it was becoming increasingly acceptable to take a less passive attitude toward mental illness. There was less resignation, recourse to prayer, or interminable confinement of patients.[5] Freud rightfully understood that an activist approach to mental illness at that time must be experimental. There were no clearly effective therapies, nor was there a coherent theory of mental function. So his attitude was one of starting from the beginning. While he was testing techniques such as hypnosis and free association, he was also making observations from which he slowly constructed a conceptual framework for understanding the formation of personality and accounting for behavior, both normal and pathological. His overriding emphasis, one that would be tempered later in the twentieth century, was on human learning from experience and how what was learned determined behavior to achieve pleasure and avoid pain. His focus was on nurture, not nature, on experience, not constitutional factors.

Freud considered his patients' relationships with others, including himself, as reenactments of relationships in the past. Analyzing those relationships, he attempted to teach his patients to do the same and uncover the original roles, acted in the present but assigned by the past. Freud distinguished between different levels of mental experience, conscious and unconscious. His therapeutic objective was to bring unconscious memories into consciousness, to bring about catharsis—a purging of old ways and expectations that would free an individual to live differently.

There were, according to Freud, three primary components of the personality: the id, consisting of primary, largely unconscious, drives; the ego, the collective thoughts used on behalf of an individual's interests, including satisfying the id; and the superego, the aggregate of society's dicta and mores, which circumscribe the activities of the ego. Less important than the scientific accuracy or demonstrability of these constructs were their profound philosophical underpinnings and their usefulness in asking further questions. For example, Freud's theories stressed that personality results from prolonged human development. An individual gradually acquires, by learning from experience, a vast collection of thoughts and capabilities that become incorporated into a unique style of behavior, particularly for relating to other people. Freud suggested that there were stages of development in which an individual could remain if he could not successfully adjust to the changing physical appearance and needs of the body. As a part of development, the dominant pleasure drive shifts from oral to genital. The ego has to acquire the necessary knowledge and control to accomplish this transition without residual conflict with the superego. Many of Freud's hypotheses about mental experience have undergone successive transformations in the practice of his successors, such as Alfred Adler, Carl Jung, and Karen Horney. Therapeutic strategies also have evolved in many directions, although classical psychoanalysis still has its adherents. Some say Freud was antifeminist, fixated on sex, too egotistical, or just plain wrong, but few can doubt the monumental impact of his thinking on twentieth-century notions of mind as an integral part of the body.

Though Freud himself made few measurements, his Weltanschauung encouraged measurements. It said look for centers in the brain that when stimulated will convey the experience of pleasure. Discover brain regions responsible for directing attention to some thoughts and not others. Tease out the physiology that inhibits the neuronal activity of traumatic memories. Reveal what happens when the brain is asleep and begins to dream. And, perhaps most of all, find out what an association means in terms of the electrical signals, structure, and internal molecules of neurons. These were the challenges he entrusted to the neuroscientists of the twentieth century.

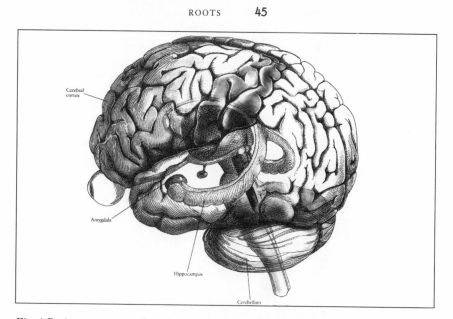

Fig. 1 Brain structures such as the hippocampus, amygdala, and the cerebral cortex are all likely to be involved in acquiring, storing, and recalling human memories. The collective experience of scientists in the laboratory and clinic over the last few centuries has implicated the participation of these structures in memory processes. (From *Brain, Mind, and Behavior*, F. E. Bloom and A. Lazerson, 1988. W. H. Freeman, N.Y.)

Fig. 2 Golgi-stained neurons are distributed throughout the brain structure known as the hippocampus. Using the technique developed by Golgi and brilliantly applied by Cajal, Miles Herkenham reveals the structures of individual neurons in exquisite detail. Golgi and Cajal shared the Nobel Prize for their breathtaking revelations of brain anatomy at the turn of the twentieth century. This slice of hippocampus has been magnified about 5x. (Courtesy of Dr. Miles Herkenham)

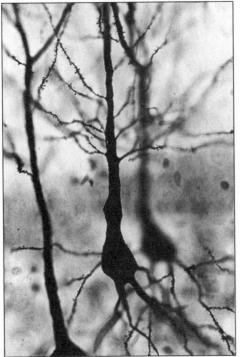

Fig. 3 Further magnification (100x) of the same hippocampal slice as in Fig. 2 reveals individual pyramidal cell neurons and their branches. The pyramid-like swelling or cell body contains the neuron's DNA and other cellular machinery for manufacturing its protein constituents. (Courtesy of Dr. Miles Herkenham)

Fig. 4 At even higher magnification (1000x), the individual swellings or "spines" are seen studding the branches of the pyramidal cell's dendritic tree. Each spine is in intimate synaptic contact with an incoming pre-synaptic branch (not stained and, therefore, not visible) which releases chemicals that carry messages across the synapse to the spine. (Courtesy of Dr. Miles Herkenham)

THE AGE OF TECHNOLOGY

It began when Galrani observed a frog's leg twitch in response to an unknown flow of electrical charge. Such electrical signaling would evolve in the thoughts and observations of his intellectual descendants into a general mechanism for communication between cells, and that communication plays a critical role in making the human brain a mind.

The nineteenth century saw the foundations of a new science built from philosophy, physics, psychology, and biology. The coalescence of so many different fields into one focused discipline, neuroscience, depended on the evolution of all human thought until that time. No age or nation was the exclusive source of this new perspective, since it derived from Aristotle, Vesalius, and Descartes, as much as from Leeuwenhoek, Galvani, Helmholtz, Cajal, and Pavlov. The culture and intellectual environment of nineteenth-century Germany, however, provided just the right ferment of ideas and observations. Here, the religious and political atmosphere conspired with the Industrial Revolution to encourage radical thinking. It was here that the conceptual underpinnings of a biological basis for mind emerged.

A new awareness was abroad—one that before could not be acknowledged with even furtive glances, without risk of ostracism, or perhaps persecution. This was consciousness-raising on a grand scale—an intellectual revolution. It did not happen without enormous resistance even among the science-oriented, let alone those who represented religious orthodoxy. Real power was at stake. Control of people and resources would shift to entirely new groups. Observations suggested that the mind is explainable by the flow of electrical signals through dense networks of cells. These networks existed in animal brains as well as human brains. What, then, made us unique? What endowed us with spiritual and moral capacities? These questions were examined now with an honesty and freedom previously denied.

It is not just culture that presides over an intellectual movement. Personalities are also important. In Germany, Johannes Müller first proposed that our different sensations, touch, vision, hearing, and taste, must activate different nerve fibers. Our sensations must arise from the responses of those fibers. Building on Charles Bell's and Francois Magendie's ideas about the function of spinal cord nerves, Müller proposed that each human sense derives from nerves with specialized properties. Müller would be proven wrong about some of the details of his claims. Individual nerves have so many fibers that they carry signals for different senses. He was also wrong in his implication that there was something unique about the fibers themselves to suit them for carrying signals about light rather than taste. But he was correct that there are sensory neurons, such as the rods and cones of our eyes or the hair cells in our ears, that are uniquely designed to convert light or sound into an electrical signal. He also understood that discrete anatomical structures, in this case the fibers rather than the fiber bundles, conduct signals into particular brain areas to create our experience of discrete stimuli such as light, pressure, or sound. This principle was important. It represented a bold departure from accepted dogma. To make and defend such a breakthrough required a personality willing to take risks, to challenge authority, to be wrong. None of this was wasted on his brilliant students, who included Helmholtz, Du Bois-Reymond, Bernstein, and even the Russian Sechenov. Nor did his call to obtain physical measurements to explain these events go unheeded.

I can imagine that Müller was tolerated, even esteemed, by his colleagues in Berlin at that time. And because of this, an innovative, sometimes radical tradition, continued by Du Bois-Reymond and Helmholtz, was encouraged. I can also imagine that in another milieu Müller might have been held in contempt. In another day, a premium might have been placed on careful, exhaustive cataloguing of all known species of plants and animals. Painstaking comparison of interspecies differences and similarities would then lead to classes of life forms. Precise quantitative measurements of where electrical signals arise in the human body in response to a touch might lead to a map of nerve fibers. Relationships of signal flow to behavior could then be slowly established by repeated observations. Not that such manner of science was without its own magnificent fruit.

Nineteenth-century England saw Darwin's *On the Origin of Species* emerge from the conceptual milieu of a place and time that included Wallace and Huxley, among others. Darwin's painstaking observations were the basis for one of the most radical theories in the history of human thought. But the intellectual atmosphere of nineteenth-century England was not like that of Germany.

Nevertheless, the English atmosphere was soon to give rise to a whole generation of brilliant scientists who were to dominate the course of twentieth-century neuroscience, just as the Germans had dominated during the preceding century. This English generation applied and helped develop a level of technology that until the twentieth century could only be imagined. It was one thing for Julius Bernstein (with Ostwald's help) to propose that an electrical signal arose from a moving wave, which reduced or eliminated the separation of charge across the wall of the nerve fiber. It was quite another for Alan Hodgkin (with the help of Cole, Huxley, Katz, and Keynes) to demonstrate that this wave arose when charged salt atoms such as sodium moved into the nerve and other salt atoms of potassium moved out of the nerve. Du Bois-Reymond had discovered the nerve signal, Helmholtz had made the first measurement of its velocity, and Bernstein had formulated a remarkably prescient theory to explain it. But the English school had the right "attitude" to uncover the route to its molecular heart. Their attitude was calm and collected, very persistent, technically masterful, but not radical. As Ragnar Granit, the great Swedish neurophysiologist, was to observe later, Charles Sherrington, the father of the English school, was not responsible for breakthrough discoveries or theories. Yet few could doubt that he was one of the outstanding physiologists of the last three centuries. His contributions arose from long, methodical investigations, which generated a synthesis. That synthesis confirmed and expanded the notions of some such as Ramon y Cajal while weakening the positions of others such as Golgi. He coined the term *synapse*, from the Greek root meaning "to clasp," to describe the functional connections he observed between neurons. He did not, however, first conceive of, discover, or demonstrate the connections themselves, nor did he reveal the nature of their messages.

Immersion in the history of one's own intellectual roots brings special rewards. It traces the origins of ideas, including one's own, right up until the present. It graces the investigative pursuit with an excitement that can only come when time is compressed and questions are answered in minutes instead of centuries. It also offers orientation, even a sense of belonging. I discover, for example, which group, which environment I find sympathetic to my own personality, my own style. It is not that the twentieth-century English tradition of electrophysiology is better or worse than the nineteenth-century German tradition. Each tradition achieved different objectives and was able to meet different challenges. Most likely, one tradition would not be possible without the other. Lacking an historical perspective, however, I might find myself surrounded by Englishmen and conclude that there were no Germans, that photographing a synapse that has been magnified ten thousand times is intrinsically more worthwhile than my recording electrical signals from a network during memory acquisition; that my constructing a computer model of associative learning is not as serious as searching for molecules that regulate the movement of sodium into a nerve fiber. Remember, real power is involved in the values that peers and authorities assign. The traditions of a place and time are perpetuated by political decisions, which impact on individual recognition as well as livelihood.

A rich inheritance was left to the twentieth century, and the beneficiaries did not squander their wealth. Simply summarized, by the end of the nineteenth century it was generally accepted that the human brain consisted of vast numbers of neurons that could be grouped into pathways and networks and which communicated with each other by transmitting electrical signals along their fibers. Although it was not accepted that these networks accounted for the mind or the soul, that possibility had become increasingly more defensible. There was no doubt, however, that the brain's networks, once understood, could account for sensations and movement. Higher functions such as speech, memory, and emotions were also thought by many to be within empirical reach. The most important contributions of twentieth-century neuroscientists, led by the English, established the fundamental biological nature of communication within these networks. There have been three major subjects of this research: the nerve impulse, the synapse, and the organization of the connections within the networks. Although outstanding investigators in many nations, including Germany and the United States, made important contributions, the

English school was particularly instrumental in arriving at a detailed understanding of how electrical signals travel along nerve fibers and how neurons send messages to each other across synaptic junctions.

By the end of the nineteenth century, the stage had been set for a drama that would ultimately take fifty years to unfold. Ramon y Cajal had established a consensus, by no means unanimous, that each neuron was separate from every other. One neuron gave rise to a long fiber or axon, which toward its end divided into many branches of progressively smaller dimensions. The branches, in turn, ended in small knobs, which were distributed along the receiving branches of other neurons. Based on his stains of neurons and other studies, Cajal claimed that one neuron signaled another at the points of contact made by the terminal knobs. Cajal and his supporters were opposed by Golgi and his supporters, who believed that neurons were connected to each other by an elaborate branching network, or "reticulum." Within the reticulum, the branches of separate neurons were continuous with each other. Signaling was accomplished, then, not across junctions between neurons but along the fibers that made one neuron continuous with another.

It had to be established that synapses—the junctions—actually existed. This issue would not be definitively resolved without new technology. The development of the electron microscope would, by the 1950s, allow direct visualization of the synapse. During the first four decades of the twentieth century, however, sufficient evidence was accumulated to make an overwhelming case in Cajal's favor. For example, studies would demonstrate that cuts across the axonal branches of one neuron caused the synaptic knobs and their branches of origin to degenerate without causing degeneration of target neurons. Charles Sherrington and others inferred delays between the electrical signals of one neuron (for example, a sensory cell of the spinal cord) and the resulting electrical signal of a target neuron (such as a motor neuron whose signals cause muscle contraction). The delay was too long to be explained by the simple travel of an electrical signal from the sensory neuron to the motor neuron. Another event, presumably the release of a message at the synapse, must, he reasoned, require the additional time. The presence of synapses could, in fact, explain a host of observations made in his pioneering studies of the spinal cord.[1]

Sherrington did most of his experiments with minimal technology by cutting critical nerves and/or administering electric currents. Yet, he was unusually artful in his technique, able to keep a dog alive for example, even in the absence of its brain. This required delicate surgery in which hemorrhage was prevented. From lesions and electrical stimuli, Sherrington moved to a series of extremely elegant behavioral experiments. For instance, he constructed a stimulus that resembled the bite of a flea: a brief mild electric current passed through a minute dissecting pin implanted in the most superficial skin layer. A sufficient number and frequency of the bitelike shocks indeed elicited a typical reflexive scratching response of the dog's leg. This behavior was exhibited even by dogs who had had their brains removed, or decerebrate dogs. There was enough of a neuronal apparatus, a network if you will, to mediate the behavior. It was as if the sensory signal received along one sensory nerve from a limb had been reflected from the spinal cord back to the limb along a motor nerve to control a movement. Thus the term *reflex* was applied to describe the event.

The complexity and profundity of Sherrington's variations on this basic experimental theme are breathtaking. He showed, for example, that a series of bite stimuli and scratch responses was followed by a period of increased sensitivity, in which fewer and milder bite stimuli were needed to trigger a scratch response. This implied another function of synaptic junctions—modification by stimulus history. A synaptic junction might have such nonelectrical properties, but a pure electrical signal along a continuous path between neurons would not be expected to change as a result of repeated stimulation. Sherrington found that different kinds of stimuli such as muscle stretch, position changes, and bites could interact or sometimes oppose each other. Within the spinal cord, choices had to be made whereby one stimulus and the response it elicited was given priority over another. Sherrington inferred that the separate synaptic signals elicited by distinct stimuli could add to or subtract from each other. The neuron served as "a final common path," in Sherrington's words, on which the incoming sensory signals converged. This, then, was another critical function of synapses: allowing the neuron to integrate the incoming signals. Information sensed in the limbs was processed by the clusters of synapses on the spinal cord neurons. As a result of the processing, a behavioral response was chosen, coordinating with other behaviors through the synaptic processing of the spinal cord. Scratching of one limb alternated with that of another. A decerebrate animal could, through its limb movements, still effectively right itself in response to a disorienting fall. Wetting the decerebrate animal's limb surfaces to simulate immersion was followed by the shaking movements so typical of dogs after a swim. Sherrington was, in effect, painting a picture of how

synapses function. He couldn't see them. He couldn't record their signals, nor did he know the molecular nature of their messages. Yet, by
observing how they processed information, he built a formidable case
for their existence. It is, therefore, fitting that it was he who gave them
their name.

In breathing life into his theory of synaptic function, Sherrington
was also creating an entire experimental approach to the nervous system. Sherrington used the spinal cord, in the absence of a brain, as a
model for the brain. The spinal cord neurons with their synaptic junctions was the first "neural network" to be analyzed. It had inputs from
the sensory nerves. It had outputs through the motor nerves to the
muscle groups. It processed information. The "reflex arc" consisted of
sensory inputs that were integrated to arrive at a choice of behavioral
response. The brain, in essence, performs the same functions, although
at a far more complex level. Sensory information is received and evaluated, decisions are reached, and actions are taken. As a model network,
the spinal cord has numerous critical features in common with the
brain. These features could be analyzed and understood in the spinal
cord long before they were accessible in the brain. Decades later, the
integrative operations of "final common paths" began to be revealed in
brain regions such as the cerebellum, the hippocampus, and the thala-
mus. Sherrington did not discover the synapse nor did he conclusively
prove its existence. But his spinal model of how the synapse works in
neuronal networks is still valued today. Sherrington's model, like most,
had limited predictive power, however. Higher brain functions are
missing from decerebrate animals, such as emotions and memory.
These features would require other experimental preparations and different search strategies.

While Sherrington was accumulating his brilliant observations and
inferences about synapses, other entirely different approaches were
being taken to the study of these still hypothetical structures. Although
the actual structure of the synapse would not be revealed until the early
1950s by the electron microscope, the electrical and chemical events
responsible for the synaptic message received intense scrutiny during
the first half of the twentieth century.[2] Thomas Elliott, then in Cambridge, England, found that the drug adrenaline (a natural neurohor-
mone which mediates our reaction to stress) could produce the same
physiological responses elicited by electrical stimulation of sympathetic
nerves. Elliott proposed that the adrenaline, which had been isolated
from adrenal glands, might be normally released at synapses every time

the sympathetic nerves were stimulated electrically. This was the opening skirmish in a scientific battle that was to last almost fifty years. The dispute centered on the nature of the synaptic message. What carried information across the synapse—electric current or chemicals? The controversy was to involve many scientists in many countries. Of these, relatively few were responsible for the major developments.

In general, English scientists played the most important roles, but a fundamental breakthrough came in 1921 with the now classic experiment of German-born Otto Loewi. Loewi was wrestling with the question of synaptic transmission. Needing to conceive a definitive experiment, he struggled with potential experimental designs, without success. Then one night, he awoke with a shout and scribbled down a plan for what seemed to be a breakthrough. Unable to read his nocturnal notes on the following day, he could not remember his scheme accurately until he awoke the next night. Taking no chances, he went immediately to the laboratory and began the experiment.

Loewi obtained two frog hearts. In one, the nerve that controls slowing of the heartbeat was intact; in the other, it was severed. He stimulated the intact nerve to slow one heart in a separate chamber. He then transferred the fluid bathing this first heart to a chamber that contained the other heart. Remarkably, the second heart slowed in response to the fluid alone. Loewi had shown that a substance in essence was the messenger released by nerve stimulation. Loewi repeated the same experiment with a nerve that caused quickening of the heartbeat and obtained the predicted result. It was left to Henry Dale, an English physiologist, to isolate and eventually identify the substance as acetylcholine.[3] Loewi and Dale had provided strong evidence that the synapse between a nerve and a peripheral muscular target used chemical transmission. They did not resolve, however, the question of synaptic messages between neurons in the central nervous system—i.e., the spinal cord or the brain.

On this question, the battle would rage for another two decades, with John Eccles, an Australian physiologist, among the leaders of the opposition to a chemical basis for synaptic transmission in the brain. This was not a subdued battle. Positions were strongly stated. Rival positions might not be cited in publications. Emotions often ran high at meetings. It was, therefore, all the more remarkable that John Eccles not only changed his mind but was responsible for the definitive experiments demonstrating chemical synapses in the brain.

Anyone who has met John Eccles must be impressed by his erudition, brilliance, and intensity. He states his beliefs vehemently and with complete conviction. In his late seventies, when we occasionally participated in symposia together, the forcefulness of his ideas and his presentations were still inescapable. At that time, in the 1980s, he was presenting elaborate theories of consciousness and memory, and the burning issue was how a synapse might change to store a memory. The thoughts he shared were largely conjectures and speculations about the future. His confidence in his own vision was so compelling that I can imagine how formidable an advocate of electrical synaptic transmission he must have been during the 1930s and 1940s. After that period, however, the full force of his intensity was diverted to the support of his former opponents' position.

Eccles poured his energies into a series of magnificent experiments to discover chemical messengers at synapses between neurons in the spinal cord. With the micropipettes invented by Gerard and Ling in 1948, he began to penetrate and record from the same neurons Sherrington had so brilliantly analyzed within reflex networks. Eccles no longer had to infer the synaptic events, as Sherrington had. His micropipette inserted into the neuron amplified the event so that it could be displayed on the face of an oscilloscope. He could see the electrical response in a target neuron when one of its incoming synapses was activated. Eccles could electrically stimulate a sensory nerve to the spinal cord and record the synaptic responses from neurons that sent their fibers into motor nerves.

Finally, Sherrington's dream had become a reality. Eccles could directly measure the delay across the synaptic junction. He mimicked the message with applications of known chemical messengers. Even the charged atoms, or ions, responsible for the synaptic signal could be identified. Some of the synaptic events were excitatory. They made the target, or postsynaptic, neuron more positively charged, bringing it closer to the threshold for triggering the large electrical signals originally described by Du Bois-Reymond. Other synaptic events inhibited the neuron by making it more negatively charged and therefore less likely to trigger the electrical signals.[4] The predominance of chemical synaptic transmission in the central nervous system had been established and would be confirmed repeatedly in the following years. A large variety of chemical messengers would be identified and even begin to be linked to disorders of movement and mood. For example, a deficiency of the messenger dopamine was implicated in Parkinson's disease, which often results in uncontrollable shaking. Other messengers, such as norepinephrine and serotonin, were implicated in altered emotional states such as depression. Although research in these directions is still in its infancy, the positive clinical benefit of even our primitive knowledge suggests the exciting promise of what has already been revealed about synapses. Supplements of the neurotransmitter dopamine can bring the shaking hand of a Parkinsonian patient under control, although relief is often temporary. Drugs known to elevate levels of the neurotransmitter serotonin in the brain can restore the will to live in the hopelessly depressed. There were, of course, always more questions, many generated by the answers just obtained.

Bernard Katz, a German Jewish refugee, spent most of his long career in England. Here he found the right environment to pursue his questions in the modest, quiet, incisive, and doggedly determined manner that characterizes his style.[5] Together with a number of contemporary scientists including electronmicroscopists such as George Palade, Eduardo DeRobertis, and Sanford Palay, Katz assembled powerful evidence that chemicals are released at synaptic junctions in the form of packets, or quanta (singular, quantum). These packets, most evidence indicates, derive from minute spherical balls called vesicles, which can be visualized in the synaptic knob—the presynaptic terminal that releases the message. The quantal theory suggests that the strength of a chemical synaptic signal depends on the number of vesicles made and released from the presynaptic terminal onto postsynaptic targets.

It made intuitive sense that experience could modify the availability of the vesicles for release and thus the strength of the chemical synaptic message. This might be critical for soft-wired, learning-dependent circuits in contrast to hard-wired neuronal pathways. Like the existence of synapses, sites of learning in neural networks would however, become the center of their own drama, one that is still unfolding and in which I would play a role.

In the later part of his career, Katz would use even more sophisticated technology to measure the flow of charged atoms that generates the quantal electrical signals. Katz's experiments were a tour de force. They were right in the tradition of the amazing technological leaps of the English school that included Sherrington, Elliott, Adrian, Dale, Eccles, Katz, and Keynes, as well as Alan Hodgkin and Andrew Huxley. These last two were part of another saga.

Theirs was the story of how a large electrical signal arises and travels along a nerve fiber. Their saga began with Helmholtz's measurement of the signal's speed of travel, and Du Bois-Reymond's identification of the signal itself. Like the question of synaptic transmission, it would require twentieth-century technology and quantitative analysis to arrive at the answers.[6] The nervous system is filled with fibers that travel comparatively great distances. Mental functions and the coordination of movement depend on very rapid signaling along the fibers running back and forth between the neurons. Yet, based on principles of conventional electrical transmission, an electrical signal should decay in a nerve fiber almost before it got started. There had to be some means by which the signal was propagated. It could not just spread down the fiber, it had to be pushed, but pushed over and over again.

It would take almost one hundred years for the mystery to be solved. But even in the middle of the nineteenth century, people such as Julius Bernstein and Du Bois-Reymond were on the right track with notions of charge separation across the nerve fiber's wall, called its membrane.[7] According to Bernstein, current flowed not simply along the core solution of electrolytes within the nerve, but across the nerve membrane in a sequence of local patches extending along its entire length.[8] The crucial experiments were only possible, however, with the development of new technology.

Kenneth Cole and Howard Curtis worked at the Marine Biological Laboratory in Woods Hole, Massachusetts, in the late 1930s with a new preparation introduced by J. Z. Young. Young, a British biologist, described a nerve fiber, the giant axon of the squid, which had before then been almost entirely unknown. Here was a nerve fiber that was at least a hundred times larger than the largest human nerve fiber. It became possible for Cole and his colleagues in Woods Hole to place one metal electrode inside and one electrode outside the giant axon. The two electrodes were long wires, which were oriented parallel to each other along the length of the axon, with the axon membrane sandwiched between the two electrodes. This arrangement allowed accurate measurements of electrical potential differences between the two electrodes. Cole and Curtis in Woods Hole and Hodgkin and Huxley in Plymouth, England, found that the inside of the axon was more negatively charged than the outside. The separation of charge across the unstimulated axon membrane produced a potential difference, when measured by both groups, that was quite close to Bernstein's predictions.[9] The passage of a nerve impulse along the axon produced potential differences that could not be explained by Bernstein's theory, however. Other ions, particularly sodium, would have to move across the membrane to explain the magnitude of the stimulated axon's electrical signal called the nerve impulse.

The proof of sodium's role required a new level of sophistication in technology, which Cole and Curtis were able to provide. They designed an ingenious circuit for their electrodes to maintain the potential difference across the axon at a constant level. For each potential, they were able to monitor the current flowing across the membrane. Cole's procedure, called a voltage clamp, in effect made it possible actually to see the sodium ions flowing into the axon across its membrane and the potassium ions flowing out of the axon during the nerve impulse.

Alan Hodgkin spent a summer at Cole's laboratory in Woods Hole, where he learned his technique. Hodgkin was continuing a tradition that has persisted at the Marine Biological Laboratory for almost a century. Students and scientists from all over the world converge on the small town on Cape Cod to learn from each other, push back the frontiers of biological research, and take in the sun. Cole as I knew him, even in his eighties, was always the gentleman. Dressed nattily, with a characteristic bow tie, he could often be heard in the laboratory humming to himself while he worked. His voice, deepened into a croak by decades of cigarette smoking, projected even in a hum beyond the walls of his own laboratory to laboratories nearby such as mine, which for some years was right next door. The impression one got was unmistakable. This was a man making his own music with his thoughts and hands and deriving immense pleasure from the process. Since it was well before my time, I can only imagine Cole's excitement in sharing his new technique with Hodgkin and their marveling at the recordings that revealed the movement of ions across the axon membrane. But I can also imagine Cole's chagrin when Hodgkin, together with such colleagues as Andrew Huxley and Bernard Katz, took a commanding lead in research on the nerve impulse. From their extensive series of experiments back in England, they accumulated enough data to construct a comprehensive mathematical model that could quantitatively explain how the flow of sodium and potassium ions across the axonal membrane produced the nerve impulse as Du Bois-Reymond first recorded it and as we know it today.[10]

For many years after these important breakthroughs, the pores, or channels, necessary to explain ion flow through membranes remained only useful constructs within the equations of Hodgkin and Huxley. No one could see a channel or even obtain enough evidence to be sure channels actually existed. It was just until that time observations accumulated could be concisely explained by their presence. Through the sixties and seventies, however, the experiments of biochemists and physical chemists made the actuality of channels increasingly more likely.[11]

Finally, in the mid-1980s Shosaku Numa and his colleagues in Japan purified and isolated a channel for sodium ions. They were able to determine enough details of its molecular structure to suggest how changes in the spatial arrangement of its atoms allowed sodium ions to pass. They were also able to insert the molecular channels into nonliving artificial membranes, which then permitted sodium ion flow like that of a living cell wall. Now Bernstein's brilliant inferences had a concrete biological basis. The nerve impulse occurred when separation of electric charge was reduced by the flow of ions through molecular channels in the nerve membrane. These channels were found wherever electrical signals were generated in the nervous system, not just in the membrane of a nerve fiber. Light controls channels in the cell wall of visual sensory neurons. Sound waves control channels in the membranes of our auditory sensory cells, and odors control channels in the sensory cells for smell. Hormones such as insulin control channels in their target cells. In all of these cases, the chemical messengers released by an electrical signal at a synaptic junction regulate channels in the membrane of the synaptic target cell. In all of these cases, changes in ion flow through the channels produce electrical signals that are then used in functions as diverse as sensation, muscle contraction, and digestion.

With the technology of the twentieth century, scientists had conclusively demonstrated a new basis for communication among the billions of cells that make up our organ systems, particularly those of our brain. Charged salt atoms move through channels of cell walls to generate the electrical language of intercellular communication. The thought that our own languages, transmitted by the sound-wave patterns of our voices, might ultimately arise from such atom flow remained fantastic, but was now far from fantasy.

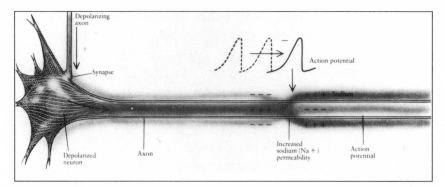

Fig. 5 An electrical signal, called the action potential, travels down the axon. A chemical message crosses a synapse on the cell body (on left) to trigger the action potential. The action potential spreads (to the right) as a wave of charged particles rushes across the axon membrane. Alan Hodgkin and Andrew Huxley shared the Nobel prize in 1963 for their measurements and mathematical description of the particle movements through pores or channels in the axon membrane. (From *Brain, Mind, and Behavior*, F. E. Bloom and A. Lazerson, 1988. W. H. Freeman, N.Y.)

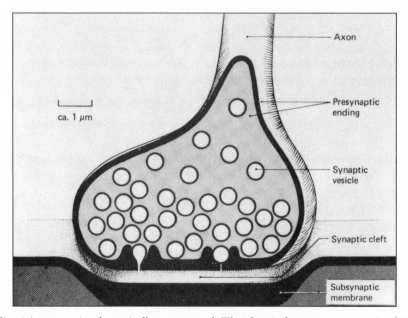

Fig. 6 A synapse is schematically represented. The chemical messengers contained in spherical vesicles are released from the branch ending of a sending neuron to cross the junction or cleft. In the cleft the chemical messengers combine with sensitive molecules called receptors that are imbedded within the membrane of a receiving or postsynaptic neuron. Bernard Katz was awarded the Noble Prize in 1970 for his measurements and mathematical description of these steps in synaptic transmission. (From *Fundamentals of Neurophysiology*, R. F. Schmidt, 1978. Springer-Verlag, N.Y.)

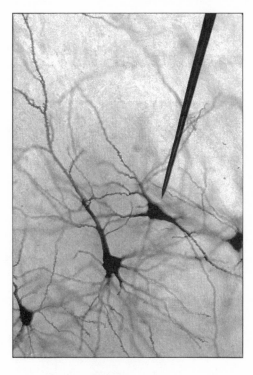

Fig. 7 A microelectrode is poised to penetrate a neuron. The microelectrode tip, too small to be seen here, can be inserted into the neuron without significant cellular damage. A minute electrical current flows from the neuron into the microelectrode and then into an amplifier that allows the experimenter to eavesdrop on conversations between neurons within networks. (Courtesy of Fritz/Goro. From "The Brain", D. H. Hubel, 1979. *Scientific American* 241 (3):9–17. W. H. Freeman, N.Y.)

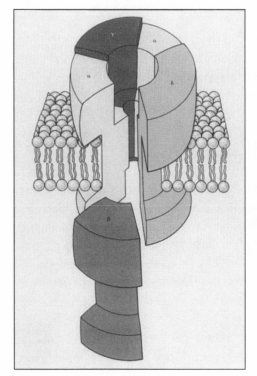

Fig. 8 Molecular model of a channel in a neuron's membrane. A chemical messenger combines with a receptor on a receiving membrane to produce a flow of charged particles through the channel. The model is based on biochemical and electrophysiologic experiments. Ernst Neher and Bert Sakmann received the Nobel Prize in 1991 for their measurements of particle flow through such channels. (From *Principles of Neuroscience*, 2nd ed., E. Kandel and J. Schwartz, eds., 1985. Elsevier Science Publishing Co., Inc., N.Y.)

OPEN FRONTIERS

In spite of the questions still remaining, many of the essential building blocks of neuronal networks in the brain had been defined by the early 1960s, when I was constructing my own research strategy. By then, the structure and function of the networks had taken on tangible meaning. Individual neuronal elements have long processes called axons, which end in a spray of fine synaptic knobs. These knobs release chemical messages onto the receiving branches of other neuronal elements. The receiving branches are called dendrites, from the Greek root meaning "tree," since dendrite branches often resemble the branches of a tree. Large electrical signals, called nerve impulses, spread along the axons by a sequence of local openings and closings of channels in the axonal membrane, which permit the passage of ion particles such as sodium and potassium. The chemical messages also elicit their excitatory or inhibitory electrical signals at synapses by analogous regulation of ion movement across local regions of membrane on the dendritic branches. These building blocks, including the channels, the synapses, the chemical messengers, the electrical signals, and dendrites, had now been defined and were beginning to be comprehensively understood.

Their use for constructing neural networks was understood in terms of the finished product, however. Once a network was formed after development, the electrical signals and chemical messages would be sent reliably and reproducibly over and over again. What was not understood was that the flow of ions through the pores, and the electrical signals that resulted, could be dramatically and permanently altered by experience, or that the chemical messages might not remain the same throughout the adult life time of a network. Ramon y Cajal knew that many synaptic connections and axons were not formed until certain periods in a brain's development. But once formed, how would they change as a function of experience? Could the patterning and frequency of electrical and chemical signals rewire the network of an adult animal by transforming the channels, the ion flow, and the chemical messages? Could such transformations be responsible for making permanent memory records in the human brain? What cellular properties of the records make them so refractory to change? What organizational features of human networks make traumatic conditioning so self-fulfilling? These were among the most exciting questions left unanswered at that time—when America was in Vietnam, blacks were demanding their rights, and I was in medical school. For answers, another series of crucial observations would be necessary.

It would not be enough to understand the building blocks of the neural circuits. The circuit designs, the architecture of the neural networks, had to be understood, too. From the time of Cajal, details were sought about the organization of the connections among neurons. To Cajal, the pattern of links between neurons in the retina, for example, was clearly different from the connection patterns in the hippocampus or the cerebellum. Cajal knew that the function of the networks in the visual cortex and in the auditory cortex was uniquely dependent on the arrangement of the neurons and their synaptic connections. These arrangements make it possible for us to see, hear, touch, and smell. In spite of important advances in our technology and knowledge of brain networks, however, these arrangements remain today one of the most challenging frontiers of science. There have been many exciting insights into brain circuitry. Yet in spite of them, we know remarkably little about the wiring of the brain. In the context of such ignorance, it is not so surprising that many careful scientists consider brain functions such as memory to be hopelessly inaccessible with our current technology. To recognize the enormity of the problem, remember that there are tens of billions of neurons in the human brain and that the number of synapses is many times greater. Even if observers had techniques to monitor all of the signals of a billion or so neurons simultaneously, how could they analyze the information in the signals? Where would they display the signals?

The likelihood is that if and when we have such technology, the information processing capability of the human brain itself will have to be integrally involved in the loop of data processing. The activity of millions of neurons, for example, might be visualized by changes of a fluorescent marker. The changes might appear as three-dimensional waves moving from one brain region to another. The human observer might then be able to recognize wave patterns that are unique to a particular experience. Perhaps such patterns could be collected, compared, and classified. Such measurements will probably some day be possible. Today they are only a glint in the eye of the neuroscientist. In the absence of such technology, insight into brain networks has been limited although still startling from the perspective of what was known in the nineteenth century.

Sherrington, his colleagues, and his successors mapped out much of the basic circuitry of the spinal cord. Here, as with almost all other mapping of the human nervous system, however, it has not been possible to determine the actual individual connections of each neuron with all other neurons. Instead, groups of neurons have been shown to have identified types of synaptic connections with other groups.[1] We have not even begun to map most of the connections of the neurons within and between the groups. What have emerged are general rules for the wiring. Certain neurons typically make particular kinds of connections with other neurons. The typical connections, however, are by no means comprehensive. They exclude untold numbers of atypical connections, innumerable variations among individual neurons. In general, the same can be said for many other neural systems of the brain. General pathways and connections have been identified, but the details of the wiring are hopelessly complex.

The flow of information along such pathways between groups of neurons was established by a combination of many different types of observations collected by many observers. Clinicians found symptoms that could later be attributed to discrete brain lesions or areas of destroyed tissue, found by pathologists. Anatomists followed the tracks of axons from one group of neurons to another. Microanatomists demonstrated that recognizable synaptic junctions occurred between neurons of identifiable clusters. Electrophysiologists recorded signals at every step, describing how information was progressively transformed and represented in neuronal responses typical of specific brain regions. Neuroscientists discovered that the brain was organized into well-defined maps of the outside world. There were cortical maps made up of neurons that received signals from touch-sensing cells distributed over the surface of the skin. Other cortical maps reproduced a version of the distribution of retinal receptors over the inner surface of the eye cup. Still others related signals of neurons in the cortex to sensory neurons of the ear.[2]

Mapping of the brain was pursued, then, with a diverse arsenal of anatomical, stimulating, recording, behavioral, and psychophysical techniques. In short, mapping was a prototypical pursuit of the new science, neuroscience, which had emerged from nineteenth-century psychology, physics, biology, and philosophy. These techniques were adapted to explore the contributions of networks to the behavior of living animals and even to the subjective experience of humans. Some investigators, such as Walter Hess of Switzerland, inserted finely sharpened microelectrodes into animal brains to stimulate focal regions and identify the networks responsible for specific behaviors, including those we recognize as characteristically emotional. Hess found cells within a brain structure called the hypothalamus that were responsible for "flight-or-fight" responses. James Olds, Sr., an American, used similar technology to uncover "pleasure centers" in the rat brain. Neurosurgeons such as the American Harvey Cushing and the American-born Canadian Wilder Penfield brought some of these techniques to the operating room. When clinical treatment required mapping to localize epilepsy or convulsion-producing lesions, these men used ultrafine stimulating electrodes to elicit responses painlessly from conscious patients. Cushing, working at Johns Hopkins University, stimulated a variety of arm, hand, and finger movements. Penfield, working at the Montreal Neurological Institute, induced a variety of sensations. They might be isolated, such as the sound of a bell ringing or a cricket chirping, or an entire experience, such as being chased by an intruder. Complete experiences could be clearly identified as having happened in the past. Penfield presumably was stimulating brain sites that stored or were connected to repositories for memories. Although his observations were anecdotal, they seemed to offer startling confirmation of the human brain's localized storage of past experience.[3]

Some of these researchers, such as Olds, Magoun, and Moruzzi, were not only stimulating brain regions but also making highly amplified recordings of the neurons' electrical signals. These recordings were ultimately perfected to the degree that they could discriminate signals of individual neurons from a population of signals and thus provide an entirely new means of brain mapping. By recording signals of neurons in different regions, investigators could assess the effects of the synaptic connections within and between neuron groups. The signals were transformed by the neurons themselves as well as by excitatory and inhibitory synaptic signals received by the neurons from other neurons.[4]

Cajal set the stage. He established the framework within which all neuroscientists have labored during the twentieth century to understand biological networks. Given the knowledge of the brain's anatomy provided by Cajal, successive generations of physiologists set out to define the function of cells within these networks. Sherrington chose the spinal cord, Eccles the cerebellum, Hubel and Wiesel the visual cortex, and Mountcastle the somatosensory (touch sense) cortex. These men, with their colleagues, students, and rivals, mapped out different territories within the nervous system. They recorded the electrical signals from distinct classes of specialized cells under standard conditions of stimulation, and sometimes, behavioral responding. In spite of differences in the anatomy and function of their chosen territories, some facts emerged as common to all biological networks. Layers of neurons are organized in an extremely precise and repeatable fashion. Neural networks are unequivocally well ordered. They fit blueprints that are specific to each functional requirement, whether it be to move a limb in response to a noxious stimulus, to maintain balance, or to see and catch a moving object. The nonrandom organization of neuronal networks is opposite to the way many artificial networks have been conceived and constructed. Natural networks are not probabilistic, but they are capable of responding to and recording probabilistic events, as will be discussed later.

Inevitably and almost imperceptibly, something else totally unanticipated emerged from twentieth-century adventures in brain mapping. The collected observations of Cajal, Sherrington, and their successors hinted at a different, more abstract way of thinking about neural networks. They could be thought of as information processors in which information, rather than just sensory stimuli, was entering a processor, rather than a brain. Physical events, which can be represented and encoded by neuronal responses, occur in time and space in certain types of relationships to each other. When the relationships occur with sufficient frequency, they become predictable. Neural networks in the brain perform operations on the information. They add, subtract, and build numerical series with the physical events that are sensed. Network operations could, therefore, be described with mathematical equations that would define the operational rules they obeyed.

Two fundamental directions opened with this new conceptualization of brain function. The first was toward understanding biological networks in the language of physics and mathematics. The second was toward understanding physical or computational networks in the language of biology. A Viennese physicist, Ernst Mach, was the pioneer of these new directions. No other nineteenth-century thinker was closer in breadth and vision to the great Helmholtz. Like Helmholtz, he was applying a physicist's methods to study the mind. Mach, however, applied principles of mind to the study of physics. Mach emphasized that the concepts of physics are still at root human. Seemingly quantitative measurements of space, time, and motion always have the frame of reference of the observer making the measurements. Physical quantities ultimately are reducible to mental sensations:

The introduction of physics of the universally comparable, or so called "absolute" measurements—the reduction of all physical measurements to such units as the centimetre, the gramme, and the second (length, mass, and time)—has one peculiar result. There exists in any case a tendency to regard anything that can be physically grasped and measured, anything that can be stated in such a way as to become common property, as "objective" and "real," in contrast to the subjective sensations; and the absolute measures appear to give some support for this opinion, and to supply it with a psychological, if not with a logical, motive. It looks as if what we call "sensations" in the familiar sense, were something quite superfluous in physics. Indeed, if we look closer, the system of units of measurement can be still further simplified. For the numerical measurement of mass is given by a ratio of accelerations, and measurement of time can be reduced to measurement of angles or lengths of arcs. Consequently measurement of lengths is the foundation of all measurements. But we do not measure mere space; we require a material standard of measurement, and with this the whole system of manifold sensations is brought back again. . . . (Mach, 1914 pp. 342–343 cf "Mach Bands" F. Ratliff, 1965 Holden-Day)

No one is competent to predicate things about absolute space and absolute motion; they are pure things of thought, pure mental constructs, that cannot be produced in experience (Mach, 1942, p. 280—cf "Mach Bands" by F. Ratliff, 1965 Holden-Day).

Albert Einstein unhesitatingly credited Mach with foreshadowing Einstein's own theories:

Mach clearly recognized the weak points of classical mechanics and was not very far from requiring a general theory of relativity—and all of this almost half a century ago! It is not improbable that Mach himself would have discovered the theory of relativity, if, during the time that his mind was in its prime, physicists had been concerned with the importance of the problem of the constancy of the speed of light (Einstein, 1916).

According to Mach, principles of physics would become more accurate if physical measurements were understood as events in human brain cells and networks. This perspective would enjoy another incarnation in the twentieth century when designs of artificial, or "engineered," networks began to be based on mathematical principles derived from biological networks.

Mach was also fascinated by sensation's influence on and sometimes distortion of the objects sensed. At the edge of a darkened area such as a shadow, for example, or an illuminated area such as a spotlight, bands of enhanced darkness and enhanced brightness, respectively, appear to be present. Mach claimed that these bands, now called Mach bands, were not actually there. They were, in his words, "not objective." The real distribution of light was more gradual—with no bands. The bands appeared, according to Mach, because of the way the changes of light intensity are sensed by the neural networks of the retina.

This was a time when networks were only beginning to be given anatomical and functional reality, before the major contributions of Cajal and Sherrington. Synapses had not yet been demonstrated. Electrical signals of neurons were largely inferred and not convincingly recorded. Yet Mach reasoned that regions of the retina separated in space exerted a mutually inhibitory action on each other. Light excited one retinal area, which in turn inhibited the surrounding retinal regions. Mach believed that his bands were perceived because of the interactions of the excitatory effects of light with the inhibitory effects of the retinal networks. What was Mach saying? He was claiming that our brain networks add features of events that we see to the "objective" world. Thus the return of the philosophical issue that has baffled thinkers over the ages—the distinction of the observer from the observed.

What kind of amazing intellect allowed Mach to infer the presence and function of mutually inhibitory networks in the retina when networks themselves were largely hypothetical! Even more amazing and astonishing that Georg von Békésy and H. Keffer Hartline would show during the next several decades that in fact the neural networks existed. Mach bands were predicted and confirmed to exist not only in our visual sensations but in hearing and touch. Synaptic connections were established among groups of neurons in each of the relevant sensory pathways. The organization of the synaptic connections could be incorporated into mathematical descriptions that quantitatively predicted the sensory experiences of humans. Psychophysics was explainable by network physics.[5]

Mach was, in effect, conducting an ongoing dialogue inside his head. One party spoke in mathematical language, the other in the language of human perception. Succeeding in translating the languages, Mach went back and forth in his mind between these seemingly alien parties using them as teachers for each other. Only in the second half of the twentieth century was Mach's dialogue actively resumed in neuroscience.

It was, of course, never entirely absent, but often it lay dormant. It could hardly be ignored in Alan Hodgkin and Andrew Huxley's studies of the electrical events underlying the nerve impulse. Hodgkin and Huxley did not know that channels existed to allow passage of electrical charge across the nerve membrane—as Mach did not know of the actuality of retinal networks—but the Hodgkin-Huxley equations were remarkably accurate in their prediction of such channels. Bernard Katz did not know that chemical messages were packaged in spherical globules and released from these globules at synaptic junctions between neurons, but his mathematical description of the signals he recorded at synapses predicted their involvement in the transmission of chemical messages. The models of von Békésy, Hartline, Mach, Hodgkin-Huxley, and Katz had their flaws. They proved, as their creators I am sure expected, to be only approximations of the "objective." They constituted, however, a method in neuroscience that was to come into vogue during the twentieth century. Network models, in fact, may represent one of the most important directions of twentieth-century neuroscience.

This was the state of affairs, then, when I started out on my own scientific journey. We had good reason to believe that networks of neurons accomplish the diverse and wondrous functions of the brain. We believed that the connections among the neurons are organized into precise patterns and that these patterns determine what we can sense, perceive, and predict about our world. The preceding generations had sketched the pathways that offered us orientation, direction, and even belief. But the sketches were rendered with broad strokes, leaving innumerable gaps. Down among the tangled mass of connections, direction and belief are often not enough. Picking our way through the jungle, it's sometimes difficult to make the very next step through the underbrush. We think we know where we are going, but getting there is another matter.

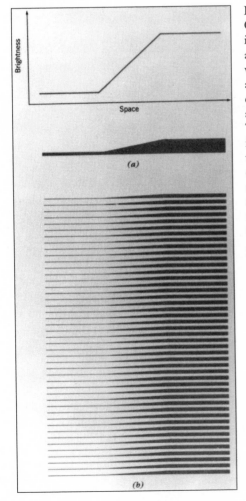

Fig. 9 Illustration of Mach Bands. Close inspection shows that lines in (b) increase in thickness from left to right as depicted over (a). At a distance where lines in (b) are no longer visible, a white band appears on the left and a dark band on the right. These bands are not actually present on the page. They appear to be present because of inhibitory connections within our visual sensing pathways. Ernst Mach explained the phenomenon more than a century ago before inhibitory connections in the retina, which account for the bands, were known to exist. (From *The Biology of Behavior and Mind*, B. Bridgeman, 1988. John Wiley and Sons, N.Y.)

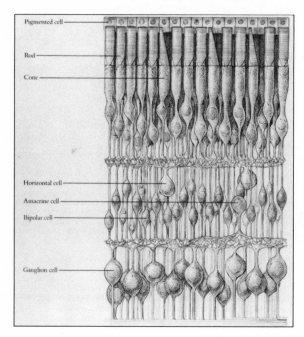

Fig. 10 Schematic model of the neuronal network in the retina. Light enters the network through the ganglion cell layer to trigger chemical and then electrical signals in the rods and cones. Signals then spread through the layers back to the ganglion cells and then through other layers to reach the visual cortex of the brain. (From *Eye, Brain, and Vision*, D. H. Hubel, 1988. W. H. Freeman, N.Y.)

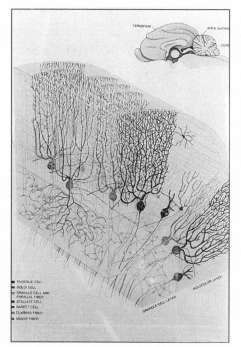

Fig. 11 Schematic model of a neuronal network in the cerebellum. Here, too, the cells are arranged in layers through which signals travel. Note the dark and large cell bodies of the Purkinje cells. The cerebellum is particularly important for coordination of body movements. (From "The cortex of the Cerebellum," R. Llinas, 1975. *Scientific American* 232:56–71. W. H. Freeman, N.Y.)

THE BRAIN'S PHOTOGRAPH

What I had read, experienced, and thought about coalesced into intuitive impressions of how the brain senses and records experience. These impressions gave me an orientation—a framework in which to work. Years of experiments, observations, and new thoughts have added a multitude of details to my mental picture of brain function. The details have done little, however, to alter the picture's essential features. Here is a rough sketch of the landscape I was soon to travel when I began my search more than two decades ago.

Secured inside its bony armor, the brain keeps informed about the outside world through sensory neurons in the eyes, ears, and nose, all strategically positioned to report to the brain about external events and objects. Millions of sensory cells are spread across the inner surface of the eye cup, somewhat like the thousands of silver grains spread across a sheet of photographic paper. Light of many different intensities from many points on an image causes chemical changes in the sensory neurons to make a distribution of electrical signals across the eye cup. Similarly, light causes a distribution of chemical changes in the silver grains to make a photograph. These changes make thousands of points on the photographic paper appear with the same dark and light patterns shown by the photographed object. In this way, the image of an object is created and stored as a photographic print. However, once the silver grains on a photographic paper are exposed to light and undergo a chemical change, they are no longer available to undergo further changes. New photographic paper with unexposed grains is needed for every new object or scene. A photograph by the sensory cells could also serve to store a memory of the image. But how and where would subsequent images be sensed or stored? Therein lies an incredibly difficult problem for evolving designs of animal nervous systems. How can a living sensing device have the storage power, subtlety, and resolution of photographic paper and still be available to sense one image after another?

For insights into some of nature's solutions, consider the systems of neurons that enable us to see. Instead of one area or sheet of neurons, mammals have a series of sheets, or layers. The functions accomplished only once by the silver grains on photographic paper are separated in the mammal and distributed through many successive layers of neurons. Receptor cells or sensory neurons are in the first layer and are the first to receive light. In response to light the molecule rhodopsin triggers a sequence of biochemical steps that ultimately generates an electrical signal whose amplitude is proportional to the intensity of the incident light. The sensory cells in the first neuronal layer, then, accomplish one important initial function. They translate light intensity into an electrical signal. Visual sensory neurons are spread in a layer across our eyes in such a way that they form a map of the outside world. The intensity of light received by these cells is translated into a distribution of electrical signals across the layer. The chemical effect of light on the sensory transduction molecule rhodopsin is transient, in contrast to the permanent effect of light on the silver grains. The electrical signal is also temporary, allowing the neuron to return to its previous unstimulated condition. In this way, the layer of sensory neurons in the eye is ready, very soon after receiving and representing one image, to receive and represent another image. Meanwhile, the electrical signals elicited from the first image are sent on to the next layer of neurons. A wave of electrical signals spreads from one layer to the next, coming ever closer to the innermost reaches of the brain.

Within biological networks, signals travel between neurons along what are essentially telephone wires. The structure of each neuron extends into a long wirelike arm. When it reaches another neuron, the arm swells slightly into a small sack containing packets of chemical messages. Electrical signals spread from the main neuron along its arm to the sack, where the signals release the chemical messages onto the next neuron. In the next neuron, the new chemical signal triggers a new electrical signal, which releases still another chemical signal onto another neuron. In this way, a wave of signals spreads through a network of neurons carrying a processed image as it goes. As this wave passes from layer to layer, it moves along a pathway within the brain. You can think of the first group of neuron layers in this pathway as fulfilling the visualizing functions of a fancy camera. The neurons in this pathway represent for us what is actually happening at the moment. I call this the real time pathway.

The neurons in this real time pathway communicate with each other in such a way that they are especially sensitive to contrast. The signals of neurons in the initial layers of the visual pathway transmit information about differences of light intensity, color, movement, and contour within an image. As the wave moves farther along the real time pathway into an area of the brain called the primary visual cortex, transformations occur in the information because it is being processed as it travels. One transformation, for example, changes a simple map of light intensity and color into a map of components—lines and edges oriented at certain angles within our eye's view. The signal wave travels from the primary visual cortex through another region called the temporal lobe which, inside the skull, is not far from the region we know as the temple on the outside.

As the wave travels from the primary visual cortex to the temporal lobe, the signals of the neurons respond to stimulation of expanding areas, rather than small spots on the map, and the components that trigger the signals of individual neurons become more complex as the map area expands. Within the final region of the temporal cortex, individual neurons fire their signals in responce to large sections of an image, such as a face in a full-body portrait. The time it takes the signals to travel from the sensory cells in the eye to the final neurons in the temporal cortex, is about one-tenth of a second. This is a bit slower than a video camera, but for most of our purposes, the trip is fast enough to represent accurately what is happening in real time.

Charles Gross at Princeton University and Mortimer Mishkin and his colleagues at the National Institutes of Health have used lesion and recording studies to improve our understanding of these pathways. The signals of neurons in the final station of the temporal lobe pathway, representing reconstituted visual images, next enter a kind of Grand Central Station in the brain known as the hippocampus. Here, and in neighboring structures, image signals can be routed for further

processing in many directions. Many of them have as their final destination the great frontal cortex. This massive structure is the end of the
second major pathway along which waves of sensory signals travel, but
only after having passed through the real time processing of the temporal lobe.

You can think of this second pathway, beginning at that complex
switching station the hippocampus, as the remembered time pathway.
The neurons in this pathway compare images we are sensing at any
given moment to those we sensed in the past. These remembered time
neurons signal similarities as well as differences among and within
images. These similarities are between what is sensed now and what
was sensed before. The job then, of this remembered time pathway is
to help recognize a visual image and the components of that image.

This pathway, then, preserves very sophisticated photographs
indeed. The photographs are generated from pieces and features and
their relationships within a visual image. The photographs are generated as well, however, from the relationships between images. We recognize a favorite candelabra not only from its distinctive filigree and
golden hue, but also from its place of honor on the living room mantelpiece over the fireplace. The family Christmas tree has its popcorn
chains, sparkling balls, and flashing lights, as well as its familiar shape
and place next to the parlor sofa. Decorative features within the tree's
cone-like shape are related to each other just as that shape is related to
other objects in the room. The brain organizes and later recognizes
these relationships.

Within and between the neuronal layers are an extraordinary number of connections between the neurons—many more connections
than there are neurons. Considering the billions of neurons in our
brains, the number of connections among them is almost impossible to
comprehend—something like a billion billion connections. No
microchip, however delicate and numerous its circuits, approaches the
intricacy and complexity of neuronal network layers in the mammalian
brain. No computer, however numerous and densely packed its
microchips, approaches the versatility for information storage of the
human brain.

Minute sites spread throughout these deep neuronal layers, like the
photographic silver grains, might be expected to undergo permanent
chemical changes to store an image. In one sense, memories are those
chemical changes within an ensemble of neurons. In another, when we
are actually recalling the memories, they are the chorus of neuronal

singers whose voices rise with precisely the right balance of volume and pitch to recreate that sound we heard in the past. A neuronal chorus can also represent visual images within the patterns of its electrical signals. If our memories are to be permanently stored, the changes at the sites for a particular memory must also be permanent. These memory sites would not change only in response to light and color patterns within the original image, however, but in response to comparison of the sensed image with many other stored images, for new memories are generated not only by new sensory experience but also by new combinations of this experience with old memories. We think of the candelabra when we think of the mantelpiece. A guest who stood by the mantelpiece on a recent visit might now enter the picture of the candelabra, along with our feelings about that guest as a potential friend. The new relationships of the candelabra's image to the image of the guest, as well as to the feelings of friendship, are also stored as memories.

For so much to be stored by the memory sites, two conclusions would be unavoidable. First, there would have to be an astounding number of memory sites. Our brains do not easily become saturated with too much information. Saturation may occur temporarily when too much information is coming in at once, but allowing for some delays, we can store much of what we can sense. Second, to accommodate such an amount and diversity of remembered information, the memory sites would have to be distributed throughout a variety of brain regions. Brain regions responsible for processing of vision, hearing, speech, touch, emotions, and movement would all store information related to a single image.

The memory sites, unlike silver grains, receive signals from other neurons rather than from the original light pattern. The permanent changes at the memory sites do not obscure the signals that continue to be sent to the brain by more recent images. Other differences also distinguish a camera's photograph from a remembered image in the brain. The camera photograph reveals its image by reflecting a pattern of different light intensities. Every time sufficient light falls on the photographic surface, the permanent record of the image is made available to us. The image stored within the brain's photograph becomes accessible in quite a different way. We remember an image, we gain access to its record, because something we see reminds us of it. An image viewed in the present reminds us of one viewed in the past. A face, for example, may be recognized because it resembles one we have already seen many times. The pattern of light intensity and color that arises from the face travels along the layers of neurons until it reaches that constellation of neuronal sites that has permanently recorded the face-pattern in our memory. These sites are then activated, making the memory accessible.

The image viewed in the present need not be completely identical to one remembered from the past. The present image may be only a small piece of the stored image. The present image may be grossly distorted, or it may be obscured by shadows or other overlapping images. Yet, if enough defining features of the original image are present and can be discriminated, the entire original image can be regenerated in our mind. At times we don't need to see any of the original image to recall it.

For example, we might see a face immediately after hearing a name. The next time we hear the name we may "see" the face in our mind. The memory sites in our brain have stored the sound of the name together with an image of the face. That sound can then activate the memory sites for the visual image. So now we have come upon a most dramatic departure of the brain's photograph from that of a camera. The camera's photograph is static. It remains constant in time. In contrast to the camera's frozen image, the brain's photograph can be a temporal sequence of images, and these are not limited to one sensory modality (such as vision). Because the sensory neurons are only transiently activated by an image, they are constantly ready for sensing the next image. So the brain can record a long succession of visual and other sensory images. Viewing only a portion of the succession can be enough to recall in our memory the entire temporal sequence of images. The thought of a candelabra might recall for us the time a new friend walked into the living room past the Christmas tree and stood next to the candelabra on the mantelpiece.

The brain's photograph, then, may be more accurately compared to a moving picture than to a still camera photograph. Light projected through a reel of moving pictures recreates the original sequence of images. The moving pictures can also be accompanied by the sounds that originally occurred together in time with the images. It is amazing what our brains can accomplish. A couple of images, with or without sounds, may trigger a talking moving picture in our brains. A motion picture lasting two hours requires thousands of sheets of photographic paper, each with millions of silver grains. Similarly, millions of sites are probably involved in our recording even a brief interlude of experience in our memory.

All of this seems reasonable, but where are the memory sites? How can we possibly hope to find the microscopically small portions of neurons in the impassable jungle of wires within the brain?

When I began my biological observations, I was captivated by an apparent paradox. How does a well-ordered nervous system, one that is not random or probabilistic, respond to and record probabilistic phenomena? Memories can never be predetermined—experience cannot be exactly predicted. Streams of sensory images are fluid, always changing. How does a well-ordered nervous system record a disorderly world? If I learned only one lesson from my own experiments, it would be that precisely ordered neural networks are designed to change without losing their orderliness. They change to record memories of the past without compromising their ability to sense the present. The only way to understand how this was possible was to find a neural network that could be mapped and analyzed completely. For such a system I would have to look among primitive animals with so few neurons and connections that they could be mapped but with sufficient number to make memory both possible and interesting. This was the delicate balance I would look to nature to strike.

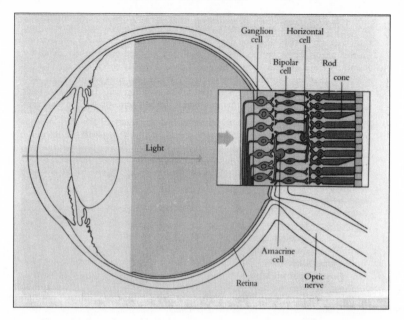

Fig. 12 The neurons of the retina (represented schematically within the inset) are spatially distributed across the inner surface of the eye cup. Light enters the eye through the cornea, iris, and lens to travel through the large volume of vitreous humor to first reach the ganglion-cell layer and eventually the light-sensitive neurons known as rods and cones. (From *Eye, Brain, and Vision*, D. H. Hubel, 1988. W. H. Freeman, N.Y.)

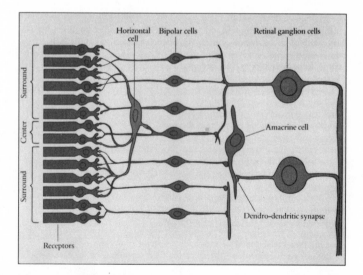

Fig. 13 Schematic model of synaptic connections among neurons within the retinal network. Each type of connection has been studied with microelectrode recordings and highly magnified visualization with the electron microscope. (From *Eye, Brain, and Vision*, D. H. Hubel, 1988. W. H. Freeman, N.Y.)

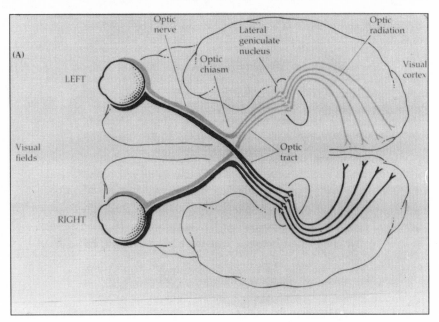

Fig. 14 Pathways taken by light patterns from the eyes (on the left) through layers of neuronal networks into the brain. Notice that the pathways cross onto the opposite side of the brain through the vast nerve bundle called the "optic chiasm." (From *Neuron to Brain*, S. W. Kuffler and J. G. Nicholls, 1975. Sinauer Associates, Inc., Sunderland, Mass.)

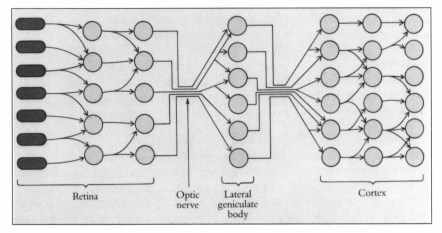

Fig. 15 Schematic representation of neuronal networks and their layers within the visual pathways depicted in Fig. 14. (From *Eye, Brain, and Vision*, D. H. Hubel, 1988. W. H. Freeman, N.Y.)

EVOLUTION'S COMPROMISE

I came to Bethesda fresh from my internship with only a primitive knowledge of electrophysiology. I had carefully chosen a laboratory that was expert at recording from neurons with microelectrodes. No other laboratory at N.I.H. was more distinguished in this respect than that of Michael Fuortes. Fuortes, with his colleague Karl Frank, had made important contributions to our understanding of networks in the spinal cord. His papers were models of rigor, logic, and elegant experimental design.

I remember reading his article "Steps in the Production of Motoneuron Spikes" with unreserved admiration. With just the right mix of compelling argument and conclusive demonstration, he traced the origin of electrical signals to a specific location on the motoneuron. He reconstructed how the electrical signal first arises right where the long wirelike axon extends from the main body of the motoneuron. Once triggered, the signal then shoots down the axon with incredible speed to reach the synaptic endings. Fuortes combined orderliness, precision, and control with a teasing wit. His neatly trimmed mustache paralleled and highlighted the clean definition of his trademark bow tie. He was, even in his fifties, lean, fit, and athletic, projecting an image of strength far beyond what his diminutive frame suggested. He seemed to draw his endless patience from an ongoing exquisite pleasure in analyzing network signals. Fuortes had been recommended as the first choice of teachers in electrophysiology. In medical school, I dreamed of learning what was then still an esoteric art under his tutelage, and now my dream had become a reality.

I remember first meeting him in Bethesda for my interview. I was competing with many other medical students across the country for what was one of the few available appointments as a Research Medical Officer at the National Institutes of Health, the nation's, and arguably the world's, premier biomedical research institution. When I arrived in Bethesda, I thought I was in paradise. The rolling landscaped campus was at the time still not overwhelmed by buildings. The spring weather of the Washington area and the soothing quiet were in sharp contrast to New York's melee of traffic and teeming crowds. The tension of New York's pace fit the unrelenting intensity I knew during my training at Cornell University Medical School, the distant Manhattan offspring of a parent long grown into the sleepy countryside of upstate New York.

Fuortes talked in a leisurely way, with an interest in who I was, what I knew, and what I wondered about. He made me feel valuable, or at least potentially so. I could not have suspected that he had just suffered the worst of tragedies—the loss of his son in an automobile accident. Did he see in me a trace of what he had lost? Perhaps I looked to him for what I had lost but never had—a father's love. He was for me, as Phillip George and Edward Liang had each in turn been, a potential model, as well as a source of guidance. Fuortes was not the first of my models to have lost a son. Soon after my success at undergraduate research under his supervision, Phillip George was dealt the same crushing blow. Phillip's son, who had been my tennis partner, was stabbed to death by a mugger in West Philadelphia. For months Phillip could hardly talk to me. It was only with the greatest difficulty that he could discuss my data in preparation for a preliminary publication, whereas for months before he had been full of enthusiasm. He never could bring himself to give it a final comprehensive review.

By the time I had arrived in Bethesda, Fuortes had shifted his interest from the spinal cord to the retina, and he had already published some elegant studies on Hartline's horseshoe crab eye preparation. The technology of microelectrode recording permeated the atmosphere of Fuortes's lab. You lived and breathed it. I could not help but acquire the art as long as I kept my eyes and ears open. The junior scientists invited me into their laboratories to watch as they visualized on the oscilloscope the electrical signals of retinal cells in response to light. We talked about the mechanisms that generated such signals in the retina, the squid axon, or the frog neuromuscular junction. This was our conversation at lunchtime, or during preparations for an experiment, or after dinner between snatches of radio shows on WWDC. From Fuortes and his colleagues I acquired much of the technology I needed to do my first work. What was not in their laboratory, I found elsewhere. It was like going to the library. If I needed a reference, I looked it up among the stacks of N.I.H. laboratories with their seemingly unlimited resources of people, techniques, and equipment.

The nervous system I was looking for would represent evolution's compromise between network simplicity and behavioral complexity. The network in the horseshoe crab's eye, for example, could be mapped, but it has not been shown capable of the associative memory so characteristic of human memory. In fact, none of the analyzable neural networks known in the late 1960s had been shown to have such a capability. So I began looking for an elementary associative network in a variety of simple creatures. Ruminations about genetically specified hard-wired networks and experience-dependent soft-wired networks were still fresh in my mind. So was the apparent requirement that two events that become associated must each first elicit signals that meet somewhere in the network. Lower animals such as snails don't have many neurons—mere thousands against our billions. It seemed reasonable, then, that I should try to find two sensory pathways that intersected. In response to a stimulus, such as light or rotation, signals traveling along each pathway would meet somewhere in the network when the two stimuli occurred together. These two pathways might lead me to a network able to learn an association.

I dissected animal after animal for months, inevitably defeated by one drawback or another. The nervous system of one species was covered by too much connective tissue, another had ganglia too distant from each other. Some animals were too expensive or were available only during certain seasons of the year. But then, a recently completed light microscopic study caught my attention. It described the snail *Hermissenda*'s two eyes, each of which contained five sensory neurons. These five neurons sent axons to a nearby cluster of thirteen additional neurons, a formation called the optic ganglion. This visual pathway was promising because of its small number of cells. There seemed to be a possibility that each of these neurons could be reliably identified in animal after animal. I might then trace the connections between each of the identified neurons to produce an exact blueprint for this visual network.

My first thought of the Pacific sea snail *Hermissenda* was how un-snail-like it was. Other snails I had examined, such as *Aplysia* and *Tritonia*, moved slowly and looked overfed. *Hermissenda* was small but glided gracefully along the glass surfaces of the aquarium. It turned its head frequently from side to side somewhat like a dog sniffing out the inhabitants of its environment. Its brightly colored iridescent coat of featherlike ceratae[1] lay sleekly flattened over its back as if neatly combed for the day's outing. The clear separation of its headlike anterior portion from its feathered coat allowed easy access of external stimuli to its sensory organs mediating "taste," touch, and "vision." And what drama followed its meeting a fellow creature.

A chance encounter by two *Hermissenda* began with a succession of rapid brief touches, which allowed each animal's pair of fingerlike tentacles to assess the size and perhaps the intentions of its potential opponent. A much smaller animal usually turned abruptly in hasty retreat, while the larger of the two might rear up and pounce as a cat might lunge to engulf a mouse. Two animals of comparable size might engage in a series of brisk rearing and lunging movements strikingly reminiscent of two stags competing for the attention of a nearby doe. Once one was clearly at a disadvantage in such a contest, it executed a violent writhing movement, thrusting itself off the aquarial wall and hurtling somewhat unpredictably toward the coral gravel below. However elementary its nervous system, this animal was capable of impressively elaborate behavior.

It took me hours of dissection to find and uncover the central ganglia of the *Hermissenda* snail. When I finally found this primitive brain, I was immediately excited. Right next to it on either side were the two eyes. Immediately below each eye was a perfectly formed transparent sphere. In the sphere's center, a cluster of crystalline structures was dancing with continuous, seemingly random vibrations. Alluring, mysterious, beautiful, the crystals sparkled as they danced. This sphere was the snail's middle ear, also called a statocyst. The constant beating of hairs that project from the inner surface of the statocyst's thirteen cells was responsible for the movements of the crystals. As the crystals press against the hairs, the statocyst senses when the animal changes position or the speed and direction of its movements. Although it had never been described, interaction of the statocyst signals with the visual signals might fulfill exactly my requirements for a primitive associative network. Two separate sensory pathways would meet at localized convergence sites in the network. Just as Pavlov's dog learned that the sound of a bell accompanies the smell of meat, perhaps the snail could learn that a visual signal accompanies a statocyst signal. The snail would learn that a visual signal "comes together" with a statocyst signal when the signals repeatedly arrive together at convergence sites in the network.

To identify the neurons, their connections, and the convergence sites within these pathways, I would have to insert probes called microelectrodes into neurons with recognizable locations and structures. Microelectrodes amplify the electrical signals within each neuron. The amplified electrical signals can be monitored without interrupting their transmission to other parts of the neuron's structure. So an electrical signal is "probed" by the microelectrode, and at the same time the signal travels down the neuron axon to synaptic junctions where it triggers the release of chemical signals to other neurons. Microelectrodes in these other neurons record the electrical signals triggered by chemical messages released from other neurons.[2]

Some say that there is a black magic to making microelectrodes. It is a matter of paying attention to the details. The smaller, more interesting snail neurons are only 10 millionths of a meter in diameter. Others, 5 millionths of a meter thick, and very much like a pancake, are 50 millionths of a meter in diameter. Even axon branches only 1 millionth of a meter in diameter can be penetrated. The shape of the microelectrode must fit the structure it will penetrate. To avoid punching through a branch, the microelectrode point should be very small, short, and stubby. To enter and penetrate the thick wall of a sensory neuron, the microelectrode should be longer and have a more gradually tapering point.

A potter must know how to shape clay keeping in mind the consistency of the material, the speed of the wheel, the form of the turning post, and the positions of her hands. Similarly, a maker of microelectrodes, an electrophysiologist, must know exactly how much heat to deliver to the glass, how quickly it should be pulled, and with what force. The shape of the microelectrode is exquisitely sensitive to the amount of heat delivered, which depends on the force and speed with which the glass cylinder is pulled through a ribbonlike filament usually made of platinum. Once fabricated, the microelectrode is moved into the neuron, whose surface is carefully prepared, its wrapping tissue gently pushed aside to allow unobstructed access. Now the microelectrode advances at exactly the right angle for optimal ease of penetration. When all of the details are attended to, recordings are almost effortless. It's like going fishing and making a catch every day. I did not believe that literally every step must be painstakingly followed. But failure is a very unforgiving teacher. The art, the magic if you will, is in these steps. Of course the steps have to be determined individually for each nervous system, for every neuron in that system, and by every worker.

I inserted these microelectrodes day after day, year after year, and never tired of it. It's like being invited to a secret club where the most delicious gossip is discussed. These experiments are not like biochemistry, where the data may take days or weeks to recover, often in the form of dry lists of numbers. The electrical signals of neurons, flowing from the microelectrode into an amplifier, can be large, fast, and frequent. There is drama in a burst of big flashes across the recording screen. The flashes can be transformed into sounds so that the signals beat out a rhythm for the spellbound listener. In the end, of course, the signals have to be quantified. Numbers have to be attached. But the process of collecting the data is great fun in itself.

Dye, injected into the cell through the microelectrode diffuses throughout the neuron's structure even to its synaptic branches. The dye reveals the physical shape of each neuron, which is also identified by its electrical signals and its connections with other neurons. A structural signature can then be established for each electrical signature. Some structures have their own striking beauty. Who could imagine the dense network of intricate branches that extends from the main trunks of certain mammalian neurons? I would never have predicted that a particular neuron in the visual pathway on one side of the snail brain sends a long process to the visual pathway on the other side, there to connect with distant neurons. The structure, of course, hints at function. This same neuron can compare signals received by each of the snail's two eyes, located on opposite sides of the brain.

The full potential of these techniques is realized only if each neuron in the network can be recognized in one animal after another. This is not frequently possible. In mammalian brains, there is no chance for identification of individual neurons. And in many so-called simple brains, the difficulties are also insurmountable. The eye of the snail *Aplysia*, for example, is comparatively simple, but it nevertheless contains 5,000 neurons, most of which cannot be uniquely identified by anatomical or electrical properties. The brain of the bee is simple by comparison to the brain of the rabbit, but 900,000 neurons are in some respects as hopeless to analyze precisely as 900,000,000 neurons. Yet an absolutely comprehensive and precise wiring diagram of a network is necessary to trace the signals that interact when a memory is acquired.

To observe and measure how a neuronal network changes, it is essential first to know how that neuronal network is constructed and specified according to the genetic program of the animal. The visual system of the snail *Hermissenda* seemed to be that rare instance where a complete map of genetically specified neuronal circuitry could be determined. By inserting microelectrodes into three or four neurons simultaneously, I extended previous observations to map out the exact interaction of each sensory cell with every other sensory cell and with the optic ganglion cells on each side of the *Hermissenda* brain. Each cell had its own unique structural and electrical characteristics.

So the visual pathway of this snail was mappable. But what about its mysterious neighbor, the statocyst? Was there any mixing of signals from the visual pathways with signals of the statocyst? I had to satisfy my curiosity. Having worked on the visual system for about a year, one day I inserted a microelectrode into a statocyst sensory cell. I will never forget that moment, sitting alone in my darkened laboratory, when I flashed a light over the *Hermissenda* eye and recorded a brisk—and lovely—electrical signal from the hair cell. I knew at once that the hair cell received signals from the visual pathway neurons. The statocyst pathway intersected the visual pathway. This, then, was the first step along the hypothesized route of my search strategy.

Once I knew that the snail's visual and vestibular pathways communicated with each other, I had the necessary incentive to painstakingly piece together the connections among the neuronal elements within these pathways. Literally thousands of experiments were required to identify each neuron and every connection it made with every other neuron in the network. This work has really never ended, even after nearly two decades of such studies. Within three years, however, I had a comprehensive wiring diagram for the eyes, the vestibular organs called statocysts, and the thirteen-cell optic ganglia, as well as for the interactions of these structures on the right and left side of the *Hermissenda* brain. Later it became possible to follow the flow of visual and vestibular information along pathways through the entire nervous system. To this extent, I had a working knowledge of some of the snail's brain from its input to its output. With this map, I could now trace the flow of signals through the snail.

With time, it proved possible to observe how each neuron within the snail's visual-vestibular system responded to patterns of sensory stimulation. There were effectively two parallel networks. One responded only to sensory stimulus patterns in the present (i.e., real time patterns). The other stored remembered patterns from the past. Precise orderliness of the real-time neural system is preserved, while less orderly probabilistic events in experience progressively transform a parallel shadow network to generate remembered time. I never cease to be awed by the intricate beauty of these systems as they function within distinct domains of time to represent the world, past and present.

Somewhere on the map, sites must change the flow of signals to store an actual memory. To find the memory sites, however, I would first have to demonstrate, without any doubt, that there was a memory to look for. All of our behavioral studies, eventually taking a decade to complete, were aimed at one question. Did the snail, like Pavlov's dog, actually learn an association between stimuli presented together? Only true associative memory in this snail would justify for me the enormous commitment necessary to reveal the network's learning mechanisms.

The networks themselves hinted at how they might be trained and tested. The snail meanders toward the source of light that reaches its eyes and away from shadows and darkened corners. This weak and indirect response suggested that light did not elicit a brisk reflex and could have some ambiguous value for the snail. In this sense it resembles the bell's sound presented to Pavlov's dogs. Similarly, the color of a flower stimulates the bee's visual pathway just as colorful objects over a playpen stimulate an infant. None of these neutral stimuli reliably cause rapid movements toward or away from the source.

The other stimulus presented to Pavlov's dog during conditioning, the smell of meat, elicited quite a different type of response. The smell caused the dog to salivate immediately. If was like pushing a button on an electric appliance—push a button and the toaster heats, the hair dryer blows, and the radio plays. Present the meat smell and the dog salivates. Similarly a bee flies straight to the aroma of a flower, and a child instantly withdraws a hand from a hot surface. All of these stimuli trigger reflex responses. They have unequivocal value, positive or negative. Shaking or rotating the snail also has clear value. In response to turbulence within its aquarial home, the snail immediately and reliably clings to whatever surface it happens to be on when the turbulence starts.[3]

The clinging response of the snail resembles the salivation response of Pavlov's dog, while light's weak attraction for the snail resembles the sound of a bell for the dog. It was obvious that I could imitate Pavlov's procedure by training the snail with light just before turbulence. I could hardly wait for the first opportunity to teach my snails. Remarkably, the training worked on the first try. The snail's response to light alone was radically transformed after training with light and rotation.[4] Most important, this response transformation depended on the light and rotation occurring together in time. I was elated. The minimal visual-vestibular network I had hypothesized and found in the snail could learn an association just as I had hoped. Maybe there were such networks in dogs, or even humans for that matter. There would be no cause for celebration, however, until the learning met a long list of behavioral criteria. And there were the even more difficult details of how such networks might be found in the much more complex brain of any mammal, let alone that of a human.

For two weeks, I was consistently able to train the snails. And then, as suddenly as the training worked, it failed. I had trained enough animals to be confident that there had indeed been learning, yet after the first twenty animals, the learning effect disappeared. I could not have imagined the effect. The data were recorded and were at a high level of statistical significance. What changed? This was the question I would ask myself an uncountable number of times over the next six months. What were the unknown conditions that I was not controlling but that had to have been just right for the animals to have learned? I embarked once more on the kind of hunt I learned during my research in biochemistry under Philip George. Ever so slowly I retraced in my mind every moment the snails experienced from the time of their collection off the West Coast near Monterey, California, to their brief stay in the collector's aquarium, to their flight across country, to their unpacking in my laboratory, to their acclimatization in our aquarium. I imagined what it was like to be jostled about in a Styrofoam container housing plastic bags of chilled sea water in total darkness; what it felt like to undergo changes of salt concentrations, temperature, acidity, length of day, and bacterial populations. As I became familiar with the variations of the conditions the snail was exposed to, I realized the enormity of my task as their trainer. For six months, I methodically brought all of these conditions under my control. Whether it was the food or the time of the day the snails were trained and tested, it all became part of a strict regimen. Then and only then, six months later, after compulsive attention to every detail of my snails' lives, could I consistently train them to learn that light was associated with turbulence.[5] By some extraordinary good luck, the conditions were perfectly controlled during those first two weeks of experiments so that I was able to observe the learning, but it took a full half-year and a near-fanatical persistence to uncover and reproduce those exact conditions again. Once known, they offered no further problem over the next eighteen years, allowing my colleagues and me to eventually observe the learning process even on a chemical level. During the course of the hunt, however, I occasionally thought that by some strange twist of fate it was the snails who were training me rather than vice versa.

Measuring animal behavior and learning is not at all like recording signals from neural networks. I am not listening to the whispers of neurons in secret dialogue with each other, occasionally injecting my own presence into their conversation. I can't be as optimistic that a result is conclusive or even typical for a single animal as I might be for repeated measurements of a single identified neuron. The initial observations of an animal's behavior can be somewhat intuitive. A total impression of how the animal reacts to its environment, including training stimuli, suggests what it is perceiving and what behaviors should be measured. In this initial period, I need to be as sensitive as possible to subtle differences of the animal's movements and responses. My initial subjective impressions, however, only set the stage for the real data collection. Automated data collection by a video camera interfaced with a computer removes me from the action, minimizing the subjectivity of my impressions. Once a training or testing procedure is begun, I am out of it, waiting in the corner to be summoned at the experiment's end. I remember many times steeling myself to wait for the results of "blinded" behavioral training and testing protocols.[6] I would not know the results until the data were decoded at the end of the experiment. And when the data come in, the story is not told only by observations of individual animals but by consideration of an entire group of animals.

Until every necessary requirement had been fulfilled without any remaining doubt, I never entirely believed that the snail's visual-vestibular network could mediate true Pavlovian conditioning. Be it for a snail, a dog, or a human, for example, true Pavlovian conditioning requires an order in the relationship of training stimuli. A snail will not learn that rotation precedes light, only that light precedes rotation. Similarly, a dog will not learn that the smell of meat precedes the sound of a bell, only vice versa. Strong stimuli, such as the smells and tastes of food, prevent attention to weaker stimuli. A dog, otherwise unoccupied, will hear a bell or feel the itch of a flea. In the midst of a meal, it may not feel the itch at all.

A child notices the cues that precede a finger prick by a doctor drawing blood. The child notices the doctor's face, voice, and white coat but pays no attention to an assistant who walks into the treatment room a moment after his finger begins to throb. To remember the white coat, the child must first pay attention to it and then learn that it occurs in time just before the painful finger prick. The doctor's coat is novel in the sense that it has no clear value until it becomes linked to the finger-prick.

We see in such ordering of remembered stimuli, the novel before the familiar, an example of the brain's conservatism. Often, the longer stimuli are stored within the memory banks, the more links, or associations, they will have formed to subsequent stimuli and the more familiar they become. The earlier we are exposed to stimuli, the more links they form, the more entrenched they are, and the more demanding they become of our attention. No wonder behavioral patterns learned in childhood are so recalcitrant to change. Older memories accumulate a richness of associations with other memories. When some of these associations are lost because of damage or death of brain cells, many associations remain. An older memory can still be recalled when the remaining links are activated. A newer memory becomes difficult to recall when most of its relatively few associations with other memories are lost. The number of associations accumulated over years of experience with a particular memory can also contribute to our sense of time. Progressively longer chains of memories linked together can correspond to progressively longer periods of time. Time must pass for the chain to grow.

These considerations suggest how Pavlovian conditioning, as a model of learning, captures some of the essence of memory links in general. The conditioned stimulus–unconditioned stimulus relationship that occurs during Pavlovian conditioning is a model for novel and familiar stimulus relationships learned throughout experience. It is therefore not surprising that such learning has been demonstrated in a wide variety of vertebrate species. But we would expect animals with only thousands of neurons, such as snails, to be able to be conditioned to far fewer stimuli than insects with millions of neurons or mammals with billions. Not only can't they sense as wide a variety of stimuli with so few neurons; the sensed stimuli have fewer network paths along which to meet. This is why I thought it best to let the snail's network guide me to the stimulus relationships it might learn.

Pavlov showed many decades ago that his dogs could learn to salivate in response to sounds within a very precise range of pitch. The dogs could learn to discriminate a pitch that was followed by meat from another pitch not followed by meat. Pavlov pressed the dogs further, however. He trained them with two very similar pitches, only one of which was followed by meat. If the pitches were too similar, the dogs could not learn. Instead, they were often left in a state of persistent, general agitation. They would begin to salivate in response to sounds of many pitches with which they had not been trained. The conditioning of the dogs had lost its stimulus specificity—another key feature of conditioning, be it of snails, dogs, or humans.

The agitation of dogs trained with demands beyond their capacity has been considered by many to resemble the symptoms of neurosis in humans. It is an example of training an organism to chronically malfunction. It is a model of how experience can in some circumstances predominate over genetics in determining behavior. It is not only trauma that leaves an indelible mark on human expectations; severe and consistent frustration may be enough to permanently influence an individual's view of his or her own abilities and perhaps even self-worth. Humans can be conditioned with hopelessly demanding standards of reinforcement. Such standards were not unfamiliar to me, but it was worse for my childhood friend Michelle. A parent's praise and acceptance, let alone tolerance, sometimes depends on performance that tests or exceeds the limits of a child's abilities. I, at least, won occasional praise. Michelle could never win. Repeated failure at winning approval teaches the child that there is no predictable relationship between effort and reward. What more effective discouragement can there be for future efforts? No invoking of genetic causes is necessary here. Even a dog breaks down when faced with problems its brain networks are not designed to solve.

Monkeys reared with prolonged periods of separation from their mothers and/or siblings become irreversibly depressed. The monkeys learn to expect isolation. Their networks respond by reducing behavioral activity in general and suppressing the drives whose satisfaction defines the animals' very purpose in life. These results of deprivation are severe enough to overshadow inherited differences in emotional makeup. Under these circumstances, nurture takes precedence over nature. It seems only logical that the same must be true of humans. A parent need not totally abandon or confine a child to impose isolation. Some parents, like Michelle's father, neglect children who are with them on a daily basis. The child waits behind closed doors, so to speak, for a moment of contact. How many years can the waiting go on before the yearning itself is impaired? The child is conditioned to expect isolation and eventually responds by no longer seeking contact. A recipe for depression has been acquired from experience, handed down from one generation to another. Trauma, chronic frustration, and isolation all stem from learned expectations, as does Pavlovian conditioning. Perhaps the same types of networks but multiplied and imbedded in a variety of brain centers record the expectations of such different behavioral and emotional outcomes. These possibilities redoubled my interest in and my caution about the snail network's behavioral capabilities.

When my colleagues and I confirmed one essential characteristic, for example, the necessity that the two stimuli be presented together during training, I became doubly anxious that the next characteristic would not be confirmed. Despite my anxiety, I wanted to know with absolute certainty whether or not the elementary neuronal network I had hypothesized, and later found in the snail could actually learn that two stimuli occur together. It would have been more painful to invest my efforts and later be proven wrong. I therefore had to be my own most demanding critic. No unexpected piece of data, no dissonant note in an otherwise harmonious hypothesis, could go unnoticed. One unanticipated observation might uncover an insight that would better reveal the core of the problem's solution.

And so I made friends with demanding critics. Dori Gormezano, for example, was not shy in expressing his reservations about our snail's ability to learn an association. Dori is an exceptionally knowledgeable and disciplined psychologist. Learning psychology is his specialty. He phrases questions about an animal's behavior with such precise focus that their answers have direct implications about underlying neuronal mechanisms. At our first meeting in a symposium at Princeton University, Dori publicly claimed that I had not yet demonstrated that the meaning of the familiar stimulus, rotation, was transferred during training to another stimulus, light. I had not yet shown that after training, light elicits the response previously elicited only by rotation. Over the next few months, I telephoned Dori many times to be sure I completely understood his objection and to plan an experiment that would unequivocally prove or disprove this property of transferred meaning, which I agreed would be convincing evidence of associative memory. Dori and I developed a collegial rapport, which over the years evolved into friendship. It would take three years for my laboratory to prove the transfer effect. By the time this question was answered, however, there was little doubt that the snail *Hermissenda* was capable of a type of memory similar to that originally demonstrated for Pavlov's dogs. Over the years I would meet and learn from colleagues as perceptive, critical, and honest in other fields as Dori was in psychology. With these people, it was never difficult to distinguish between critical rigor and hostility. Their questions, though demanding, were always sincere. I identified with their commitment to a scientific esthetic and a shared sense of purpose. I also identified with their uncompromising intolerance of arbitrary, unfounded judgments.

To continue the experimental strategy I had mapped out sometimes required confronting such unfounded judgments. Not long after I had obtained the first evidence that the snail could be trained with paired light and rotation, I noticed a marked change in the attitude of one of my senior scientific supervisors. As long as I worked on quantitative details of the visual-vestibular network, I was treated with respect and considered to have considerable promise. But when it became clear that I had an interest in memory, the atmosphere grew chilly. At first I was gently warned with jokes. Later, more direct advice was volunteered. "Leave memory to the Russians. Here, we are realists. We work with hard science, not fuzzy pipe dreams." I never for a moment considered complying, but when the time came to publish my first report on associative learning in the snail, the most negative of my supervisors raised a prospect that took me aback. He felt my report should not even be submitted for publication. Unwilling to take full responsibility himself for censoring my publication, he formed a board of review. I cannot forget the shame and indignation of having to defend my science before that board.

I remember trembling with anger at those who mindlessly ridiculed the idea that a snail could be capable of associative memory. They were not questioning the data documenting features of the animal's learning behavior or the neuronal network which made it possible. There were no doubts about my objectivity or the highly significant behavioral differences produced by the training. But to some, using the word *learning* to describe any part of a snail's behavioral repertoire was absurd. They disputed the possibility that the snail training or its underlying cellular mechanisms could have meaning for other species, particularly vertebrates. According to some of my senior colleagues, any intelligent investigator should know that such phenomena would never be generalizable. They had only contempt for the possibility that mechanisms of memory storage could be conserved and therefore ubiquitous among species. Such heretic notions, they claimed, should not go unchecked. Other voices were raised in counter protest, however. A majority of the board supported my view, and my work escaped the censors.

Many years would have to pass before I could conduct my experiments once again without looking over my shoulder. It also took time for the debate inside my own head to be resolved. Only an exhaustive examination of the snail's learning behavior finally demonstrated virtually every major feature of Pavlovian conditioning so well known in mammals including humans. Nevertheless, perhaps, my ordeal served a purpose. It showed me clearly that science was all too human an enterprise. Intellectual positions could be as inaccessible and emotionally charged as other learned patterns of behavior. Colleagues might vigorously disagree not because of personal animosity, but because beliefs that formed the underpinning of their own experimental approaches were threatened.

In retrospect, the attitude of some of my supervisors was in the mainstream of twentieth-century neurophysiology so ably led by the English. Their focus was on the origin of electrical signals from the flow of ions through membrane channels. Some believed the only reasonable approach was to analyze transmission of chemical messengers across individual synapses or, at most, a finite group of synapses, as in the eye of the horseshoe crab. Problems such as memory in a mammal's brain, they felt, were beyond the scope of present technology and should be left for the future. To attack such problems now was at best foolhardy, at worst grandiose.

The Russians, indeed, had a different tradition, one forged by Pavlov. Pavlov, too, in the early nineteen hundreds was confronted with a chorus of discouraging voices. It took considerable courage for him to shift his experimental emphasis from studies of gastrointestinal physiology to learning behavior. But didn't the study of concrete "real" phenomena win him the Nobel Prize? Memory mechanisms were categorized as "psychic" phenomena. Leave such vague intangibles to others, he was advised. I, too, had formulated an intellectual position that others might find limited or distorted but to which I felt compelled to be true. The power of experimental verification is that slowly, sometimes over many decades, the accumulated observations of generations help us to accept new and different beliefs and positions. In this slow, sure way, we continue to demonstrate our capacity to unlearn what was learned and remembered so long ago in the past.

Fig. 16 The snail *Hermissenda*. Note the anterior projections that sense touch and chemical stimuli. The coat of featherlike appendages over much of its length provide increased surface area for respiratory and digestive functions. This animal is about 3 cm. long. (Courtesy of T. Crow and J. Forrester, 1991. *The Journal of Neuroscience*, V. 11, cover. Oxford University Press, N.Y.)

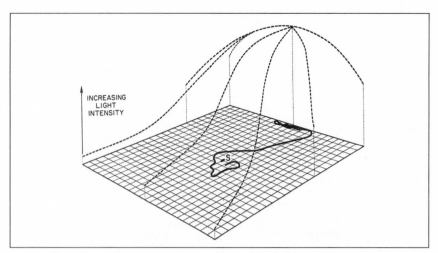

Fig. 17A The trail of the snail. The black line across the checkerboard traces the path of the snail as it moves toward a source of light at the peak of the radiating lines. Pavlovian conditioning transforms this response into a powerful contraction of the snail's muscular undersurface causing the snail to cling to the surface that supports it. (Courtesy of Dr. Izja Lederhendler in *Memory Traces in the Brain*, D. L. Alkon, 1987. Cambridge University Press, N.Y.)

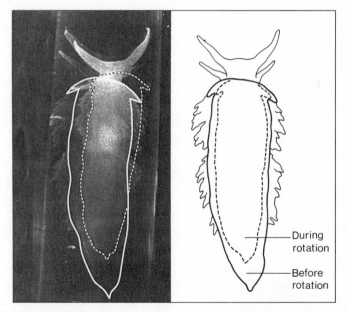

Fig. 17B The snail clings during rotation. Time-lapse photographs just before (solid outline) and during (dashed outline) rotation visualize the contraction of the snail's muscular undersurface, called its "foot." The contraction causes the snail to grip and hold on to the surface over which it is moving. The length of the snail is about 3 cm. (Courtesy of Dr. Izja Lederhendler, formerly of the author's laboratory.)

DISCOVERIES

To follow the flow of signals through the snail's brain, I made thousands of microelectrode recordings from neurons that talked to each other across synaptic junctions. But to analyze memory in these networks, new as well as classical recording techniques were often necessary. Still, there was always the pressing question: did the experiment justify the time necessary to develop the technique?

Once, for example, I decided it was important to monitor the neurons while the network was actually learning. I wanted to watch the network go through the steps of change required to store a memory. This meant keeping a microelectrode inside a neuron while the entire network was being rotated at 50 to 70 r.p.m. For months I rebuilt my recording apparatus so that the microelectrode would not slip out of the cell. When the snail's nervous system rotated, the entire recording apparatus rotated with it. Still the microelectrode kept falling out of the neuron during rotation. This was due, I reasoned, to the movement of the sea water against the microelectrode. I had to devise a chamber in which there would be no movement of the sea water during rotation. My new chamber would be like a jar filled with sea water but with no air space between the water's surface and the jar's lid. Then there would be no possibility of the water sloshing about during rotation.

The stability of the microelectrode during rotation improved enormously, but it was still not good enough. After spending almost half of a year on this problem without success, I came to a difficult decision. As worthwhile a project as it was, I could not invest much more time. I could still continue my strategy without this technique, although a valuable piece of the puzzle would remain missing. I gave myself one more week. Feverishly, I worked under my self-imposed time limit, experimenting with different ways of holding the snail nervous system immobile. Tiny pins through the tissue kept tearing it, allowing the nervous system to move ever so slightly during rotation. Finally, I came on just the right configuration. The pins no longer penetrated but instead lay across the nervous system. Two thin strips of vaseline, in turn, held the ends of the pins, and thereby the nervous system, onto the glass. Now I could train the snail's nervous system, but without the snail. Microelectrodes positioned through tiny holes in the transparent lucite lid of my chamber "jar" monitored the transformation of the neuronal signals during learning.

This was only one of the many experimental configurations we would have to use, but it was a crucial one. I would not have to guess what happens when a network's signals progressively changed during learning. I could watch it happen. Later we would want to record from the neurons in the living animal during learning. Other measurements required isolating single neurons and/or their membranes or even molecules associated with their membranes. Each question would require its own technical answers, which would have to justify the required commitment of time and resources.

I was not playing a game. To me it was all a serious business. I was not responsible for patients, but while I satisfied my curiosity, I was in my own way fulfilling an obligation to those who, like Michelle, were beyond the reach of modern medicine. During those first years while I launched my search strategy at N.I.H., Michelle probably enjoyed her best times. Just finishing college, she married, worked sporadically and looked forward to having children. Her hypersensitive, overactive, often aggressive, and slightly out of control manner hadn't changed on the few occasions when we met during these years. Yet she seemed to have achieved something of an equilibrium. I never gave up hope that she might realize some fulfillment in her life, but I had known her too well and for too long to be optimistic.

When I came to the N.I.H., I left clinical medicine with great regret. Though I loved science, I also loved caring for patients. I was particularly interested in their psychological orientation as a cause or consequence of their physical symptoms. What better opportunity could I have to learn about human behavior than to enter their lives by forming a therapeutic alliance? In the laboratories of N.I.H., without such opportunities, I consoled myself with the plan that one day I would combine basic research with clinical practice. After a few years, I knew I could not do the type of science I aspired to and also have clinical duties. Although it might have little direct impact on patients, science would be my mission as well as my pleasure.

I did, however, have other opportunities to work closely with people as my science entered a new phase. I had laid out a large canvas for myself. Even for a lowly snail, mechanisms of memory storage encompassed many research disciplines from experimental psychology to electrophysiology to biochemistry to molecular biology. I could not be a master of all. To carry my strategy further, I would have to work together with colleagues who shared my interests. I began by accepting responsibility for one or two postdoctoral fellows, but soon my single laboratory grew into a small department. I built this department, keeping faithful to my mission orientation. My determination to get the science done provided a powerful incentive to modify my isolated ways. It forced me to learn a whole new set of skills for working with people, which I did not have. It was, in fact, a process of socialization. In order to pursue my search strategy, I would have to train younger colleagues to become productive. Making them productive, however, was not just a matter of assigning a task, enforcing discipline, and checking on job completion. I was not showing someone how to use a cash register and then assuring myself that a sufficient number of customers were amiably accommodated in a day. I had to discover how someone thought. What were their questions, insights, values? We would spend long hours discussing protocol designs, necessary equipment, and the practicality of planned experiments. Eventually my involvement with a member of my laboratory would become total. I learned of their strengths and weaknesses, their personalities, and their reliability.

Often, this meant working in the laboratory directly with an individual. There are few opportunities to obtain more complete knowledge of a person than from doing experiments together on a daily basis. A person's attitude toward work, self, and others ultimately becomes transparent. It might take a few months, but by then I could gauge an individual's scrupulousness, persistence, creativity, technical adeptness, and, most of all, honesty. Supervisors who have enough contact with their younger colleagues need not be watching over their shoulder to suspect wrongdoing. Intimate contact over a prolonged period provides an abundance of clues about trustworthiness.

I recall, for instance, one postdoctoral fellow who had an obvious command of the neuroscience literature. He understood current theory and he was always informed about the latest developments. He was technically above average, able to record from neurons and to analyze the data he collected. He was excited about the experiments and he seemed willing to work hard. Some months after he had come to the laboratory, he brought a few complaints to me that made me a bit curious. He claimed he didn't have enough of the most modern equipment. In order to do the experiments he planned, he needed to buy more than what we had agreed on. Now this in itself was not a cause for alarm, but it seemed to me that the extra equipment, though desirable, was not essential. He didn't have to wait for the equipment to do his experiment. If I were he, I wouldn't want to wait for months for new equipment when I could be making observations. He also complained that a few of his co-workers weren't taking adequate care of shared resources and interrupted his privacy too often. Again, the complaint in itself was ordinary. Yet there was a quality to his concerns that hinted at distortion. The world around him was not treating him well. It was not his behavior that was causing him trouble, nor was it the inherent difficulties of doing his experiments. External forces, particularly people, were conspiring against him. This was, to be sure, quite subtle. He did not come with any theories of conspiracy or persecution. There was, however, a quality to his complaints that made me suspect the possibility that he was attributing control over his life and actions to everyone but himself. This would let him off the hook. If he failed, it would not be his fault. It would be the negative conditions in the laboratory, his colleagues, and, of course, I, his supervisor, who made him fail. Some months later, my suspicions, which had already made me vigilant, were not only confirmed but expanded.

One day he came to me excited about an observation he had made. An electrical signal of a particular neuron changed when he injected a molecule well known to be affected by synaptic messages. His finding could have potential importance since this might be a mechanism by which synaptic messengers caused long-lasting changes of neuronal signals. I asked him how many times he had repeated this observation. He said that although he had done the experiment with this particular neuron only once, he had seen similar effects with many other neurons. He presented the other examples, which showed great variability. None of the signals were exactly the same to begin with, nor were the effects of injection the same. Some injections had no effect, some had the opposite effect. I suggested that there was simply too much variability to draw any conclusions on the basis of the data he had collected. I recommended that he choose one single, recognizable neuron in the snail and repeat the injection under exactly the same conditions enough times to determine whether or not the effect was real. I watched the expression on his face change as I insisted on an extensive and rigorous protocol. His unusually handsome features became twisted. How could I not see the obvious? Why was I not sharing his excitement? There was even an indication that my reaction was born of jealousy. Nevertheless, he would follow my advice and we would then discuss it further.

Months passed. Experiments that should have been straightforward were not finished. When we finally talked again, he had added only a few neurons to his sample, with no clear trend apparent in the data, yet he remained convinced that the finding was unequivocal. Now I was sure he was not to be trusted. Every observation he had made in the past was now in doubt. There was no way I could clearly distinguish between data he had actually collected and data he had completely manufactured. I had no choice but to repeat with my own hands every measurement he had made. I permitted none of his data to be published unless I had collected all of the data over again myself. This did not endear me to my young colleague.

There are few, if any, generalizations I can make about the scientists, senior or junior, with whom I have worked over the years. While very few are overtly dishonest, some can fool themselves. While most are careful, a few are so compulsive that they become immobilized, unable to complete an experiment. Some are interested in the science, others the imagined prestige. Some are active, others passive. Some love the equipment and the techniques for their own sake and care little about questions and their possible answers. To make my laboratory productive, I learned to limit my goals. I did not aim to shape the interests of an individual who had already finished college and graduate school. My goal was to help create conditions in which young scientists might discover what they were best suited to do. To me, it was less important whether they were question oriented or technique oriented than that they knew and acted on their real orientation. There is always a need for new ideas as well as better technology. What would work for the individual would often work for the research.

We were engaged in exploration of inner as well as external worlds. I doubt that Phillip George knew exactly what I needed in my first independent experience in science, which was to be left alone with occasional advice and reinforcement, but he happened to provide it. Once in a great while, I will see myself in a young person coming through the lab. One graduate student, for example, decided he wanted to record from neurons in brain slices. This fellow was ruggedly independent, bright, overly assertive, and compulsively honest. He wanted only a certain degree of supervision and needed to feel he was in his own laboratory. Not that I wasn't welcome to record with him, discuss and analyze data, and interpret results. It was just that he needed plenty of room. I gave it to him. Supervising him was not always the most pleasant experience. Nevertheless, he turned out to be one of my most productive colleagues in the laboratory.

Self-awareness helps in finding one's scientific niche. I saw this in action when another young scientist approached me with his concern that he was playing too much of a collaborative role. He was facilitating the experiments of so many other people that he was neglecting his own particular interests and he was not publishing enough papers. He decided he should become a bit more selfish in order to find his own direction and express his individual perspective. In the past, I had often thought of this young man as the glue that held many of the laboratory members together. He was, indeed, a facilitator. Not only gifted in diverse technologies of the lab, he was never confrontational, always accommodating. His eagerness to please sometimes worried me, although I found it difficult to refuse his amiable assistance. Thinking his self-assessment entirely accurate, I encouraged him to pursue a more self-oriented research program. Aware of his own behavioral patterns, he enlisted the support of others, including myself, to change those patterns. We don't often have the privilege, in science or in any other life pursuit, of seeing clearly what we are doing, what we're after, or where we're coming from. Yet success often depends on some such perspective, even if it is only partially conscious.

I sometimes catch myself being disturbed or saddened when I have not met with approval from a director, a colleague, or someone I supervise. There may be valid reasons for the disapproval, but the reasons may also be due to differences of style, taste, and personality. These differences are, I believe, best accepted, for better or for worse. I happen to be animated, enthusiastic, emotional. I am interested in scientific questions that don't readily admit to definitive answers. I am willing to take risks. I don't like beating around the bush and I am not accomplished politically. In many ways I don't fit into the often sedate, English-led traditions of quantitative twentieth-century neurophysiology. But it won't help to try to become what I am not. There isn't that amount of freedom in life. I was formed and shaped by my experiences to work on certain experimental problems. It has been my immense good fortune that what I was suited to do, and what I became passionately interested in, converged with the needs and interests of the times in which I live. Whatever success my science has had and will have derives from that fortunate match.

UNEARTHING THE RECORD

According to my search strategy, the blueprint of the snail's visual-vestibular network would serve as a map to find the site(s) of memory storage. Some form of memory record should be preserved at such a site. My task was now to find the records. But what should they look like?

Many guesses were reasonable. The record could be located at synapses, the junctions that connect one neuron to another and tightly regulate the flow of information throughout the network. The amount of chemical message released at a synapse could be altered during learning and remain permanently altered as a memory record. Or possibly, the chemical message would be unchanged, but the receptors, sensitive spots on a neuron that receive the messages, would be transformed during memory formation. A change in the physical structure of the synapse was another alternative. Maybe the synapses themselves don't change during learning, but the long wirelike branches leading to the synapses are altered. Perhaps learning changes electrical properties or the transport of ingredients down the axon to the synapse. I knew what memories looked like inside my head but not what they looked like in neuronal networks. Perhaps recordings of electrical signaling within the network would lead me to sites where the memories could be revealed.

I inserted microelectrodes into neurons along the path followed by electrical signals through the visual-vestibular network. The portion of the neuron's electrical signals that flows into the microelectrode is negligible, but it can be amplified and viewed as phosphorescent traces on an oscilloscope. Microelectrode recordings are like wiretapping, which monitors a telephone conversation by drawing off very small amounts of the electrical signals that carry voices without altering those signals or the voices. Microelectrodes allow us to eavesdrop on the discussions within a neuronal network without the neurons knowing. Microelectrodes can also eavesdrop on the signal conversations at synaptic junctions between the visual and vestibular pathways. With simultaneous impalements of sensory neurons, intermediate neurons, and motoneurons, my colleagues and I followed the light-triggered changes of electrical signals from input to output of the snail's brain. Rotation, the stimulus we used together with light during Pavlovian conditioning of the snail, causes its own sequence of electrical signals in the networks.

Learning was immediately apparent in the electrical signals of a particular type of sensory neuron called the B cell. Each signal is very short, lasting from 1 to 20 thousandths of a second. For all known neurons in the snail and the vast majority of neurons in mammalian brains, such explosive signals are the basic alphabet of a network's language. Somewhat like Morse code signals, they cluster together to form words and sentences. The signals carry information in their frequency, duration, and clustering as they are transmitted along the axon at great speed to reach the terminal synaptic branches. At the synapses, the frequency and duration of the electrical signals determine the chemical messages released.

The electrical signals of the type B cell tracked the snail's learning with amazing precision. The snail's learning improved, for instance, with repetition of the training stimuli. Exactly the same improvement was evident in the B cell responses. With practice, the learning improved and the B cell response improved. When the animal remembered to contract its foot in response to light, the B cell remembered to increase its signals. When the animal forgot its Pavlovian response, the B cell forgot.[1] Furthermore, the B cell communicated what it learned in conversations with other neurons. These neurons in turn passed on the information to other listeners.

Although the B cell's electrical signals were correlated with changes in the snail's learning, a closer relationship, one of causality, was still in question. If the B cell was in fact a storage site for the snail's memory, then the changes in B cell signals should *cause* the learning and not simply be related to it. Were the B cell changes only passively reading out what was stored somewhere else? Perhaps learning caused permanent changes at some unknown sites in the snail's brain, and these sites caused both the learned behavior and the changes in B cell signals. Here the network map proved essential to follow the route of the light stimulus effects within the B cell,[2] as well as through the nervous system.

To prove that the learning changed the type B cells themselves, I removed the same exact type B cell from each of many animals that had learned to associate light with rotation. The type B cells were isolated, with all compartments intact except for their synaptic junctions, on days after the animals' training experience. Now, no other neurons anywhere else in the brain could influence the type B cell responses. Days and even weeks after learning, light triggered enhanced signaling in type B cells isolated from trained animals, while no changes occurred in the responses of cells isolated from untrained animals. Only animals that had learned to associate light with rotation had B cells with an enhanced electrical response to light. Therefore, the memory record had to be inside the cell. This memory could not be due to some other unknown cell signaling to the isolated B cell or to some unknown hormone or chemical released from the brain. No other cells were present. This result was the second major clue in the hunt for the memory record.

Now my pursuit assumed a relentlessness over which I seemed to have no control. This was no longer simply a matter of mission, curiosity, or esthetics. It was a battle. I was matching my wits against the hidden complexities of this network maze. And I was beginning to win. The first clue was the close relationship of the B cell signal changes to the changed behavior of the living animal. The second clue was that these changes were still present in type B cells completely isolated from the snail's networks. An additional compelling clue came from tracking all other signal changes along the mapped pathways. By following the wiring map, my colleagues and I were able to show that other learned changes measured within the snail's visual-vestibular network were a direct consequence of the type B cell changes. Electrical changes at each station along the pathways, from the input, where the information was sensed, through the brain, where integration occurred, to the output, where behavior was controlled, were reflections of the changed type B cell itself. Changes of other neurons in the pathways did not persist if the neurons were isolated.[3] These other neurons were not storing, therefore, but reading out what was stored in the type B cell.

Joseph Farley, working with me at the Marine Biological Laboratory in Woods Hole, provided additional support for the type B cell's memory record by inserting microelectrodes into B cells of living snails that had not been trained with light and rotation. By injecting electrical current shortly after a light flash occurred, he artificially enhanced the B cell responses and thereby mimicked the effect of learning on the type B cells. After allowing the animals to recover, he found that they showed evidence of learning the light-rotation association just as if they had been conditioned with natural stimuli.

We were, therefore, at a storage site. At this site the memory record "looked like" more signals in response to light. More electrical signals send more synaptic messages to other neurons and therefore store the memory. But what in the neuron makes more electrical signals? We knew that the flow of charged particles through channels in the neuron's wall produced the signals. Perhaps learning regulated channels? Memory-regulated channels would in turn alter the charged particle flow, the signals, and the synaptic messages.

We had to look at the channels. This would require another level of acrobatics with microelectrodes. One microelectrode in the type B neuron would not be enough. I now inserted two or three into the same cell. Inserting each microelectrode without knocking the others out or tearing the cell wall apart proved to be a nerve-wracking balancing act. Yet I eventually managed to record this way for hours on end, sometimes with one of the microelectrodes within the wirelike axon, only a millionth of a meter in diameter. The signals recorded by such microelectrode ensembles revealed the flow of charged particles through the channels in the neuron's wall.

Soon after I began measuring particle flow across the neuron wall, or membrane, something peculiar caught my attention. Once activated by the light flash, the flow of certain charged particles, those of a potassium salt, across the membrane could not be entirely reactivated for many seconds afterward. It was as if the potassium flow had a memory of its prior activation. I remember sitting in the dark marveling at the slowness of this recovery (originally observed by John Connor in other neurons) and thinking how different this was from the classic story worked out for electrical signals, which spread down axons at fantastic speeds. Each of these axonal signals, also present in the type B axon, was completed within a few thousandths of a second and ready to be reactivated almost immediately thereafter. Maybe, I thought, the prolonged recovery of the potassium flow was in some way related to the prolonged nature of memory storage. Maybe a recovery lasting many seconds could, during memory acquisition, be extended to many hours, days, and longer. When all was said and done, this would prove to be the case.[4] A permanently altered flow of potassium particles through membrane channels provides a memory record for later recall not only in the snail, but also in mammals.

Now the words *memory record* and *memory trace* took on a new and exciting meaning. A memory record "looks like" altered molecular channels in neuronal membranes. Channels in a mature neuron's membrane remained changed for weeks after the light occurred together in time with rotation. Nothing comparable had ever been encountered in any fully formed cell known to science. This was not what I or anyone else had expected. Since Helmholtz first measured its speed, Bernstein theorized how it was generated, and Hodgkin and Huxley measured its underlying flow of charged particles, no one imagined that a neuron's electrical signal could remain transformed for days or even weeks. True, the signal developed along with the neuron. But once development is complete, a neuron's signals were thought to be just as constant as those that pace the heart. Yet our observations in the snail's brain and later the rabbit's hippocampus violated our expectations and led us to a new way of thinking about particle flow. Experience could produce long-lasting changes of particle flow. Nature heard nurture's voice in the movements of particles through membrane channels.

Memory-altered channels in a cell membrane are in a sense like altered molecules within a magnetic tape. A tape deck transforms a voice's sound patterns into patterns of magnetic force. Patterns of molecule alignment on a tape winding through the tape deck are permanently shaped by the voice-controlled magnetic force. The tape, or even a portion of it, can be physically removed from the recording machine. Years later, the alignment patterns of the tape, once again within a machine, determine electric current patterns, which are transformed back into the sound patterns. The recording is preserved on the tape within the molecular alignment, but the machine is required to make and later to play the recording. Like a tape deck, the snail's visual-vestibular network first makes the memory record in response to an elementary stimulus pattern: light followed in time by rotation. The memory record is then preserved within the type B neuronal membrane by the alteration of potassium channels. Later, light sensed by the visual network replays the memory record when it activates the altered channels. Only light makes the type B membrane positive enough to open the potassium channels. During recall, light addresses the memory of its association with the second event, rotation. This is how the natural magnetic tape is replayed.

This mechanism of memory storage should not be peculiar to the snail. It should, perhaps with some modifications, also store memory in more advanced animals. It should tell us what to look for and where to look. Perhaps the potassium channel changes in the snail would be a basis for memory storage even in humans. The elementary, isolated biophysical transformation in the snail might occur thousands, even millions of times when a memory is stored in the mammalian brain. Maybe this memory code, multiplied a thousand times over in layers of neurons within regions of mammalian brain, serves as the basis for recognizing not one, but the millions of memory links within a remembered pattern or image. My experimental game plan was designed to test just that possibility. But the snail results already pointed to the need for rethinking popular notions of memory storage.

Ramon y Cajal imagined, as did many others after him, that memory was stored by the growth of new synapses, the junctions of communication between neurons. This notion was partially derived from previous observations that synapses and branches proliferate during early development. The branches of a dendritic tree, which receive synaptic signals from other neurons, become much more complex during the first one to two years of postnatal life. Wasn't it reasonable to suppose that the proliferation of synaptic sites that occurs in development also occurs during learning? Deprived of experience, didn't the neurons lack some of their usual structural complexity and functional integrity? Many other related experiments demonstrated that prolonged exposure of animals to sensory-rich environments, particularly during critical developmental stages, increased the number of sites of synaptic contact while sensory deprivation reduced their number. It was reasonable to suppose that learning changes networks in the same way sensory enrichment does. More learning produces more synaptic sites. However, we had found that remembering associations between stimuli does not result from the amount of sensory stimulation, but from the timing of the stimulation. Maybe the developmental growth of synaptic sites, which is susceptible to deprivation, is in fact not directly analogous to the neuronal changes that store memory. Maybe the initial changes of learning don't involve any new synapses at all but only changes in the effectiveness of synapses that already exist. Perhaps learning changes the *strength* of existing synapses but not their *number*. Long after mammalian brains are no longer developing, long after their neurons have stopped dividing, long after their branches have stopped becoming recognizably more complex, isn't the brain still able to store vast quantities of new information?

The potassium channel changes that stored the memory of the light-rotation link in the snail were telling us, then, not to look for an increased number of synapses or greater complexity of branches but for modified membranes distributed throughout systems of neurons that already existed—that had already developed according to genetic blueprints. They were telling us that the neuronal code for memory has its own unique features, quite distinct of codes that allow for development of the neurons themselves. The initial changes during snail and, later, rabbit learning were saying that cellular expressions of remembered time that are due to an individual animal's experience are different from expressions of evolutionary time that are due to an entire species' experience. And to understand memory, particularly memory as complex as that of humans, these differences would have to be sorted out.

So far, we had seen that a memory "looks like" more electrical signals and reduced flow of potassium particles across a membrane. But the revolution in science during the past two centuries had demonstrated that life depends not only on the functions of whole cells but also on the molecules within the cells. Somehow molecules were colliding and recombining in such a way as to change the potassium flow and thereby the electrical signals. Now I had to use a "microscope" with power enough to "see" molecules. Therefore I began to use the microscope of modern biochemistry to visualize memory records at a molecular level.

There is one formidable problem that any molecular memory mechanism must overcome. This has been one of the most fascinating and impenetrable mysteries of memory storage. Almost all proteins in a neuron have their own individual lifetimes, which may be a few seconds or a few days. Protein lifetimes are generally too short to permit them to store long-term memory. If a molecule has been modified during learning, shouldn't this modification be lost forever once the molecule is degraded during the cell's normal cycle of protein break-down and synthesis?

Several scenarios have been proposed to explain how the cell might get around the mortality of its own constituents. DNA, for example, which orchestrates the cellular machinery for making proteins, might be altered. This would be a change at the source, so to speak. The genetic template, once altered, would alter all subsequent proteins made from that template. It has so far been impossible to demonstrate a memory-specific DNA change, however. Then there is the difficulty of how information stored in the inner sanctum of the cell, its nucleus, targets remote branches of an elaborate neuronal tree. Another sce-nario, not mutually exclusive of the first, localizes permanent memory storage in the physical structure of the neuron. A branch that contacts specific neurons might be eliminated, never to return again. Or new branches might be added. The shape of existing branches might be changed so as to make some incoming signals larger. Changes of cell structure do not reverse easily. The structure itself influences the avail-ability of new proteins to different regions of the cell. Twisted arrange-ments of molecules in space may be self-perpetuating, because the newly synthesized molecules will take on arrangements according to what is already there. This self-perpetuating characteristic is common to all scenarios proposed for making the memory records permanent. If the DNA is altered, it then directs the subsequent synthesis of proteins so that the DNA remains altered. If the structure of the neuron is altered, the structure will channel the entry of new proteins and the removal of old proteins so as to maintain the altered structure.

Francis Crick proposed a different variation on this theme. Perhaps the self-perpetuation begins within the cytoplasm of the cell. An altered protein signals to the DNA or to its RNA targets to change the synthesis of other proteins, which then act on the original protein to keep it in its newly altered state. Alternatively, an enzyme once acti-vated during learning might act on itself to keep activated. The enzyme would then be its own target. Memory storage would initiate a cycle in which an enzyme becomes activated and then activates more enzymes. If these scenarios sound like pure speculation, that is just what they are. They are interesting, provocative possibilities with only a few hints of substantiation.

To sort out molecules that store memory and leave the world of speculation, my colleagues and I followed biochemical pathways within individual neurons just as we had traced a map of pathways among the neurons in networks to unearth electrical records. Once again, the snail provided the first clues. During training, stimuli are translated first into a molecular as well as an electrical language of the neurons. The light stimulus is represented by a burst of calcium particles within the type B cell. Rotation, the unconditioned stimulus, is represented by increases of another molecule, diacylglycerol, or DAG for short, near or within the type B membrane. The right timing of the training stimuli causes the right combination of the molecules calcium and DAG to throw a molecular switch inside the type B cell membrane.[5]

Just as water and cement powder interact to form concrete, a material with new strength and permanence, the combination of calcium and DAG produces a memory record that begins to harden. The combination of light and rotation throws the switch by causing an enzyme called protein kinase C (PKC) to move to the neuron's membrane. At this new location near the cell's membrane, the enzyme is potently activated to reduce the flow of potassium particles through the membrane channels.[6]

Louis Matzel in our laboratory obtained evidence that this enzyme appears to retain its activated state even weeks after the snail has learned the light-rotation link. But it is not clear how the cell's molecules accomplish this persistent activation. Almost all proteins, including our enzyme switch, are continually resynthesized and broken down into constituents. A shift toward increased synthesis of the ingredients responsible for activation (such as DAG) could help explain long-lasting effects on the PKC. Alternatively, there might be increased synthesis of a protein that mediates PKC's effects during learning. In fact, Thomas Nelson in our laboratory isolated and characterized just such a protein.[7]

When the snail learns the light-rotation link, the modified "conditioning" protein appears to act on the channels within the type B cell membrane. Carlos Collin showed that injection of this protein into the type B cell immediately alters the flow of potassium, storing short-term and eventually longer-term memory. Did other effects of this protein mediate long-term and perhaps permanent memory? It remained for a Japanese colleague, Manabu Sakakibara, to provide evidence that this conditioning protein also causes a structural rearrangement of neuronal branches, just as we found occurs during long-term learning.

Years before, Manabu had come to our laboratory in Woods Hole as a postdoctoral fellow, although he was already an assistant professor in his home university. When he first arrived, he concentrated on every

step as I dissected the snails, isolated their nervous systems, and prepared their neurons for recording. During the first few days, he just
watched and took notes. Later I would stop toward the end of the
preparatory procedures and he would finish where I left off. Gradually
he took over the experiment earlier and earlier in the protocol. Within
three months, he was conducting his own protocols. None of the hundreds of people who have worked in my laboratory ever mastered the
techniques with Manabu's ease and success. During his brief appren-
ticeship he became my arms and legs, but then he was once again his
own man, with new abilities and new experimental horizons open
to him.

Manabu never talks loudly or insistently, but what he says, he says
with a conviction and a firmness that command attention. His persistence appears almost fanatical, but he remains open. He can change
direction based on sensible criticism or a different perspective. Within
his first year, he was predictably productive. Then his professor sent
him a message that it was time to return. The relations among faculty
in Japanese academia are such that the wishes of a superior are followed
without question. Yet Manabu and I felt he was just in the midst of har-
vesting the fruit of his training. Manabu suggested that as his American
supervisor, I might write to his professor to request that he spend
another year. So seriously was this suggestion considered that his professor journeyed to the United States. There in Woods Hole, Manabu,
his professor, and I met around a large conference table, methodically
examining why it was important for Manabu's scientific development
to stay longer and what he had done to deserve such a privilege. The
discussion was gentle and fact-finding, not adversarial. Manabu's professor was dignified, kind, and apparently open-minded. Not long after
his return to Japan, we received his positive reply. But it was no surprise. This was the type of man Manabu had somehow found for his
supervisor. Nor was it surprising that his parents showed the same
quiet dignity and confidence on their visit to Woods Hole.

To an American among the crowds on the Japanese subways, the
visible similarities of the people are at first more noticeable than their
differences. The same is true of their customs and manners. A first
exposure suggests a common concern with respect, and indirection in
expressing emotions. Smiling and bowing, they bring gifts to establish
contact. Conversation is formal, often humorless. Yet among the many
Japanese who have worked in my laboratory, no typical personality has
emerged. Still, Manabu was unique in his steadiness, maturity, and

competence. He was equally at ease with equations or electrical recording, microdissection or behavioral measurements. He could work with
an excitable colleague as well as an excitable membrane. And the people who mattered in his life reflected his maturity, whether it was his
parents, his wife, his students, or his teachers. These were the patterns
of experience he had learned and continually recreated. The behavioral
conditioning involved seems almost contagious—or self-propagating.
He was taught to expect certain behavior and, through his actions, he
lives that behavior, is drawn to it in others, and fosters it in others as
well.

But where did I fit in this pattern of conditioned behavior? Perhaps
there was something in me, too, that mirrored Manabu's expectations.
Manabu found me quite far into my life. He did not know my loneliness as a youth or the emotional origins of my driven search. By the
time we met, I had established my own equilibrium. I had already
found firm ground. By that time, my laboratory was my own world,
which to some extent I could transport intact to wherever I migrated
and settled. Within this world, all of the rules and procedures were
familiar. Not only had I amassed a large collection of experimental
tools, but I was used to asking questions and getting answers—publish-
able answers, which, although not always profound, were slowly filling
in a previously empty canvas. I had acquired a process I had come to
trust. I believed in my ability to make this process work, and to some
extent I could offer guidance to others who also wished to acquire it.

Now, in the summers, Manabu and his colleagues join us annually
to renew a partnership very much within the long tradition of collaboration between Japanese and Americans at the M.B.L. It is part of the
human puzzle that two nations locked in mortal battle less than five
decades ago now join forces in a struggle with nature's mysteries. Getting to know a Japanese colleague, I wonder where his parents were
during the war. There are no clues in the face of the son to the father
who served in a factory just outside of Hiroshima when the bomb fell,
as a foot soldier in the Pacific, or as a diplomat in Europe. As delicate
as the subject is, it is never that far from their minds. Decades later,
they still remember an almost universal resolve to change direction. It
is not fortuitous that the same Japanese Emperor who endorsed the
war would decades later visit the American laboratory by the sea that
shared his love of marine biology. Nor is it wasted on any summer visi-
tor, Japanese or American, that a parchment affirming these values in
the midst of the war is framed in a visible place of honor in the labora-

tory's library. Written at a Japanese marine station about to be occupied by American soldiers, the parchment asks that the peaceful pursuit of biological research be spared. At the end of this respectful plea for the station's preservation is the haunting signature "the last one to go."[8] Manabu feels welcome in Woods Hole, and that, along with the continually unfolding opportunities to satisfy one's curiosity, is why he, and I, keep coming back.

Two summers ago, Manabu knew that our snail's learning was accompanied by rearrangement of neuronal branches. He also knew that learning was accompanied by a prolonged chemical change in the protein that we had isolated and purified from the snail's eye. To test the hypothesis that the protein's change triggered the neuron's structural change, he injected the protein into an identified snail neuron through one microelectrode, and then through a second microelectrode injected a dye that spread from the cell body down the axon into all of the fine branches on which the synaptic junctions are located. The injected dye stains the cell's entire structure. Manabu found that the protein caused the stained branches to contract, or focus, just as we had found with the snail learning. Furthermore, in collaboration with others in the laboratory, he found that this focusing was accompanied by an alteration in the flow of protein particles within the branches. This one little protein, then, was able to trigger a number of different effects within the neurons that stored the memory record. The protein altered the flow of potassium across the neuronal membrane, altered the arrangement of its branches, and seemed to change the transport of particles within the axon and its branches. Later, Tom Nelson was able to demonstrate that the same protein also increased the actions of the RNA molecules that read out the directions of the DNA for manufacturing neuronal proteins.

From all of this, a possible molecular scenario for memory storage emerged.[9] In the early stages, the training stimuli act locally on particular neuronal branches. The resulting chemical messengers then change the electrical signaling of the neuron, as well as the movement of protein particles within its branches. As the memory record begins to gel and becomes longer-lasting, the protein we identified activates the machinery for making proteins in the neuron's nucleus. Still later, when the memory starts to become permanent, the local branch that originally received the training signals begins to undergo structural alterations in response to proteins transported from the cell body. Within the last few years, another scientist in our laboratory, James Olds, has revealed in the rabbit hippocampus the same type of dialogue between the neuron's synaptic compartments and the main bodies of neurons.

When I was a medical student, I was fascinated by experiments in which scientists blocked learning behavior by blocking the synthesis of proteins in the brain. Though fascinated, I was also frustrated. How could these scientists tell what significance protein synthesis has for the learning process without knowing what cells are making the proteins or what impact those proteins are having on the actual formation of the memory traces? Maybe protein synthesis is absolutely necessary for the animal to maintain its awake state and thereby sense the stimuli that occur together during training. Maybe without protein synthesis, the sensory cells cannot convert the stimuli in the external world into electrical signals inside the brain. Maybe the synapses in general do not function as well. Maybe the animal's muscles are less able to execute the learned behavior when synthesis of proteins is inhibited. Protein synthesis might be necessary in a variety of cells to permit learning and memory, therefore, but might not be specific to forming the memory trace. It was clear to me that molecular steps during learning had to be identified and analyzed for their exact contribution to functional changes within those cells that stored and expressed the memory. This had proven possible with the snail *Hermissenda* and later with the rabbit.

The molecular steps we had identified may only hint at an as yet unknown biochemical universe within the cell's memory apparatus. Nevertheless, they were inroads I had not expected to make in a lifetime of searching, no matter how much I wanted my quest to succeed.

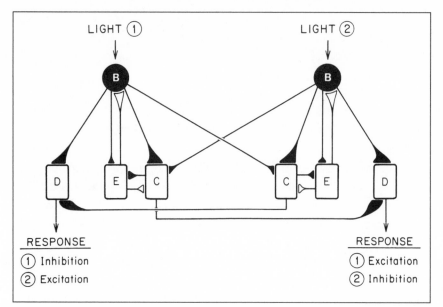

Fig. 18 Schematic representation of the snail's visual pathways. The intensity of light (1) stimulating the left eye is compared to the intensity of light (2) stimulating the right eye within the signals of neurons in the next layer. Open triangles signify excitatory synapses; closed triangles signify inhibitory synapses. This network tells the snail in what direction to move to reach the light source of Fig. 17. (From Tabata and Alkon, J. *Neurophysiology*, 1982. V. 48, 174–91)

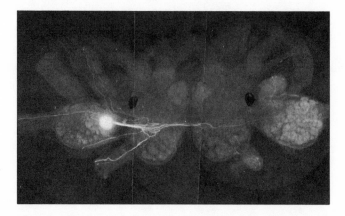

Fig. 19 A fluorescent dye injected into an identified neuron fills its most delicate branches which extend throughout the snail's central nervous system. The eyes and statocyst are located on each side next to the large ball-like neuron collections called ganglia. (From Jerussi and Alkon, J. *Neurophysiology*, 1981, V. 46, 659–71)

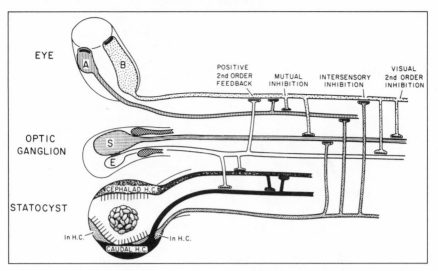

Fig. 20 Schematic representation of the snail's visual-statocyst network. Points of synaptic contact allow signals from the eye to meet signals from the statocyst. Stimuli and the signals they send linked in time adjust the weight of certain synapses and thereby change the flow of subsequent signals through the network. (From D. L. Alkon, *Science*, 1979. 205, 810–16)

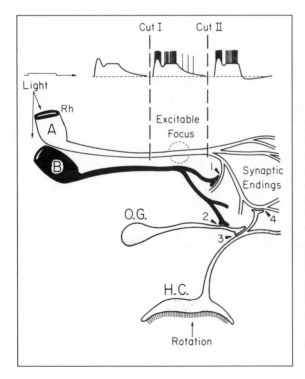

Fig. 21 Sketch of the visual and statocyst neurons' structures. Well-placed cuts (dashed lines) remove compartments of the neurons such as their connections or the origin of the large electrical signals (excitable focus) on the long axons. Such cuts isolate parts of the electrical responses recorded at the top of the figure. (From D. L. Alkon, *Memory Traces in the Brain*, 1987. Cambridge University Press, N.Y.)

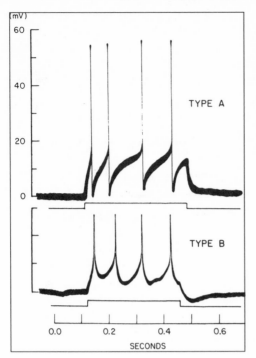

Fig. 22 Electrical signals of the snail's photoreceptors. The large signals of the type A cell provide an electrical signature which is characteristically different from the smaller signals of the type B cell. The number, frequency, and pattern of the signals express a kind of Morse Code in the language of neurons. (Recorded by the author in 1970)

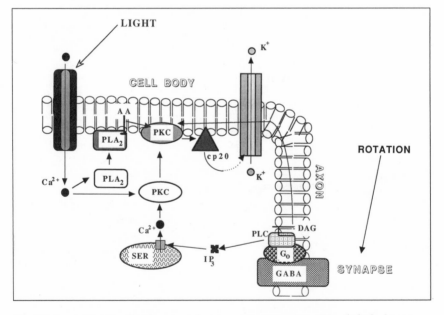

Fig. 23 A model of molecular steps during memory storage. Stimuli linked in time, light and rotation cause molecules to interact with each other in a cascade of events beginning at the wall or membrane of the cell. Ultimately, the sequence adjusts the weights of synaptic connections made by the neuron. (Courtesy of Dr. David Lester from the author's laboratory)

WANTING RESULTS

I wanted the snail *Hermissenda* to learn an association just as I later wanted to find the memory sites in its networks. For results, I would first have to separate wanting from measuring. The more automatic the data collection, the less opportunity for hopes and preconceived notions to bias the results. We could, for instance, train and test the snails and record their behavior automatically with time-lapse photographs. Frame by frame, the details of the snail's responses would be entered into and measured by a computer. Still we might, in our eagerness, inadvertently alter the measurements. We eliminated this possibility by using at least two observers. One knew the training experience but was "blind" to the testing measurements, while the other knew the testing data but not the training. Only at the very end of such a blind protocol did the two observers break their codes to each other. Automation, blinding, and careful analysis enable investigators to have their cake and eat it, too. They have their ideas, but to test them, they must use a different part of their cognitive capacity, a discipline that is not suited for generating ideas, but for testing them.

No single experiment or its replication was enough to know with complete certainty that the phenomena we observed were in fact real. We depended on a collection of such experiments, with a variety of manipulations and physiological contexts. The consistent replication and predictive power of the data eventually convinced us, as well as others. Inevitably, of course, there were some who, with or without the data, would never be convinced.

I have, on occasion, been told it simply is not possible to measure changes of membrane channels during learning. There is too much noise in the data, it is asserted, to detect a reliable signal. No matter that we had quantified a change for a specified neuron, that the change was shown by blind and automated protocols to occur only after training with light linked to rotation, that it was reproducible and even generalizable to other species. When I began my scientific career, I had certain expectations of standards by which people, including myself, would behave. My experience in science has taught that such standards are by no means universal.

Early in my research career, I worked with a professor who had taken a strong position about how chemical messengers carry information at the synapse. We designed experiments to test his hypothesis. After working intensely for more than a year on this project, my results became reliable. They also unequivocally contradicted my professor's hypothesis. He immediately dismissed the results, telling me the work had become uninteresting. The preparation was now functioning beautifully, and the planned protocol could be completely implemented, but I was told to discontinue the experiments. There wasn't any choice for me. I refused to stop, finished the protocols, and became persona non grata with a teacher I formerly admired. I soon found another mentor who did not have a vested interest in the results. Perhaps in another country my career would have been ended by such insolence. In our system, flawed as it is, I survived.

As a young investigator, I began to serve on review panels that evaluated programs for fundability. Senior reviewers sometimes made it clear that it would be simply unacceptable for particular investigators not to receive funds for their research. On other occasions ranking reviewers might suggest that so-and-so was not in the mainstream, not to be trusted, or was a bad academic influence. The signal having been given, attacks were launched without compunction.

I have witnessed humiliating interrogations of individuals in which the quality of their science was completely lost as an issue, while their personal integrity, originality, and rigor were attacked. First one of the pack nipped, then another took a bite, and soon it was a feeding frenzy. The poor victims were defenseless in a situation where their interrogators had the power to cut off funds, not only for their research funds but sometimes even their salaries. It is difficult to act with dignity and clearheadedness under such conditions. But some do.

The pressure within and outside of those committees can be overwhelming, and it is not limited to the awarding of grants. It influences decisions about the publication of scientific articles, about appointments to faculty positions and the awarding of prizes. It isn't always as I have described it. There are many contrary examples. But I have been disappointed more often than I could have imagined when I started out. I would never have believed, for example, that even scientific discussions are often carefully orchestrated. Orchestration can be implemented through the choice of topics, speakers, discussants, and attendees. The order of presentation, time allotments, and number of speakers are chosen in advance to influence the message. I am often reminded of politicians maneuvering for photo opportunities and sound bites. One biopolitician may determine, like a presidential candidate, that it would not be in his interest to appear at a public forum with his opponent. The polls show him too far ahead, so he stands to lose more scientific supporters than he might gain.

When a meeting is held, the dialogue can also be manipulated. Advocates of one point of view arrange to be in the majority in a discussion group and then belittle what appears to be a minority opinion. I have on occasion knowingly participated in such a group, prepared to confront a consensus entirely contrived beforehand. It can be a painful experience. I have done this in the hope of reaching a few neutral participants, some of whom have later become valued colleagues and even friends.

A scientific meeting can, of course, be the opposite of coercive. It can, and many times does, offer a real exchange of perspectives and results. It can be personally and intellectually rewarding when the atmosphere is not charged with potential hostility and when one need not hesitate to speak out for fear of contradicting the party line. The process is one of sharing conceptual and experimental experience. There are few barriers among the attendees because of differences in status.

When successful, such meetings are not idle exercises or privileges offered for the enjoyment of the invited; they are essential to the scientific enterprise. Whether it is economics or archaeology, mathematics or biology, physics or chemistry, accumulated knowledge in a particular area is so vast that it acquires a language of its own. Each discipline has its own terms and symbols, rules for organizing them, grammar for expressing them, and protocols for testing their reality. These languages are not acquired overnight. It takes years of thinking and speaking about the quantitative studies of behavior that make up experimental psychology before their language becomes a natural form of communication. Biophysicists who have devoted their lives to figuring out how charged molecules pass through the pores of a membrane need not, and usually do not, understand how to describe, let alone measure, the behavioral changes that conclusively demonstrate learning. A biochemist may suggest parallels between immunological recognition of an infecting organism and brain recognition of remembered images. But unless the biochemist demonstrates similar molecular events within the immune system and nervous system, the suggestion will remain largely within the realm of poetic license.

The cardiologist studies molecular and physical properties of the heart muscle, which control the distribution, strength, and rhythm of the force that pumps blood throughout the body. In parallel, the geneticist hunts for chromosomal abnormalities that produce a heart without a chamber or with a defective valve. Such different sciences, given their common interests, can learn from each other, but a dialogue among disciplines thrives only with mutual respect. The participants must really want a dialogue. The clinicians cannot dismiss the mathematicians because they have no appreciation for a functioning organ system. Nor can the physicists look down on the physiologists because they can't handle complex equations. No research is more in need of interdisciplinary dialogue than that on memory and cognitive functions. These subjects, by definition, span a range of disciplines from molecular biology and biochemistry to biophysics, mathematical modeling, and experimental psychology. It is easy for the dialogue to break down, and it often does.

Learning a new language, particularly when you already have one of your own, requires some humility. There must be a willingness to start over, to be and appear ignorant and therefore at a disadvantage. The new arrival in a strange land seeks acceptance from people who don't need him, at least not at first, the way he or she needs them. An expert on membrane biophysics, armed with a command of equations that describe current flow during neuronal signaling, is not going to suddenly solve the problems of learning and memory without knowing what learning and memory are. These are phenomena involving intact living organisms, their movements and their responses to stimulus patterns. Learning and memory, by definition, are not cellular phenomena, although they are potentially explainable by cellular and subcellular mechanisms. All of the equations in the world of membranes will not explain learning and memory unless those equations are put into a context of behaving animals. The biophysicist must learn to think and communicate in what must seem at first an alien and somewhat frightening language if he or she wants to solve problems formulated in that language.

I suppose many scientists experience some of my reactions while listening to scientific stories told by colleagues in their own languages. First, my curiosity is piqued. The initial remarks in the lecture, an introductory slide, invite me into the world of the speaker. I think about the questions being asked and their potential significance. A context begins to be created. The accumulated observations, taken together, make an extraordinarily compelling story. As I listen to the story, I want to believe it. Believing it brings satisfaction, a sense of mastery of the unknown, the solution to a mystery. I identify with those who are telling the story. I admire their brilliance, technical virtuosity, persistence, and accomplishment. There is, however, another side to my feelings as I listen. A part of me compares what the speaker can do with what I can do, competes, rather than identifies, with their accomplishment. I want to criticize, to find flaws, and show how I could do better. These feelings make me open to other observations not entirely consistent with the proposed hypothesis. Mistrust feeds on the urge to compete. The competitive feelings are useful in the demands they make for rigor and conclusive demonstrations. The tension between my positive and negative emotions, between admiration and jealousy, can be constructive; I can't be snowed, but I won't be hostile. The tension is resolved as the evidence becomes persuasive or obviously shaky. I imagine many of my own listeners have similar reactions. They want to be convinced, but they are ready to appreciate the beauty in a scientific story.

Listening to a music recital, I want to have confidence in the soloist. I want him (her) to bring me to a state of belief where I trust his (her) commitment to the perfection of the notes and their rhythms. I expect delivery on that commitment so that I can gradually give myself over to the music, no longer conscious of the musician. A musician's greatest gift is to give the music an independent life. This is also what a scientist can aspire to, accepting the inevitable separation between the observer and his observation, and, as with his child, ultimately entrusting it to others.

THE KINGDOM
OF REAL BRAINS

As much as I was fascinated by the snail's learning networks, I was never interested in them for their own sake. Their secrets were important to me only for what they might teach me about the way the human brain works. I knew that the snail's networks themselves could never reveal the brain processes that underlie human memories of trauma, unresolvable conflict, or isolation. I had no illusions that a tinkertoy network afforded experience which remotely resembled that of the brain's intricate wiring among billions of neurons. It was not even clear that the snail underwent anything that might be called "experience." Yet, I thought it possible that there was a kind of memory code locked within the snail's networks. This code might appear in its simplest and most recognizable form in lower animals but might be used in vastly more complex networks within the human brain. Such a code written in electrical and molecular alphabets might someday help us to read our own minds.

It is not possible with present technology to track human memory accurately. At any one instant, it is like a tidal wave of associations spreading through the brain, engulfing a multitude of neuronal signals in its wake. A human's conditioned emotional response cannot be reduced to an elementary association. An absolutely massive bank of memories may be recalled before the emotional response is triggered.

For a human, recognition begins with a few familiar fragments of a scene. In rapid sequence a shower of other memories comes into consciousness. Finally, a chain reaction culminates in an explosion of memories. So diverse and numerous are the memories within a single recognition experience that hosts of brain regions must participate in the process.

By the time I could even begin to test the generality of the snail's memory mechanisms in brain regions of higher species, it was much too late for Michelle. Long ago she had arrived at and acted on her own generalizations about what to expect from her relationships. Long ago I had made my peace with the certainty that no discoveries I could ever make would influence the outcome of her desperate course. I had no illusions, either, that the findings of colleagues throughout the field would in our lifetimes have a significant impact on people like her. Over the years, Michelle had acquired countless memories that confirmed her original traumatic abuse. Because of her learned expectations, she had sought and helped shape relationships that failed in family settings, school, and the workplace. Failed relationships, in turn, shaped her expectations and feelings about herself, her abilities, her physical appearance. By the time I started working on "real brains," such as those of rabbits and guinea pigs, Michelle was already generalizing her expectations of failure to her children. Not that there was any reason to. Her children were bright, physically beautiful, and devoted to her. But they were of her, and anything of her and with her, to Michelle, must be tainted.

What manner of technology could unravel such seamless layering of life's defeats in her responses even to everyday experiences? Today, imaging techniques reveal regions of increased blood flow in the brain during human perception of an object, or remembering a word or event from the recent past. However, we find scarcely a hint of the signal patterns that must exist among the millions of neurons in one region after another for even such rudimentary experiences, let alone experiences emerging from years of layered memories. What would be the signal patterns in Michelle's mind responsible for unloading her heavy emotional baggage onto everyday interactions with her children, husband, and employers? What unknown techniques will allow us to follow the mental ruts that forced her eternally to retrace the hopelessness of her past in spite of whatever she sensed in the present? These ruts cannot stand out in bold relief like tumors or hemorrhages. And even when they do, as I believe they someday will, knowledge of their intricate twists and turns through the brain will not reveal how they are created in the first place or how we might change them. No, long ago I made peace with the enormity of that challenge, but not without concessions. While I accepted the reality of the limits of the possible, I did not submit to denial or passivity. For me, it was simple. I cursed the darkness but also lit a candle by identifying a code in primitive animals. And by the mid 1980s, when that candle shed its first flickering light on the complex brains of mammals, Michelle had only a few years left to her.

For the snail's network to be useful in decoding memory within the hieroglyphics of brain circuitry, its mechanisms would have to have been preserved over the eons during which animal species evolved. There were already many examples of such preservation. The genetic code itself was deciphered in such lowly organisms as bacteria. With essentially minor modifications, the code applies to houseflies as well as humans. Along the helical structures of DNA, sequences of molecules called amino acids are arranged to encode the protein building blocks of cell structure and function. Once this code was created in nature, it was never recreated. Not that this would be impossible theoretically. But in our particular niche of the universe, species could become infinitely more adaptive and sophisticated and still be derived from the same code. A similar story is true for the channels in cell walls.

Traffic of charged ion particles through these membrane channels generates the electrical signals we have come to know as the language of neuronal networks. The unicellular organism called a Paramecium has been shown to have channels remarkably similar to those observed in snails, frogs, the mammalian spinal cord, and even humans. Once the molecular template for this channel was fabricated by nature, it changed minimally in an entire parade of animal species. If membrane channels are essentially the same from Paramecia to Homo sapiens, then perhaps the memory records assume a form, i.e., altered channels, that is not very different in snail and human. Perhaps the special arrangement of neurons and their connections that alters its channels in the snail's visual-vestibular network is repeated throughout the networks of "real" brains.

We entered this territory of real brain circuitry with the advantage that some of the basic functions of the brain and its centers had, over the last two centuries, been brought together into a conceptual framework. For every human sense there are brain regions whose neuronal signals correspond to the spatial distribution of signals in the outside

world. In each of the brain regions, signals sensed from the environment have a collective representation, which to some extent recreates
their original arrangements, such as in a face or a landscape. In other
neurons, representations of body movement occur before and during
an animal's behavior. One structure, the cerebellum, is particularly
important for coordinating movement. Another controls the levels of
general arousal and attention. Still other neuronal collections are active
during emotional experiences, such as pleasure, pain, fear, anxiety, or
anger. Higher brain functions such as language are relegated to one
side of the brain, again involving certain regions more than others.
These distributed brain regions are physically and functionally joined
to each other by large bundles of nerve fibers, some extending for great
distances across the brain.

Until a few decades ago, the most interesting clues about how and
where memories are stored in these structures came from the clinic.
Numerous deficits described by clinicians during the past 150 years are
related to localized destruction of regions of the brain. Specific memory deficits result from lesions of brain regions responsible for specific
senses, such as vision, hearing, touch, or smell. Others involve speech
and/or language usage. Still other deficits are more general, such as the
loss of all recent memory. One particularly interesting patient known
as H.M., lost most of the structures known as the temporal lobes,
which include another structure, the hippocampus, on each side of the
brain. H.M. is able to carry on what seems to be a perfectly normal
conversation, recalling past incidents and interests in his life. An hour
later, he will have absolutely no memory of this conversation having
occurred.

Complaints and symptoms help identify the nature and location of
a disease process, often a lesion, within the brain. The lesion may be a
tumor, which whether benign or cancerous can displace normal brain
tissue and derange function, possibly causing paralysis of a limb, loss of
touch sensation, visual impairment, poor coordination, muscle twitching, declining memory, or mood disorders. Ruptured blood vessels
hemorrhage into local brain regions, causing specific deficits or giving
rise to slowly collecting blood masses beneath the coverings with
which the brain is enveloped. Larger masses may cause headaches, confusion, nausea, drowsiness, and even coma. Clogged arteries no longer
sustain brain centers, which begin to fail and, in some cases, die. When
such patients are taken to surgery, pathological tissue can be related to
the symptoms it generated. Other tissue is examined at autopsy. These

are definitive means of linking symptoms to brain lesions. Collections of symptom-pathology links help classify diseases as well as implicate brain locations in specific mental functions. Such and such a deficit is related to a certain lesion in a specific brain region. In this way, a correlational data base accumulates.[1]

The development of brain imaging techniques has dramatically expanded correlations of pathological changes in the brain to memory deficits. Three-dimensional X-ray analysis with CAT-scanning, for example, permits very precise localization of lesions in the brains of living patients. Harmless radioactive isotopes injected into the bloodstream and incorporated by billions of cells within the brain also reveal localized areas of functional deficits in brain tissue. These are more sophisticated ways of making the same kinds of correlations accumulated over the last one and a half centuries. These new techniques tell the neurosurgeon where to operate, and, in some cases, how to effect a cure.

Inferences about memory storage from imaging studies, however, like those obtained from autopsy or removal of diseased tissue on the operating table, suffer from inherent uncertainties. We know that the diseased brain region is involved in storage of certain types of memory, but the nature of the involvement is obscure. The lesioned brain area could be an actual storage site, or it might have no memory records at all. For example, it could be simply a relay station through which electrical signals travel to reach the memory records in some other brain area. Or perhaps the lesioned area only receives signals from an area that stores records and then relays the signals to express the memory.

To better understand these uncertainties, think of a memory record as a piece of microfilm hidden in a distant capital. To be of use, the microfilm, which includes photographs of enemy bases, has to be retrieved and analyzed. To gain access to the file, a diplomatic courier is dispatched to the distant city to find the microfilm and transport it back to his country of origin. The courier might never get to the microfilm because all travel routes to his destination are blocked. The microfilm would remain, but the courier just couldn't reach it. A lesion could block the electrical signals trying to reach a memory record without actually destroying the record itself. Alternatively, the courier might recover the microfilm but never make it out of the country, so the sought-after information would never become accessible to the courier's homeland. A lesion, to continue the parallel, might still not destroy a memory record but only block the route traveled by electrical signals to produce behavior that would verify that the record is still intact. When destruction of the hippocampus eliminates recent memory, we don't know that the hippocampus is the repository for recent memory. It may only be a route through which electrical signals must pass to reach the repository. Or the hippocampus might be both a route and a repository.

In short, the lesion literature, although immensely valuable, is necessary but not at all sufficient to establish where memories are stored in the forbiddingly complex pathways of the brain. Just as with the elementary visual-vestibular networks of the snail, the flow of information has to be tracked step-by-step as it makes its way through the nervous system. Thus far, few, if any, brain pathways and networks of neurons are mapped in sufficient detail to allow this kind of analysis. A blueprint cannot yet be made for the networks of the hippocampus or the cerebellum. What can be done can be done only with broad brush strokes.

An entire layer containing the pyramid-shaped CA1 cells, for example, can be identified within the hippocampus. The CA1 pyramids are lined up in a row so that distinct cellular compartments occupy identifiable bands of tissue within the hippocampus. The cellular compartments known as dendrites, which receive incoming signals, occupy a horizontal band immediately above the horizontal band in which the cell bodies reside. Stations that relay information from one group of neurons to another via synaptic interactions can also be identified. The cerebellum, a brain region vitally important for coordination of body movements, is also composed of groups of neurons, synapses, and axons arranged in orderly rows and arrays. Similar general knowledge is available about other brain regions, although few show the well-ordered patterns of neuronal alignments occurring in the hippocampus and to a lesser extent in the cerebellum.

Confronted with this sort of general knowledge rather than the detailed circuitry of mammalian brain regions, a number of pioneering workers asked what they might add to the limited, albeit intriguing, insights gained from the lesion literature. People such as James Olds, Sr., Robert Galambos, Robert Doty, and, later, Richard Thompson began making electrical recordings from brain regions at different stages of information flow during learning. They recorded electrical signals from whole populations of neurons rather than from individual cells, as was possible with the snail *Hermissenda*. Olds and Thompson made what in retrospect were some remarkable observations. They found that as an animal became conditioned, the electrical signals elicited by the conditioned stimulus became larger. It was as if these signals might represent a memory record. Why did training with two discrete stimuli enhance the signals of so many neurons? Some of the colleagues of Olds and Thompson did not believe the data. It did not matter that the results were confirmed repeatedly in different laboratories. To some skeptics, the results did not make sense, so there had to be some hidden errors to account for them.

Results obtained later by Richard Thompson and his major collaborator, Theodore Berger, seemed even more improbable, perhaps even ridiculous. Berger and Thompson recorded electrical signals emanating from individual CA1 pyramidal cells in the hippocampus. The signals of about 50 percent of these neurons were enhanced in response to a stimulus tone, only after conditioning. Why on earth would so many neurons show changes when just one simple link between two stimuli was being learned? After all, if 50 percent of neurons changed for one simple association, there could very quickly be no neurons left to store the millions of other associations that can occur in a mammal's experience.

Accept for a moment, as I did, that there could be an explanation for this paradox. Accept that it is possible that a large fraction of an entire neuron population could change for each of millions of different associations without ever using up much storage space. If this were true, would it not then be possible to conduct experiments analogous to those we had been conducting with the snail? With the snail, we were able to isolate the membrane of the type B cell body and measure electrical changes produced only with learning. The flow changes were permanent and robust enough that they survived isolation of the neuron from the nervous system and even isolation of membrane patches from the neuron. The memory record was preserved. Was there a similar memory record in the CA1 pyramidal cells? It was well known that the channels in the membrane of the CA1 pyramids were strikingly similar to the channels in the snail's type B neuron. Could memory-specific differences in channels be the record that explained enhanced CA1 responses, just as they explained the enhanced electrical signals of the type B cell in response to light?

The available recordings from CA1 neurons and even individual neurons provided the kind of correlational data we first obtained for the snail's learning. As the snail learned the light-rotation link, the electrical response of the type B cell to light was progressively enhanced. Similarly, the pyramid cell responses to a single-toned sound increased as a rabbit learned that the sound was associated with a puff of air on its eye's corneal surface. On the basis of these observations, I came upon an experiment that I felt had to be done. It was an experiment with little likelihood of success, but if successful, it would be extremely revealing. Why not remove thin slices of rabbit hippocampus on days after the animal was shown to have learned the link? One group of animals would have learned the association. Another group would receive the same tone and air puff stimulation but with no consistent temporal relationship between the stimuli. A third group would have received no tone or air puff stimulation. We would then insert microelectrodes into the pyramid cells to measure membrane channels. Would there be changes of particular CA1 channels only in animals that had learned the link? John Disterhoft was my first colleague to show an interest in this question. Shortly thereafter, a brilliant, fiercely independent graduate student, Douglas Coulter, bit into the project.

At the time, my laboratory, still part of the National Institutes of Health, was located year-round at the Marine Biological Laboratory in Woods Hole. Here we had the optimum sea water conditions to raise our own strains of the snail *Hermissenda* and to keep them healthy for long-term learning experiments. But now we wanted to look for parallel learning mechanisms in the mammalian brain. Coulter, as a graduate student, was entitled to a small cubbyhole, an offshoot of a main room filled with the necessities for marine organisms including aquaria, flowing sea water, and dissecting tables. Sensitive electronics for recording from neurons in brain slices don't like sea water. The most essential feature of his cubbyhole was its solid oak door. Once the door was closed, most sound, sea water spray, and human distractions were shut out. Coulter emptied every square inch of his little room and filled it with the most carefully chosen essentials of neurophysiology. He left just enough space to ease his large frame into a chair perfectly positioned so that he could comfortably control the equipment surrounding him in every corner from the floor to the ceiling. Eventually we were able to find the resources for as technically sophisticated a recording apparatus as was available anywhere. Coulter recorded lovely electrical signals from the hippocampal brain slices for up to ten hours at a time. As far as his fellow students were concerned, Coulter's rabbits were sufficiently inconspicuous among the lobsters, squid, crabs, and snails that he was just another typical member of the Boston University Marine Program. At least the rabbit experiments although not on marine animals were motivated by marine biology.

John Disterhoft, a visiting scientist from Northwestern University Medical School, found a corner in my laboratory to set up behavioral training and testing of the rabbits. There, in the ninety-year-old Lillie Building facing Martha's Vineyard across the sound, I could walk from one lab for recording signals in the snail's visual-vestibular networks to a behavioral lab next door for teaching the rabbit to associate a tone with an air puff to its eye's corneal surface. People were adventuresome at the M.B.L. It was here that K. C. Cole invented the voltage clamp and showed it to Alan Hodgkin, who later described specific channels within axonal membranes. It was here that Hartline demonstrated that visual neurons in the horseshoe crab's eye inhibit each other. This inhibition enhances the contrast perceived by the cells at light-dark borders just as predicted by Ernst Mach. It was here that Robert Allen visualized particles moving down axons with video-enhanced microscopy for the first time. It was not exactly traditional to train rabbits in these tall dark rooms with drains in the concrete floors to catch the sea water spilling from aquaria and buckets of exotic specimens from the deep. But though not traditional, it was acceptable because this institute by the sea was an international enclave of biologists who just often happened to use a marine species with some particular experimental virtue. And if some scientists didn't use marine organisms, they enjoyed meeting with colleagues and teaching students who did.

Disterhoft and Coulter were like oil and water. Coulter was intense, unsmiling, hardworking, and sometimes brusque. Disterhoft was unflappable, friendly, relaxed, and given to mixing a measured pace of research with the trappings of the good life. Without Disterhoft's expertise in rabbit training and testing we would have spent untold months acquiring the experience necessary to measure the rabbit's learning behavior in a carefully controlled and quantitative way. Without Coulter's dogged persistence in recording from thin slices of the rabbit hippocampus, we would not have been able to relate changes of neuronal signals to stages of learning and memory storage. It was always an uneasy truce, but one I managed to keep until we finished our first study and each had learned something of what the other had to offer. For my part, I tried to make the electrophysiological analyses of the rabbit neurons as exhaustive as those I had made for the snail cells.

Decoding the first blinded results, we were torn between hope and anxiety. From the pilot study, we already had our first taste of changes in the rabbit's neurons. They had been beyond our expectations. Our hope was that we would be able to observe differences in channels somewhere within the CA1 pyramidal cell membrane. Our initial results suggested that not only did cells from the trained animals show such a difference, but the difference was remarkably similar to what I had found in the snail. This similarity made us doubly careful to avoid inadvertently biasing our observations. The full study had a blind design; Disterhoft did not know the electrophysiological measurements made for a given animal, and Coulter did not know the behavioral learning scores. Only after we collected the data did we match the behavioral score to electrical properties for each animal.

Each week, we would sit together to reveal and then match behavioral scores to neuronal electrical properties for each animal. At what seemed to be an intolerably slow pace, we accumulated electrical values for conditioned animals and controls. The data showed the hoped for tendency but were still not conclusive. One problem after another seemed to delay the study's completion. Equipment broke down. The chambers in which the brain slices were bathed with solution mixed to resemble that bathing the brain became contaminated with microorganisms and had to be sterilized. We were plagued by coursework, lectures, and travel obligations. Finally, I knew we were close, but I was obligated to a speaking tour in Europe and the Middle East. Someone else would have to substitute for me to decode the blind experiments.

Just before a lecture at the Weizmann Institute in Israel, I grabbed a moment to telephone Disterhoft and Coulter at the M.B.L. I tried to prepare myself for disappointment. It doesn't have to work, I told myself. There will be other experiments on other brain regions with other techniques. Over the phone, Coulter in a brusque but friendly manner broke my bubble of anxiety. "The data held up," he told me. There were now statistically significant differences between the conditioned animals' pyramid cells and those of both control groups. In spite of my relief, new anxiety flashed through my mind. Could the study be replicated? And what did such channel changes mean about how information is stored by the pyramid cells?

Like Berger and Thompson's earlier recordings from living animals, our studies showed that 40% to 50% of the cells in the population were affected. Even for this simple conditioning of the rabbit, a large enough number of its hippocampal neurons were changing for us to find them. Both Coulter and Disterhoft are impeccably honest and careful. With the blind procedure, I had no reason to doubt their findings. Still, for a number of years, I would reserve judgment. Many additional experiments would later dispel my doubts. Coulter repeated the entire experiment himself, introducing further refinements and additional measurements in his protocols. Disterhoft went back to Northwestern to repeat the experiments with new colleagues and make his own refinements. They found, for example, that the changes of channels were not as large in undertrained animals, which showed poorer learning. Still other investigators confirmed the original observations and found new changes consistent with those originally found. The accumulated weight of many studies by different workers in different laboratories finally brought me to the conviction that our results were indisputable. To understand their significance, however, was another matter.

When I proposed the experiment, I not only thought it was a long shot, I also thought it too high a hope that the same channels would change after learning in both the snail and in the rabbit. Yet this turned out to be the case. Coulter showed further that this memory-specific change was intrinsic to the pyramid cell itself. In strict parallel to the type B neuron changes in the snail, the CA1 pyramid cells themselves had stored some sort of record of the learned association. A number of subsequent studies suggested that the channel changes were located in the neuron's dendritic branches, where messages are received from other neurons.[2]

The main dendrite, somewhat like a tree trunk, fans out into a host of branches, which in turn divide into smaller branches. This dendritic tree is particularly well suited to receiving messages. The large number of branches provides an extensive surface area on which great numbers of synaptic interactions can occur. For example, there are 100,000 to 200,000 synaptic contacts within the dendritic tree of each single CA1 pyramidal cell. Local communication between contacts on the same branch can be somewhat like a telephone connection occurring between two parties but without a party line. The conversation occurs along a branch somewhat isolated from other branches of the dendritic tree. Stimuli occurring together during training can converse privately on a particular dendritic branch. This compartmentalization provides a plausible resolution to the apparent paradox that so many cells change with learning a simple association.

By compartmentalizing incoming calls, a large fraction of neurons can participate in storing each association and still leave sufficient room for storing many more associations. Each pair of stimuli sensed together by the animal during training could affect different branch compartments of a large number of pyramid cells but leave millions of other compartments for other stimuli. After an animal has learned to associate two stimuli, only one of the stimuli will be necessary to activate specific dendritic branches on a combination of many pyramid cells. The number of possible combinations using 40% to 50% of the CA1 cells is literally astronomical. So the same pyramid cells can participate in endless combinations without even beginning to tap the storage capacity of their entire group.

Coulter, Disterhoft, and later Joseph Lo Turco, then a graduate student at Yale University, had accumulated a convincing body of evidence by penetrating the CA1 pyramid cells with intracellular microelectrodes. The evidence said that electrical changes of snail neurons were conserved and similar to those of mammalian neurons during memory storage. Our next question was obvious. Were the molecular changes of snail learning also similar to those of mammalian learning? Barry Bank found preliminary evidence that the molecular "switch" that we had found in snail neurons, the enzyme protein kinase C (PKC), was also thrown in the rabbit's hippocampus during memory storage. But it was James Olds, Jr., who developed the imaging technology to "see" where and when this switch was thrown during learning.

Olds's father and mother, James and Marianne Olds, Sr., had recorded from a number of brain regions, succeeding as no one else had in tracking changes of electrical signals during rat learning. James Olds, Jr., continued his parents' quest but with his own modern technology, some of which he had acquired from Louis Sokoloff, developer of the first useful biochemical labels of brain activity. Sokoloff scanned the distribution of radioactive biochemicals that generate an image of the cells most active during a particular experience. Olds, Jr., and I wanted to do the same kind of scanning, but as a measure of memory storage in neurons rather than just their electrical activity.

All of our studies in the snail and the rabbit had implicated activation of the enzyme PKC as an important step in laying down a memory trace. It seemed possible that this molecular event might be ubiquitous among animal species and throughout brain regions during learning. Why not find a radioactive chemical that would bind only to PKC after it had been activated? The chemical might then mark neuronal spots where a memory was being formed. Low concentrations of just such a chemical had been successfully used in Solomon Snyder's laboratory to label activated PKC.

To our amazement, Olds found that, just as we had predicted, cells in the hippocampus showed increased labeling only in rabbits that had learned to associate the tone with the air puff. The label provided the first glimpse of a memory record that could be visualized as an image. In other words, a primitive image of a brain region being transformed during learning could be visualized and transferred to an observer's brain. This image was not entirely static. One day after the rabbit learned the tone-puff link, the label was concentrated in the region of the bodies of the cells and, to a lesser extent, in the dendritic branches. Three days after the rabbit had learned, the label distribution between the cell compartments was radically different. Now the label was concentrated in the region of the dendritic branches, with less in the cell body region. The memory record appeared to pass through different phases as it became progressively more permanent, conforming to the same scenario we had proposed for the snail. In the initial phase, training stimuli would cause chemical messages within the space of a dendritic branch. Activated dendritic sites would send chemical signals to the cell body, perhaps via the "conditioning" protein.[3] The cell body, once signaled, would increase its synthesis of critical proteins, which when transported back to the original site would induce more permanent changes of excitability. In this dialogue, the cell body would be operating like a factory, delivering its manufactured proteins on order to any one of a multitude of remote sites distributed throughout the branches of the dendritic tree.

In the snail brain, the meaning of the memory records could be directly assessed. With the blueprint of the visual-vestibular network, we could trace how the memory was acquired, stored, and expressed. Channel changes at a site of memory storage explained how the snail's clinging response to rotation had been transferred to the light stimulus. Memory records within CA1 pyramidal cells of the rabbit hippocampus defy such close scrutiny with present techniques.[4]

If there is such uncertainty about the networks in the rabbit's brain that learn when two stimuli occur together, imagine the uncertainty as the number of stimuli occurring together increases. How does a rat's hippocampus or its visual cortex represent a sequence of twists and turns within a maze by electrical signaling within networks of neurons? What is the pattern of information flow among the memory sites? What other structures of the brain are involved? Presumably, with complex patterns of information, there is communication among many different brain regions. Electrical signaling, perhaps from groups of neurons, might flow from one structure to another and then back. We haven't begun to reconstruct these patterns of electrical signals with reference to identified groups of neurons in distinct brain regions. And if maze learning is not easily explained by network function, what about even more complex memories? What happens in a monkey's brain when it learns to use rules and not just to recognize images or patterns, or a human brain as it learns mathematical operations?

What enables brain networks to construct new image combinations that have never been experienced? How does an Otto Loewi imagine, from what he remembers, that a chemical is secreted by a nerve to make a heart muscle beat faster, when he doesn't know what the connection between the heart and muscle actually looks like? When and how did Michelle imagine her fantasy of a paramour who would whisk her away from a world of abuse? What were the integrative operations performed by her brain centers that synthesized the obsessive thoughts from her memories to distract her attention from her depression and self-loathing? How do such synthesized obsessions became displaced by elaborate delusions and hallucinations, which, though divorced from "reality," usually include remembered snatches of actual experiences and people from the past?

The network representations of scientific theories, fantasies and delusions must each have unique features as aggregates of signals spread over the brain and continued over a period of time. But to the degree that they call up memories stored throughout the brain's networks, they may depend on the same basic electrical and molecular mechanisms. The integrative processes performed by the networks must be different, but the basic storage principles, like the chemical-electrical switches on a computer chip, could be the same. That sameness—for example, the protein kinase switch we found in the snail, the rabbit, and the rat—might be tagged in living humans and not just brain slices. A camera with enough power might see those tags wherever and whenever a memory was being stored or recalled, revealing new pictures of what memories look like. Studding the impenetrable thicket of network branches, memories might look as different as the face of a baby from that of its grandfather. Memory sites, themselves, however, may be no more different from each other than the silver grains of a thousand photographs.

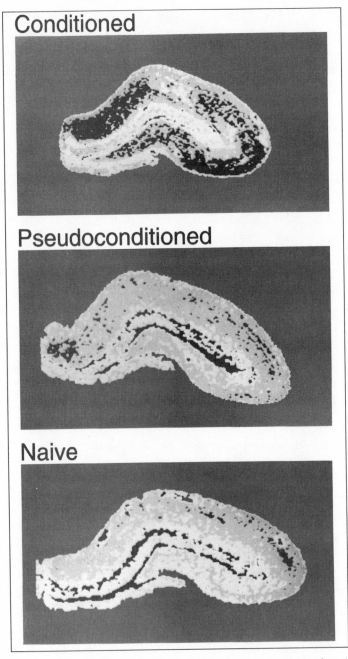

Fig. 24 Visualizing molecular changes in the rabbit hippocampus during learning. Photographs show the distribution of a labeled enzyme (protein kinase C) which has been activated (darkened areas) during learning. The upper photo shows a hippocampal slice taken from a rabbit that has learned a Pavlovian response. The other two slices are from animals that were trained with control procedures and therefore did not learn and did not show activation of the enzyme. The sizes of the slices reflect the size of the animals and not experience. (Courtesy of Dr. James Olds, Jr. of the author's laboratory)

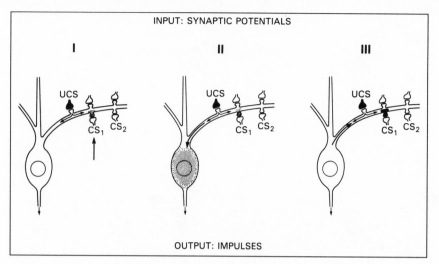

Fig. 25 Model of stages in memory storage. Signals linked in time meet on a branch (upper part of each panel) of the dendritic tree in the first stage (1). In second stage (11) a signal travels to the cell body to regulate the manufacture of protein constituents. During consolidation of the memory in the third stage (111) proteins travel back to determine the function and structure of the original site of memory storage. The memory is recalled when later signals (input, above) trigger a new combination of output signals (impulses, below) sent by each neuron. (Courtesy of J. Olds, from *Science*, 1989)

A STORY NOT YET TOLD

There is a special irony in brain science: On the one hand, the complexity of brain circuits defies our efforts at understanding and to this day remains invulnerable to our cutting, probing, and recording. On the other hand, we rarely hesitate to draw conclusions about how our own and others' brains work. Everyone seems to have a laboratory in the backyard. You need only to observe your neighbor to formulate the next hypothesis. So and so is just as insecure as his father. Such and such a trait runs in the family. Since he was in Vietnam, he hasn't been the same. She still hasn't gotten over the loss of her son.

Intuitive, personal, arm chair insights are no less prevalent among professional scientists. Uncovering mechanisms of learning and memory is not like purifying growth hormone from the pituitary gland or finding the virus that causes an encephalitis. It's not like discovering that penicillin can cure pneumonia or that a vaccine can prevent polio. There are no definitive answers; in fact, even the questions are difficult to agree on. Some might say true memory is only cognitive. It is one thing to study memory of two simple stimuli related in time. It is quite another to study the memory of a feeling, a mathematical process, or a rule of grammar. Others might say that any long-lasting change of behavior constitutes a memory. Taken to a further extreme, any long-lasting change in a nervous system, even in the absence of behavior, is thought by some to be memory. With such disagreement about definitions, it is not difficult to understand the ease with which workers confuse or mislead colleagues and students, and even themselves. There is often plenty at stake. Definitions that catch on affect judgments about which experiments are worthwhile, what research should be funded, and what results are considered "meaningful." Rewards can be based on the right definitions, the correct passwords.

While I was pursuing my own game plan, there was no lack of players with their own definitions and strategies, all reaching for the same brass ring. Terjé Lomo of Norway and, later, Timothy Bliss of England began one strategy by pulsing positive current outside a bundle of hippocampal axons. A period of high-frequency current pulses enhances the synaptic signals transmitted from the axons' branches. The synaptic signals become more "potent"—i.e., they are larger and more readily trigger target cell spikes. This "potentiation" usually lasts one to two hours in brain slices isolated from the hippocampus. Its persistence suggested the label *long-term* and thus the name *long-term potentiation*, or LTP. With enough current stimulation such enhancement, or potentiation, of synaptic signals (LTP) can last for much longer periods in living animals.

There are some interesting similarities between the sequence of cellular events that leads to LTP and the sequence we implicated in snail and rabbit learning. In both LTP and learning, an initial step is a prolonged elevation of the calcium ion within the target cells. In both cases, the elevated calcium appears to work together with other biochemical signals to cause long-lasting activation of the same enzyme (protein kinase C). To its credit, LTP is a fairly straightforward neuronal change to induce. It is dramatic, robust, and available in a dish, so to speak: a slice of brain can be isolated and immersed in nutrients within a culture dish so there is no need for a living animal, for coping with the myriad of other stimuli to which the animal is responding and the torrent of cascading signals forever entering and exiting brain regions. From the secure vantage point of a quantifiable, reproducible effect such as LTP, ambitious claims can be made, and they have been, most with sincerity, and some with the support of elegant experiments.[1]

Learning, however, unlike LTP, does not arise out of currents injected from outside thousands of axons simultaneously. During learning by neural networks, patterns of electrical signals recreate the patterns of stimuli received by the network from the outside world. A shock to a thousand axons at once does not cause such a pattern. Given the drastic differences of stimulus conditions in which they arise, therefore, LTP and memory storage are also likely to be fundamentally different in at least some of their underlying mechanisms.

Although many have tried, no one has been able to show that LTP occurs when an animal actually learns. The vast majority of LTP studies are made within a period of one to two hours after the current is applied. So precious little is known about mechanisms that might be responsible for LTP lasting long enough to become permanent. To psychologists, LTP is an interesting cellular process whose relevance to memory storage is purely a matter of speculation. There are some neuroscientists, however, who consider behavioral criteria far less important than a measurable and lasting synaptic change. Their emphasis on the sophistication of electrophysiological measurements is within this century's tradition of the English school. Minimizing the importance of psychological constraints continues the awkwardness of the dialogue begun between physicists and psychologists more than 150 years ago. Fechner, Helmholtz, and Mach were physicists as well as brilliant psychologists. Even the great Helmholtz was uneasy, however, when he theorized about the illusions of perception. He was ambivalent about clearly identifying himself as a psychologist. And with good reason: he was no longer on terra firma. There were no equations that could be unequivocally verified or disproven. This is what investigators of memory, which has psychological as well as cellular features, let themselves in for.

Eric Kandel is another player with his own definitions and strategy. Kandel, director of a large group of neuroscientists at Columbia University, writes and speaks with unusual eloquence. The textbook on basic neuroscience that he coedits with a long-time colleague, James Schwartz, is the recognized standard in its field. His way with words can be almost mesmerizing. Listening to him at the M.B.L. and viewing his elegant recordings of neuronal signals, I remember feeling the pull of his personal magnetism. Even when I found myself disagreeing with what seemed to be an oversimplification or tenuous generalization, I could not help being carried along by the excitement and dramatic sweep of his story.

As a medical student, I was captivated by the work of Kandel's teacher Ladislav Tauc. Tauc, an expatriot in France from Czechoslovakia, understood the potential of the snail *Aplysia*'s nervous system. Some years before, the husband and wife team Arvanataki and Chalzonitis first introduced this snail to electrophysiologists. Tauc analyzed synaptic interactions among neurons within the *Aplysia* ganglia. In the tradition of other brilliant electrophysiologists of his day, he studied in a step-by-step fashion not only how the presynaptic endings released chemicals to cause postsynaptic electrical signals, but also how these synaptic signals were modified as a function of use. He showed that the strength of signals at a certain synapse progressively decreased if the synapse was used with enough frequency over a brief time interval. The signal strength of other synapses was enhanced with sufficiently frequent use. These effects resembled use-dependent changes of synaptic strength that had been observed in a variety of other preparations.

Use-dependent synaptic modification was central to one elegant hypothesis proposed by Donald Hebb. Hebb postulated that synapses would not just change during memory storage as a function of use. Memory would also require that the postsynaptic cell fire when it was receiving chemical messages from the presynaptic cell. The more often the chemical messages occurred together with the postsynaptic firing, the more the synapse would be modified during learning. Tauc examined such possibilities with real neurons in living networks. Kandel took the next step of relating changes in the snail's synapses to changes in its behavior. This was a logical but innovative extension of an experimental tradition dating from the time of Sherrington. Electrical signals of neurons were evaluated in terms of their impact on the behavior of living animals. Kandel realized that the snail *Aplysia* both exhibited interesting behavior and had a nervous system that was analyzable in great detail. In this respect, the snail ganglion was like the eye of the horseshoe crab, *Limulus*, which had interesting sensory capacity and also a potentially understandable neuronal network. Similarly, Adrian Horridge emphasized potential learning behavior–network relationships in his pioneering studies with the locust.

Kandel and I differ about what type of behavior in a snail would be most helpful as a model, in revealing cellular insights about human learning. To my mind, human memory is in essence an associative process. As I have attempted to illustrate, it permanently records how frequently events occur together in time. Although Kandel would not dispute the importance of associative memory, his emphasis is entirely different. Kandel remains deeply rooted in the use-dependent tradition of electrophysiologists.

The stimulus, touch, causes the snail *Aplysia* to withdraw a part of its body known as a gill. With frequent use, gill withdrawal rapidly weakens, or habituates. This weakening can, like associative memory, last for days or longer. Unlike associative memory, however, habituation does not depend on distinct events occurring together in time, and it only lasts if the animal's subsequent sensory experience is severely restricted. The instant the snail receives a single shock to its tail or pinch on its neck, for example, the habituation disappears forever. As long as the *Aplysia* is not aroused or "sensitized" by other important stimuli, its gill withdrawal remains weak. But humans cannot be protected from receiving information. They must be able to store one set of information after another. More like moving pictures than single photographs, our memories must consist of a continuous flow of images, none of which excludes the others.

The arousal caused by shocking the snail with an electric current is an example of a prolonged behavioral change produced by a single stimulus. No links of stimuli in time are necessary.

A single electric shock to the *Aplysia* tail not only erases habituation, it also increases the response of the animal to almost any sensory stimulus. The nonspecificity of sensitization illustrates another issue on which Kandel and I place different emphasis. To my mind, a memory must be addressable by the particular stimulus or stimulus pattern that recalls it. Otherwise, the information is not very useful for the animal's behavior. The animal's ability to predict and thereby adapt its behavior to future events is only enhanced by addressable storage. When the *Aplysia* has been shocked or pinched, how does it know which response should be enhanced? Should it withdraw its tail or its gill to avoid the shock? Should it turn its head to move away from the shock? Should it ignore food in order not to be shocked? What behavioral change is adaptive? If there is no specific address for the memory, there can be no specific adaptive behavioral response.

Furthermore, a response remains sensitized for many days only if the sensory stimulus that elicits the response is restricted. Like habituation, sensitization must be protected by limiting the subsequent sensory experience. This is not memory as we know it, which is relatively resistant to erasure in spite of an entire lifetime of subsequent sensory stimulation.

Kandel has devoted most of his career to these two examples of behavioral change. Reading his initial reports on these two effects when I was a medical student, I was impressed by the lovely parallel of the behavioral change and the change of synaptic signals he and his colleagues recorded from *Aplysia* neurons. A group of sensory neurons released chemical messages onto a group of motor neurons in the

Aplysia abdominal ganglion. The synaptic messages received by the motor neurons from the sensory cells decreased in amplitude as the gill withdrawal response decreased in amplitude. Similarly, the same synaptic signals increased in amplitude as the gill withdrawal response was enhanced by shocking the animal. But while this was behavioral change in an animal with identifiable neurons and synapses, it was not associative learning. Nor did the sensory-motor neuron synapses constitute a neuronal network likely to learn an association. The findings of Tauc, Kandel, and their colleagues encouraged me to look at snail preparations for a neural network with more promise for true memory capacity. I would then let the network and the animal's behavior suggest stimuli that were effective in its natural habitat and could therefore be used for training the animal.

Kandel's use of an artificial stimulus such as electric shock highlights another difference between our experimental philosophies. I was convinced, and remain so today, that the wiring of a network has evolved to sense a limited group of stimulus patterns and learn from what it senses. The simpler the nervous system and the fewer the neurons, the fewer the stimulus patterns that can be learned. The human capacity to learn whatever can be sensed is unique in the animal kingdom. Other animals are far more limited in the possible stimulus combinations they can record. They have, for one thing, fewer sites in their brains where electrical signals representing different stimuli can meet and thereby interact. It seemed only logical to me that to find what an animal can learn, one begins by determining what the animal can sense and then finding where sensed information meets within a network. The snail *Hermissenda*, for example, has light-sensitive eyes and statocysts, vestibular organs, that sense changes of the animal's orientation in space or changes of movement velocity. As described earlier, electrical signals representing these stimuli travel along pathways that meet within the visual-vestibular network. The touch stimulus applied to the *Aplysia* falls into the same category of natural stimuli. *Aplysia* would be expected to encounter such stimulation regularly in its natural habitat, and it has sensory cells that have evolved to respond to touch.

Electric shock is another matter. The animal virtually never encounters electric shock in its normal habitat. The networks of the *Aplysia* possess no cells to sense and then record the shock by electrical signals. The shock will produce other effects, such as stress, tissue damage, and organ dysfunction, as well as electrical signaling within neural networks. The behavioral changes may be due to any one or some combination of these effects. The same can be said of biochemical changes that may accompany and/or contribute to the behavioral changes. If shock does produce a behavioral change, it seems less likely that the underlying mechanisms will be similar to mechanisms that have evolved and might be conserved within the networks of other species. Again, this is a difference of experimental philosophy. Use of a global, artificial stimulus seems to me to reduce the likelihood of tapping into principles of memory storage that might be general and, therefore, relevant to humans. Kandel, still active after a long and productive career, seems to have some awareness of such problems. In recent years, he and his colleagues have tried to combine the two nonassociative changes, habituation and arousal, into something with associative properties. The result shares some features with associative learning, but there are some fundamental differences.

Kandel and I, although rivals, share a common interest in human memory and have each committed a major portion of our scientific careers to studying snail learning and networks. In spite of our differences in experimental emphasis, we both believe that learning mechanisms in simple creatures have potential relevance to those in species with real brains. I imagine that in some other world our ghosts will greet each other as soul brothers who shared the tradition of common intellectual ancestors. In our ethereal forms of Descartes's "unextended substance," we would laugh at the pettiness of our rivalry and the waste of what we could never share while we were alive.

Despite the similarities of the snails *Aplysia* and *Hermissenda*, I feel closer in philosophy to a number of other scientists who have used only mammals to study associative learning. In the course of their research, these scientists have tracked the electrical representation of natural stimuli along neuronal pathways that have evolved and are genetically specified within the animals' networks. If I could have, I would have used Kandel's observations to pursue my own search strategy. This is what I was able to do, for example, with the research of James Olds, Sr., Dori Gormezano, and Richard Thompson.

Thompson, together with his brilliant young colleague Theodore Berger, built on Olds's electrophysiology and Gormezano's quantitative behavioral analyses. They demonstrated that electrical signals of pyramidal cells in the hippocampus changed in close parallel with a rabbit's learning to link a tone to an air puff on its corneal surface. Pavlovian conditioning in a mammal, therefore, might produce neuronal changes similar or identical to those produced by Pavlovian conditioning in a snail. The odds were helped by the fact that both experiments caused electrical signals within neuronal pathways that had evolved to respond to the training stimuli.

My colleagues and I did not have to work out the Pavlovian conditioning for the rabbit. That had already been beautifully documented by Gormezano, his colleagues, and his predecessors. We didn't have to establish that there were electrophysiological correlates of the learning in the hippocampus. That had been demonstrated by experiments of Olds, Thompson, Berger, and their colleagues. Nor did we have to guess that the channels of hippocampal neuronal membranes were similar to the channels in the membranes of *Hermissenda* neurons. That had been established by David Prince, Philip Schwartzkroin, and others. Nor did we have to start from scratch to trace the flow of information along neuronal pathways into the hippocampus and the cerebellum. This work was already well advanced through the efforts of Masao Ito, Rodolfo Llinás, Richard Thompson, Christopher Yeo, and others. My experience with these colleagues was mutually reinforcing and complementary. We didn't want to do the same experiments, not even the same type of experiments. Yet the findings of these mammalian physiologists contributed to my own search strategy, and our results from the snail and rabbit confirmed and extended the previous work of Olds, Sr., Thompson, and others on Pavlovian conditioning.

Whether assembled together, or conversing through the literature, the community of scientists reports its experience from different angles and gradually brings into view what can only be seen by the mind's eye. The progress of research is inevitably toward agreement. There is an inexorable reconciliation of apparently contradictory observations, interpretations, and beliefs. But the periods in which conflicts persist may seem interminably long when measured on the scale of a single lifetime.

A collaborative team spirit can often characterize scientific exploration. For example Marine Biological Laboratory scientists of varying levels of seniority and expertise sit together at lunch with students, exchanging stories of adventures in the laboratory. Ideas bounce from one individual to another, acquiring new twists and turns as they move around the table. Results are reported long before they are published. Methods are documented and challenged. Interpretations are volunteered, questioned, revised. The diversity of intellect and talent generates a synthesis, a unique blend of individual and group expression.

Once, for instance, I was talking about our protein, which appears critical for memory storage. I mentioned how this protein, similar to related proteins we found in mammalian hippocampus, potently regulates membrane channels, as well as the flow of protein particles within the axon and its branches. I voiced my suspicion that somehow this memory protein was also responsible for the changes of branch structure measured only in neurons that had learned the light-rotation link. I thought that perhaps the protein's alteration of the axonal flow of particles precipitated the structural changes. Reflecting for a moment, a biophysicist at the table replied that he had a somewhat different notion. Maybe, he suggested, the protein was reducing the number of membrane fragments incorporated into the outer membrane wall, which defines the shape of the neuron itself. Maybe these membrane fragments, which were continually recycled as part of the cell's normal self-renewal, contained the channels that regulated the neuron's excitability. Training might activate the protein to reduce the number of membrane fragments being incorporated. Fewer membrane fragments might lead to fewer channels and also less extensive branching, just as we had previously observed. He then suggested a straightforward electrical measurement to seek evidence of a reduced quality of membrane in the cell.

Excited, I suggested that we could make the same membrane measurements after learning as well as after activating the protein. Some one else suggested different measurements using labels of membrane constituents. A student at the table volunteered that the high-resolution video microscopy developed at the Marine Biological Laboratory might be used to watch the protein change movement of labeled fragments into the membrane. And so ideas bounced around the table. My initial story now included totally unexpected molecular actors and events. The story not yet told was being born in the minds of those bound together for a moment in a common quest and a shared adventure. From the interdisciplinary repartee emerged a rough notion of what might be happening at a molecular level when memory is formed. Although it was a hypothetical image, it had plausibility. It was an attempt to get at a biological truth.

Ten years before, in the late 1970s, I had been in a similar meeting but in the legal rather than the scientific world. Here, too, there was a shared quest to unravel a mystery, but a mystery of human actions and responsibility. Here also an image emerged from the dialogue among those assembled, an image of what had happened. Only what had happened was medical malpractice. I had my own observations and ideas, but until those meetings, I never really understood how my father died.

On his final day, I was telephoned by one of his doctors. I was told that my father was in stable condition, that his recovery was slow, but he was being successfully treated to bring his diabetes under control and to improve his heart's ability to circulate blood through his body. Something about the nonchalance, even complacency, of the doctor's manner frightened me. Although I was an intern on hospital duty that weekend, I hurriedly arranged to travel with my brother to be at my father's bedside.

When I arrived, still in my intern's uniform, I asked to see my father's medical chart. I was aghast at what I saw. Throughout the preceding week, the results of critical laboratory tests either had not been recorded or had never been obtained. Blood sugar levels essential to follow his diabetes were missing. Levels of blood potassium were not continuously monitored although they had become dangerously high. These and other measures of metabolic, cardiac, and kidney function had been grossly neglected. A second-year medical student would know better. None of his doctors was present. Only after my insistent phone calls did they request the tests that should have been done all along.

At this point my father was already moribund. His kidneys were failing and his heart seriously compromised. No reassurance dissuaded him from his already formed conclusion that death was imminent. My father's last words for me were about my future, about my health and safety, not about my performance. Our parting was in keeping with the way our relationship had mellowed during his last few years. But my grief at his passing joined with fury at the way he had been treated. On the following day, I commissioned a detective to photocopy the hospital records. Years later, when the malpractice trial was finally heard, there were two sets of hospital records, one as photocopied, the other, entirely different, as altered afterward by hospital staff. It was in the preparation for this trial that I was struck by the science of my lawyer and his colleagues.

Each morning during the week before the trial, my lawyer assembled witnesses, including relatives and friends, the legal staff, and medical experts. Seated around a table, under the brilliant direction of the lawyer, the group first reviewed the experience of witnesses. Family members painstakingly retraced the events of my father's hospitalization. Who had been his doctors and nurses when he had an episode of sweating, tremulousness, and anxiety accompanied by abnormally low blood pressure? How did this fit with the level of sugar in his blood? Was this an episode of hypoglycemia, and did he experience chest pain at that time? How did the medical staff respond to his complaints of symptoms? What precautions had been taken to minimize the stress of his situation? Had anyone become aware that he had been so overmedicated with insulin as to produce hypoglycemia, hypotension, and possibly further damage to his already weakened heart? Had anyone considered the possibility that the level of potassium in his blood was so high that it might block the natural pacemaking signals that kept his heart beating?

The first-hand experiences elicited by the inspired questioning of the lawyer reverberated around the table. It was like taping a video with ten different cameras, all directed at a scene from different angles. When the tapes were replayed, a multidimensional picture sprang to life. We were at a séance recalling my father's spirit and asking him to tell us his story. "What happened to you?" we asked. He told us more than enough to convince the jurors. It was also an opportunity once again to say good-bye.

It is impossible to separate emotional reinforcement and confirmation from experimental confirmation. Research from many different angles generates a multidimensional image of memory, but the image arises from whole people who receive confirmation along with their observations. So much of my professional life has been spent with only a secondary focus on approval and confirmation that I have grown accustomed to following my own tastes and setting my own standards. Critical reactions and suggestions of teachers, colleagues, and students are not unimportant to me. Through the years, I have gained perspective from the opinions of critics, even when hostile. Nevertheless, the momentum of my research efforts has always been channeled in directions that I, and not others, determined. I have rarely depended on others for confidence. Occasionally, with someone of Bernard Katz's stature, this modus vivendi was temporarily suspended.

Bernard Katz, an outstanding figure in the history of neuroscience, happened to be sitting next to me during a lecture at the Marine Biological Laboratory. After we exchanged a few pleasantries and comments about the lecture, I suggested that sometime he might like to see some of our work in the laboratory. It was about 9:30 in the evening. Katz said he was ready to visit immediately. For almost two hours, I reviewed our latest experiments. Despite his age and undeterred by the lateness of the hour, Katz took in every detail, raising one question after another. Katz's interests and towering achievements concerned membrane channels, sensory receptors, and, most of all, synapses. He had never studied memory. But nothing escaped his intense interest and keenly critical eye. Why this particular snail? Why associative memory? What was the role of intracellular calcium, and where were its sites of action? How was it possible to record with microelectrodes inside of neurons while rotating the preparation to stimulate the vestibular organ? Since he had pioneered analysis of very small signals at synaptic junctions, he was especially interested in very weak stimulation of the sensory cells. Katz no longer conducted his own experiments, yet he listened and questioned as if my experiments were his. Honored though I was by the great man's attention, I felt a certain camaraderie. I identified with the steeliness of his will and the immersion of his whole being in pursuit of answers. We didn't finish that night, and he said he would return the next day. He didn't say when, but the next morning, before most of the rest of the scientific community was out of bed, he was knocking on the door, and we went at it for another couple of hours.

As I explained our experiments I could hear my voice, not as an adult, but as a child. His presence, his attention, recreated my feelings as a boy seeking my father's blessing. I could feel my throat constrict and my voice assume almost plaintive notes. If Katz was aware of my apprehension, he showed no signs of it. He was neither effusive nor negative. He indicated his general approval and appreciation for my review and left. His most generous compliment was the time he spent with me. But when he left, I was unsatisfied. My ancient need for approval was exposed, but not assuaged.

A few years later, lecturing at Harvard University, I saw Katz sitting in the front row of the audience. He smiled briefly in greeting. In this setting, there was no room for hesitation and no need to be confirmed by higher authority. I spoke with a sense of control as well as enthusiasm. At the end of my lecture, as I mixed with the audience and answered questions, I approached Katz where he sat. He rose slowly and shook my hand vigorously. With obvious pleasure and in a voice that seemed to echo throughout the hall, Katz commented that my story was truly beautiful. He remarked further on how much progress there had been since we last talked. We would meet again on subsequent occasions, in his old department in University College, London, among other places. He did not forget me or our discussions, but I could tell that his memory was failing. In just a few years, he declined rapidly, but not before he had imparted his gift. That moment at Harvard, I felt a relief of tension which never returned again with quite its familiar intensity. My search strategy was still under way. The questions that drove me remained unanswered. Yet the loneliness of the race had begun to dissipate.

VARIETIES OF NEURONAL EXPERIENCE

It's easy to get lost among the molecules and the channels, easy even for the investigator who thinks he can see them. However distant their invisible lives are, they are still related to ours. Hearing their stories can be a bit like listening to your grandfather talk about his ancestors' trials and tribulations. Part of the fascination comes from the thought that these people you are hearing about are connected to you and that in some remote way it is *you* who are having the adventures as you listen. Channels and molecules, neurons and networks take on meaning when we consider them in the context of our own experience.

Although learning can occur at any stage of our lives, the type of learning it is and its importance to us will depend on where we are in our developmental or aging cycles. When we are younger, for example, it is less difficult to learn a new language, to commit long lists of historical facts to memory, or to acquire a tennis stroke. It is also likely that emotional contexts, highs and lows, are experienced in childhood with an impact that is rare later in life. Other types of learning, however, particularly of abstractions based on complex categories of information and long sequences of rules and logical steps, often must wait for young adulthood.

We have been discussing until now how memories are stored in neuronal networks of mature animals, which had stopped developing long before the animals were trained. Yet training rerouted the flow of signals through the networks to store memories. Presumably, this must also be true of our own brains since, even as adults, when the number of our neurons is actually decreasing day by day, we retain a remarkable capacity to learn new tricks. A network need not be developing in order to learn, nor need aging prevent it from learning. The network changes that we measured during learning—changes of ion flow, chemical messengers, and structural arrangements—occur in the absence of development and in the presence of aging. In fact, I chose to study young adult animals to more easily distinguish memory mechanisms from those of development and aging.

In the early stages of human development, our brains undergo dramatic changes independent of experience. The DNA, a constellation of helically arranged molecules grouped in the nucleus to transmit heredity, does not have space to encode all or even most of the specifications to construct the neuronal networks of the brain. It encodes, instead, a program, or set of rules, according to which neurons develop, differentiate, and become connected. Through changes of its DNA, a species evolves adaptively to pressures in its environment. Although such changes, called mutations, originate randomly, they nevertheless become a permanent record of the link between a particular cluster of environmental stimuli and an adaptive change of the organism. An adaptive mutation is itself a kind of memory record, which functions during the lifetime of a species rather than of individual animals. During evolutionary time, a mutation allows the species to learn and remember design improvements in the circuitry of neuronal networks that should be replicated in future generations. Such evolutionary memory records are preserved in the molecular structure of DNA as it replicates in dividing cells.

Adult neurons in the brain rarely divide and replicate their DNA, but although a neuron often lasts for an animal's lifetime, its component parts, its proteins, are continually being synthesized, degraded, and resynthesized. The DNA orchestrates this ongoing renewal of the cell as well.

Very early in its lifetime, a neuron is an unidentifiable member of a cell cluster located in an identifiable region of a primordial embryo. Cells in this cluster are fated to become the heterogeneous collection of cells that makes up the brain and peripheral nervous system. A balance of precise genetic specifications and pressures from the neuron's physical and chemical environment determines where the embryonic neuron migrates and what shape it assumes. Whether the primitive neural element is at the top or at the bottom of the cluster may influence the direction in which it migrates as the embryo develops and therefore where in the mature organism it finally resides. Molecular signals outside the primordial neural cluster help determine when a major developmental transition will occur. At this very early stage in the neuron's lifetime, genetic controls dominate its fate. Signals from the microenvironment surrounding the neuron, though important, play a subordinate role, and stimuli from the external world surrounding the embryo are so tightly buffered that they have little impact. The odyssey of a neuron through its experience is accompanied by a progressive shift in these roles. With time, genetic control is markedly abridged as environmental signals gain influence.

At early developmental stages, some genes can even activate other genes in a cascade of growth regulation. A number of such genes and gene products control how a neuron begins to assume the shape and cellular properties that equip it for its later special functions. Some neurons will have elaborately branching processes ideally suited to receive thousands of chemical signals from other neurons. Other neurons will be endowed with an intricate apparatus to receive one form of energy, such as light, from the environment and to transform that energy into electrical signals. Some neurons will develop long wirelike axons ending in minute branchlets whose chemical secretions onto muscle fibers control movements of the organism. Still other neural precursors are fated to wrap themselves around the long axons or the main bodies of neurons to insulate them and provide metabolic machinery for their nourishment.

Long before the postnatal period, the precursors have become committed to their lifetime roles. All of the information for these commitments is not explicitly provided in the DNA, but even at this stage, cell clusters follow rules as they react to their microenvironment. The final location and relationships of the mature neuron, and even some of its shape and function are quite dependent on the interaction of the juvenile neuron with its neighbors and its chemical environment. As the developing neuron dances in slow motion, its pose, steps, and rhythm are exquisitely orchestrated by the DNA. The full complexity and beauty of the choreography only emerge, however, when the whole company of neurons coordinates its movements to bring the brain to life.

Much of the dance occurs in the mammalian brain before birth. Yet much still remains. While a neuron is still traveling to its final destination, it has already begun to send out its long transmitting branch, or axon. Once it has achieved a stable location, the neuron begins to elaborate its main receiving branch, or dendrite. During postnatal development, the dendrite begins to send out many other branches of progressively greater complexity. Small protuberances or spines proliferate throughout the branches to provide sites where synaptic junctions with other neurons can occur. During the earliest months and years, the number of synaptic junctions increases dramatically. During the next stage, the number declines as synapses are eliminated and the circuits become more precisely wired. Purkinje cells in the cerebellum, for example, initially make synapses with many ascending, or climbing, fibers. Later in development, each climbing fiber is synaptically connected with only one pyramidal cell. The same is true of synapse number in many brain regions. For some structures, however, neurons crucial for the mature network are still missing in advanced developmental stages. Small neurons in the hippocampus of the postnatal rabbit arrive later to provide alternate paths of information flow among the large pyramid-shaped cells. In other structures, neurons present early on later disappear entirely. For example, some smaller neurons in outer layers of the immature cerebral cortex are absent from mature brains, apparently no longer needed.

As the neurons make their way in the postnatal world, their fate becomes increasingly determined by communication with their neighbors. Axons that reach target neurons compete with other axons to make synaptic connections. Once a certain number of connections are formed, the target neuron prevents new connections and eliminates connections that have not been completed. The target neuron has become committed and is no longer available. Electrical activity of target neurons helps choose which synapses remain. But electrical activity in developing neuronal networks increasingly depends on sensory stimulation received by the postnatal animal from its environment. At critical developmental periods, signals triggered by sensory stimuli can radically transform entire regions of neurons.

David Hubel and Torsten Wiesel showed, for example, that if one of a kitten's eyelids is kept closed throughout a critical period of development, its visual pathway is permanently altered. Neurons of visual centers within the kitten's brain no longer respond normally to signals sent from retinal cells in the eye. Even the anatomy of these visual neurons and their connections is altered. During later developmental or adult stages, closure of an eyelid has negligible impact on visual function and neuronal organization. Furthermore, the changes of function and anatomy are less dramatic if both eyelids are kept closed during the critical period. The imbalance of stimulation received by the two eyes causes the most drastic changes of the visual pathway. The genetic program requires a certain level and pattern of stimulation during a developmental period for the visual networks to reach completion.

Many other elegant experiments have since confirmed the profound influence experience can have on network development. In the rat brain, neuronal networks representing whisker touch sensation can be transformed by restricted stimulation of some facial whiskers and not others. Again, the networks are vulnerable to such stimulation only during a critical developmental period. Similarly, an owl localizes sounds in space with networks that have to adapt to the growing size of the animal's head. The visual and auditory experience of the owl shapes the networks in this way only during a restricted period of the animal's growth.

In this phase of a neuron's experience, it has become a member of a network, but the network's wiring has not been completed. It is still forming, and experience of the animal actively participates in the wiring. This is a very specialized participation, one that cannot occur during maturity. In maturity, the neurons are already connected within the network. Now the effect of experience on network wiring is more subtle as it adjusts the weight of the connections to store memories.

The difference between developmental formation of networks and adult learning's adjustments of the networks might help explain some of the power of childhood memories. Perhaps associations learned during critical periods of development not only adjust the synaptic weights but actually help choose which synapses live or die. Memories in childhood then, would become doubly imprinted in the brain. They would not only be stored in networks already present in a child, they would actually be stored in the network *designs* they helped to create and structure.

The power of childhood memories probably also derives from the fact that later memories often build on earlier ones. We cannot write words before we have learned the letters of an alphabet. Somewhat like learning a written language, learning to recognize the concept of depth probably requires some history of seeing visual patterns that include surfaces near and far. Presumably, an infant's experience of touching and moving over surfaces as they appear contributes to the interpretation and classification it learns for the images. Enough images, together with its touching and moving experience, are collected to build the concept of depth. This building has the appearance of development. It is as if the infant's depth perception is developing. Development in this case, however, may involve few if any developmental changes in the infant's brain. The necessary changes may only be those that store learned information within neural networks, whether those networks are in a 5-month-old or a 50-year-old. An infant's conceptual maturation, however, also involves development of its brain. It may very well be that some of the synaptic connections are not sufficiently complete to allow the infant to do the information processing necessary for depth perception. In all probability, the staged capacities of the infant and young toddler depend on the interaction of both developmental and learning changes within the networks. Later, when the brain is no longer developing and growing, the stages of intellectual development depend more exclusively on learning-induced network changes.

These two interactive classes of network change, developmental and learning-induced, are extremely difficult to tease apart. We do know that developmental changes not only require a critical period, they typically require very prolonged stimulation, often weeks and even months. Learning, on the other hand, can begin to occur within seconds and minutes at any period in an animal's life. Developmental changes often involve extensive travel of axonal branches to sites where new synapses are formed. Other axonal branches may undergo marked degeneration and withdrawal from sites where they failed to form synaptic junctions. Learning, however, even in the absence of new synaptic connections or the loss of old ones, begins by adjusting the weights of synaptic connections already present in the neuronal networks. Weight adjustment begins immediately when the first stimuli associated during training trigger molecular events that regulate channels within the neuron's membrane. When for example the flow of potassium ions decreases, the excitability of that membrane in response to synaptic stimuli increases. In this way, synapses already wired into the snail and rabbit networks can change their weight during memory storage.

A large body of behavioral research conducted over the past thirty years suggests a dynamic interaction of development, learning, and brain organization. Since the pioneering studies of Robert Fantz, we have come to understand that an infant, like other animals, doesn't come into the world as a tabula rasa. The infant's brain is shaped by genetics, development, and experience, but the brain also shapes experience. Infants pay attention to and thus receive increased stimulation from certain sensory patterns in preference to others. Fantz found that a face attracts the infant's interest and thus has maximal opportunity to stimulate its networks. The same parts of the sensory pattern in the face rearranged into a nonface pattern will not command the infant's attention. Similarly, baby chicks, before they have had any other visual experience, will peck at spherical particles in preference to cubic or pyramidal particles. Preferences built into the chick's and infant's networks help determine what stimulation they will seek. The stimulation, over time, however, will help further determine the network by affecting the network's development and by inducing changes that store memories. The network continues to go through this cycle. Now another level of sophistication in the genetic blueprint becomes apparent.

I mentioned earlier that the DNA simply does not have enough room to specify the details of a brain's networks. Instead, a set of rules is provided by which neurons form themselves into networks. The interaction of these rules with developmental and learning-induced changes allows a delicate but powerful dialogue between genetics and the environment, nature and nurture. Through this interaction, the experience of the species from eons past is reconciled with the experience of the individual animal during its lifetime. The interaction cannot, of course, be limited to sensory perception. Harlow showed that it must also include emotional experience. Monkeys, for example, deprived of their own mothers, become attached to dummies with just enough visual and textural similarities. There can be no doubt from the monkeys' behavior that they bring their emotional needs to the dummies. Dummies that feel right to the monkeys attract their attention and their affection. A cloth-covered surrogate will consistently attract, while a bare-wire surrogate will not. The baby monkeys will choose the cloth-covered surrogate even when only the wire surrogate has a nursing bottle. Here again, genetics has predesigned the monkey's brain to prefer and attend to a certain pattern of sensory stimulation. What it finds will satisfy or fail to satisfy established emotional needs for nurturance and protection. This dialogue, too, has critical periods of impact. The monkey will learn that its needs are consistently unsatisfied by the surrogate. The effects of this experience during such critical early periods will cause developmental and learning-induced changes in the monkey's networks to expect consistent satisfaction or deprivation.

The networks, now so shaped, will then help determine all of the monkey's future interests and experience.

Animals, and presumably humans, deprived in these critical periods never have quite the same expectations of satisfaction. Reared in isolation, animals expect solitude and never successfully mix with other animals. We might infer that their networks have now become sufficiently wired by developmental and learning-induced changes that they can no longer be rewired by socializing experience. This seems to be an example of what is generally true about the development-experience dialogue. The networks achieved at any particular developmental stage set the limits on what can or cannot be learned. Learning, presumably through adjustment of synaptic weights, can fine-tune the networks and sometimes functionally alter them, but only under the ground rules set first by the network.

The intricate mixing of genetic, developmental, and learning determinants of networks does not persist into adulthood. By this stage, the ground rules are no longer changing. Now it is learning's game, with development and aging on the sidelines. These observations suggest a biological basis for the importance of early childhood experience to human behavior, normal and pathological. We face more than the simple problem of distinguishing early learning from later learning when we wish to retrain an individual into more satisfying, less self-destructive behavior. It is not simply a matter of learning new habits and forgetting the old. The adult brain's networks, formed by the interaction of genetics, development, and learning, are to a significant degree hard-wired. The wiring is presumably expressed in the constitutional features that characterize individual personality. Behaviors that are shy, passive, or depressive rather than aggressive, intense, or hostile are imbedded in the wiring of millions, if not billions, of neurons. They permeate life's every aspect, from childhood play and schooling to athletics, from relations with the opposite sex to performance in the workplace. One individual has the temperament to be an airline pilot, another to broker corporate mergers. Some of us get into art, others mathematics. There are those who need to be engaged physically for most of the day, while some can sit at a desk for hours without jumping out of their skins. These are not styles that can be trained. They are ingrained, built into a permanent template. When we wish to counsel change in others or consider it for ourselves, it seems essential, therefore, to know the basic terrain of the behavioral landscape. New training and radically different experience may be able to modify familiar behavior, but the networks will not change with learning in adulthood as they can when we are growing up. The chemistry of personality has already been determined.

Once the formative years have passed, who can say what in those hard-wired networks is genetic, developmental, or learned? From the perspective of adulthood, personal style might as well be genetic because it is no longer open to change. This is not to say we retain no flexibility. Our networks still have soft-wired portions. We still have choices—at least, that is our hope, as well as our gamble. But these thoughts do recommend an attitude of humility toward the possibilities of change for people. We listen to memory's voice with new respect not only for its cultural origins but also for its biological roots.

This was not what I expected to find when I set out, energized by a sense of mission to wrestle with trauma's grip on the human psyche. In those adolescent days which I remember as the dawning of my own consciousness, I adopted a kind of rugged individualism. I thought it possible that I might be able to transfer my own hopeful ambitions to a friend in need, Michelle, and later to patients. Still developing myself, I little understood that as developmental milestones came and went, doors, though not closed, could be opened with increasingly greater difficulty. Still in high school, Michelle, too, had ambitions, not just fantasies, of intellectual growth, professional independence, and loving relationships. She seemed then to be reachable. Over the years, I watched helplessly as she missed opportunities and withdrew into herself. At the same time, increasing familiarity with brain networks tempered, but did not dispel, my optimism about the power of psychotherapy. Even in medical school, I knew that although early experience is formidable, in therapeutic settings we try to create later experience that can compete for a patient's attention. But I didn't understand then, as I do now, that the actual biology of experience's influence on our brains is not the same in most of adulthood as it is in early childhood.

To be sure, there is evidence of some overlap in basic mechanisms between developmental and learning-induced changes. Activation of the chemical messenger pathways we had found during learning apparently also occurs as a neuron sends out its axon to develop sites of synaptic contact with other neurons. Channels within membranes of some developing neurons are modified in ways we had found when a memory is stored. There is even a suggestion that as memory becomes more permanent, it requires some structural alterations which resemble some of those during development. But networks can change during critical developmental periods in ways not possible later on. We can begin to store a memory in seconds, while development takes much longer in response to more repeated and profound sensory stimulation. Once certain design choices are made during development, no redesign is possible.

Some of what is learned even in childhood can be unlearned. Bad grammar can be corrected. Proper attire and etiquette can be substituted for socially unacceptable habits. But the trauma and fears of abuse cannot easily be swept away once certain expectations have been imprinted during formative years. Attitudes of helplessness or prejudice inculcated with mother's milk are not easily erased by the teaching of an enlightened professor, clergyman, friend, or lover. More likely, those attitudes will determine the choice of friends and lovers, limiting them to people who share those attitudes or at least offer little threat to their tenability. Sadly, it seems, the emotional importance of what has been learned in critical periods determines its permanence. If only the brain changes of adult learning were more like those of childhood. Perhaps then we could be more ambitious. As it is, for now, these differences limit our freedom and, to a degree, seal our fate.

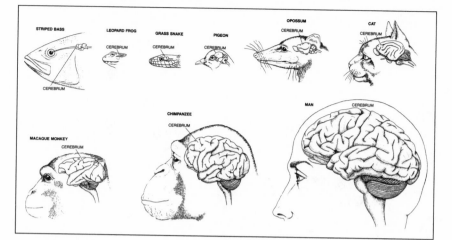

Fig. 26 The size of vertebrate brains, drawn here to scale, increases in vertebrates. Mammalian carnivores, particularly primates, tend to have the largest and most complex brains. (From "The Brain", D. H. Hubel, 1979. *Scientific American*. V. 241 (3), 9–17. W. H. Freeman, N. Y.)

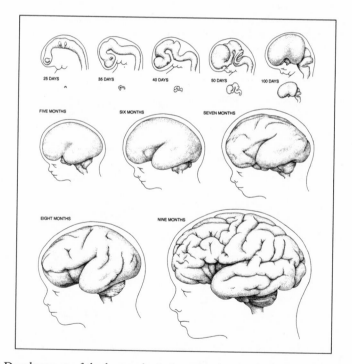

Fig. 27 Development of the human brain in successive prenatal stages. Cowan points out that neurons are generated in the developing brain at a fantastic average rate of more than 250,000 per minute. Few neurons are added after birth beyond the already incredibly large number of 100 billion. (From "The Development of the Brain," W. M. Cowan, 1979. *Scientific American*, V. 241 (3), 106–117)

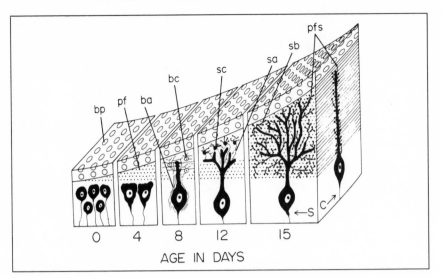

Fig. 28 Development of Purkinje cells in the rat cerebellum. This schematic model suggests rules whereby fibers running in perpendicular planes form synaptic connections during the postnatal development of the cerebellum. The volume and complexity of the Purkinje cell dendritic tree in the plane of the page continues to increase even many months later into development. The labels indicate known neurons and axon fibers in this structure. S and C indicate two planes of development. (From J. Altman, 1976. *Comparative Neurology*, V. 165, 65–76. The Wistar Institute Press)

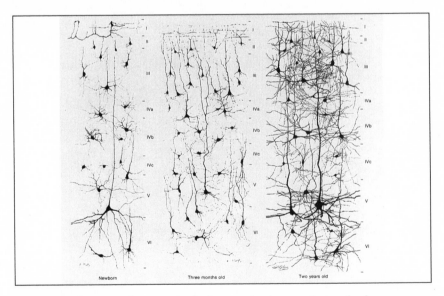

Fig. 29 Development of neurons in the human visual cortex during the first two years of life. The number and complexity of dendritic branches as stained with Golgi's technique increase dramatically during this period. (From *The Postnatal Development of the Human Cerebral Cortex*, J. L. Conel, 1959. Harvard University Press, Cambridge, Mass.)

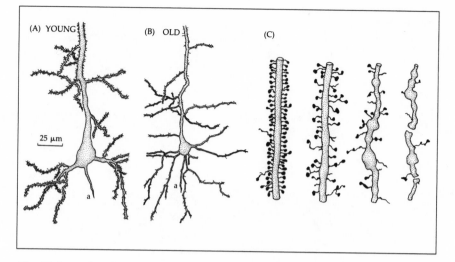

Fig. 30 Age-related changes of neuronal structure. A pyramidal cell in a three-month-old rat is larger and has many more spines (A) than such a cell in thirty-four-month-old rat that has entered senescence (B). A similar reduction in spine number can be seen at higher magnification from left to right with increasing age (C). Connections or synapses are located on the spines. (From *Principles of Neural Development*, D. Purves and J. W. Lichtman, 1985. Sinauer Associates, Inc., Sunderland, Mass.)

BRAIN CHILDREN

I had a hidden agenda as I teased apart neuronal networks. My will to understand was inseparably linked with the will to change human behavior. I scrutinized blueprints of neural circuits with radical notions of revolutionizing psychotherapy. My vision went beyond simply talking about problems with patients or prescribing mood elevators and tranquilizers. I aspired to develop more specific and gentle manipulations that would cause the brain's circuits to relinquish their buried records and make room for new expectations and patterns of behavior. Perhaps a psychiatrist could become more like a surgeon. I didn't think any of this through, of course, when this undercurrent first held its greatest sway on my thinking, as I dreamed of answers for Michelle. The flavor of these notions did influence my experimental questions, however. Naïve, presumptuous dreams combined mission with a touch of madness. I never for a moment contemplated rewiring a troubled brain. But this was among the Frankensteinian extrapolations of knowing how the brain rewires itself during learning.

Going even further, engineers of the future would incorporate brainlike circuits into artificial networks that would endow robots with powerful intelligence. Such is the promise of computer-based networks, but today they still cannot recognize a face or learn a language. My own interest in artificial, computer-based networks has less to do with designing intelligent machines than with gaining insight into the brains of humans. I am concerned with how well artificial networks serve as models for brain networks because a model that successfully mimics brain function helps bring ethereal abstractions about inaccessible brain wiring down to earth. This is particularly true if the model is derived from actual properties of brain networks. Starting from biological networks of the snail and the mammalian hippocampus, then, rather than principles of physics and engineering, my collaborators and I set out to construct computer-based learning networks.

Theorists in the past had constructed artificial networks with no more than a few trivial features of real neurons. For almost four decades, in fact, mathematicians and engineers have worked with little success to create "artificial intelligence." Like aircraft designers inventing their own machines to fly, "cognitive engineers" have used very few of nature's own solutions. The ancient designers of the first flying machines dreamed of doing what nature had not done—endowing human beings with the capacity to fly. Birds provided their inspiration, but only a few principles of design.

Network designers have constructed their own "intelligent" devices which achieve a few limited brain functions, but not in the way the brain does. It is not surprising that their engineering shows minimal attention to the wiring of actual brain circuits. After all, despite the exciting breakthroughs of the last forty years, we still know relatively little about how the brain processes information. Until the recent past, we knew even less about how the brain recognizes patterns or images. So what guidance could the cognitive engineer take from biology when biological systems were a mystery? A view to the world of computers, on the other hand, gave a different impression. Here were devices created by mathematicians and engineers to accomplish limited tasks, but with superhuman performance. Over the years, the tasks became increasingly sophisticated and the performance beyond all expectations. This was more than enough encouragement to take computer design a step further—to create de novo designs of computerlike instruments with brainlike endowments. If such designs were successful, they might be considered possible models of brain function. Many ambitious mathematicians and engineers were drawn to the challenge of creating such designs.

The current interest in network models probably began in the early 1940s. Alan Turing had recently hypothesized a computing machine based on a simple code of sequences imprinted on a tape. At each position in the sequence, the switch was either on or off. Turing claimed that the most difficult computing operations could be encoded by the appropriate sequences of on-off switches. In 1943, Warren McCulloch and Walter Pitts were able to mathematically model a hypothetical group of neurons that could mimic some of the computing functions of Turing's machine. The McCulloch-Pitts neurons had few biological properties, but they were connected, and they did respond to inputs with an on-off signal. They could sum inputs, but they could not encode the magnitude of inputs by responding with varying frequencies of signals. Their connections were fixed and were not organized according to any scheme derived from a real biological network. Yet, with their artificial features, they could do some computation.

The thought that networks could perform computational tasks was novel but in itself did not go far. In the years that followed, many such artificial computer networks were created to incorporate additional features. One program, called the perceptron, for example, included one layer of receiving neurons whose signals converged onto output neurons of a second layer. The strengths of connections between the first receiving layer and the second output layer were not fixed. They could be adjusted so that the perceptron was able to "recognize" particular patterns. Such artificial networks were more interesting than the previous generation of artificial computing networks, but they were extremely limited in their capabilities. Yes, they could learn patterns, but only a few patterns. Furthermore, the number of artificial neurons and the number of connections among them was prohibitively high. Existing computers could not overcome such limitations by simply repeating billions of simple computations. In the last twenty years, more attention has been paid to the operations performed by the networks. Rules of operation, also called algorithms, were incorporated to endow models with new problem-solving and pattern-recognition capabilities. In spite of these new designs, however, the important limitations of these artificial networks remained. They required enormous computational power, and they could store relatively few patterns.

For more than two millennia, those who would fly failed. So thirty or forty years of failure in developing artificial intelligence is no reason for discouragement. New biological insights into neural networks may offer quicker paths to design solutions. But what's missing?

Vast amounts of information can be entered and stored in a computer. In this respect, a computer and a brain are alike. But punching the proper code into a computer can call up and print out an entire book of text or a complete file of telephone numbers. The human brain cannot approach this kind of sequential recall. Nor can the human brain perform the almost unending sequence of mathematical operations of which a computer is capable. Computers, but not brains, can perform these operations with great speed. The brain can focus on only a limited number of events or functions at once. It can perform and store a sequence of only a few operations before its attention is no longer available for further operations. A computer can simultaneously take into account the velocity of a rocket hurtling through space, its fuel reserves, its current trajectory, and the mass and atmosphere of nearby heavenly bodies. The computer can integrate all of these factors to yield a predicted trajectory and, if necessary, advise a course correction. The human brain cannot quickly calculate how all of these factors and their interaction will sum together to produce a resulting flight path. There is too much data for the brain to attend to at once. A single X ray of a human organ such as the brain contains a complicated pattern of silver grains whose exposure varies with the density of the tissue. The resulting light-dark pattern is a cross section showing the spatial relations of brain structures. A computer can store one such section after another and then, on request, put them together to generate a three-dimensional picture of the brain. We cannot even begin to hold in our short-term memory all of the spatial relationships for these cross sections and then calculate how they fit together into a three-dimensional object. As a calculator the brain is a poor match for a computer.

While the computer excels at some of the tasks it shares with the brain, like most artificially intelligent machines, it is a virtual idiot when it comes to tasks that tap the cognitive potential of the human brain. For example, let us look more closely at what is called computer memory. Does a computer learn? How does it acquire new information? The programmer types it in. The computer knows nothing that hasn't first been learned, stored, and transferred by a human brain. It is true that endlessly repetitious operations may yield a result that the programmer did not know. But the operations and the decision to repeat them were first in a human brain. Sufficient information was then entered and stored in the computer to achieve goals selected by that brain.

The actual physical process by which the information is stored in the computer is in some respects no different from the way information is stored in a phonographic record, a tape, or a photograph. A pattern of physical events is represented by and preserved within another pattern. For the phonographic record, a pattern of sounds at a particular moment in time results in a pattern of structure within the record's grooves. On a tape it is a pattern of molecular alignments. On a photograph it is a pattern of chemical changes within the silver grains spread across a sheet of paper. The information is the pattern of events. To store a sequence of patterns changing with time, there must be a sequence of records, each representing a different pattern. All of these recording techniques are simply translating one type of pattern into another. A television camera translates a pattern of light signals which are then transmitted as patterns of electromagnetic waves or electrical signals which travel along cables to receivers. The receivers translate the pattern of electrical signals back into a pattern of light signals, which we view. The computer also translates patterns. Patterns of coded language in the programmer's brain are translated into patterns of current flow within the computer.

There is, however, a crucial difference between the kind of information that can be recorded by a computer and all of the other recording devices just mentioned. The computer can record simple patterns, but it can also record patterns of patterns. As directed by the programmer, it can process information grouped in classes. Mathematical operations and logical statements involve such processing, just as do ledgers of financial transactions or vocabularies of languages. All income entries are added to one class, all payments added to another. All nouns are grouped together, like all verbs or all vowels or consonants. The computer, as directed by the programmer, can store and access information according to similarities, differences, or relationships in time and space. These examples of computer-recorded information are all on a continuum leading to the kind of processed information we remember from our experience. It is from our experience, however, that our brains sense and store event patterns. In marked contrast, it is only from us, not experience, that the computer stores its event patterns. The computer has no way of determining whether or not a list of cash sums belongs in an income class unless the programmer signals it by placing a plus sign before each sum. Similarly, the computer acquires its language from us, while we acquire ours from experience.

There is no one predetermined language for the brain. Language is acquired from what we hear, see, and speak. When combinations of consonants and vowels are encountered with sufficient frequency, they are stored and thus expected in the future. A sequence of such combinations will be learned as a word whose sound pattern is linked in time to a visual sensory pattern such as the appearance of a ball, a table, or a face. Progressively larger groups of sensed events become linked to each other in time as the language develops. Soon the word sequences also become linked. A ball bounces. Food is on the table. There is a smile on the face. Each of these clusters of words is sensed together with sufficient frequency to be entered into the brain's memory banks. Now conventions are learned to ease communication. These conventions are learned according to the frequency of their use by other people. Words linked to action are always heard after words linked to things. Words that characterize actions, such as *slowly* or *quietly*, occur together with action words. Such conventions for grouping words to describe events are learned and in this way determine a grammar. Children learn to recognize and say letters of the alphabet long after they have learned a good deal of grammar. A vowel's sound is heard as its form is seen. The more frequently this occurs, the more likely the sound will become permanently identified with the appearance of the letter. In China, one set of sound-sight links is stored in a child's mind, in France, another. No programmer enters these links into the brain. They are entered only as a result of how frequently they occur together in the child's experience.

Language, as well as the capacity for more abstract thinking, develops as the child learns to classify events and groups of events together. Classes might arise from events that are similar, but not identical. One event might remind a child of a similar event in the past. At first the child's grouping may be quite imperfect. It sees a moving furry object with four legs and calls it a dog, although it may be a cat, a rabbit, or a squirrel. But the process of grouping by similarity is apparent from the name. The child may have first learned to link the sound of the word *dog* with an actual dog. Later, the child sees a cat that is enough like a dog that the visual pattern of a dog and the sound pattern to which it is linked are remembered. Certain physical aspects of the cat, resembling those of a dog, trigger the memory of the rest of the dog. When a critical mass of a sensory pattern—for example, the image of the dog—reoccurs, the memory links fill in the missing portions to complete the pattern. The frequency with which events occur together, as well as their similarities and differences, programs the child's brain, allowing it to classify, categorize, complete patterns, learn languages, and build abstractions. Only some of these abilities can today be programmed into a computer. Very little is generated within or by the computer itself.

Given these limitations, some designers of artificial networks have looked to the brain to exploit its secrets. In the 1940s and 1950s, the look was a passing glance, a dutiful nod. It was, however, a beginning. The first step was to recognize that the brain contains large rows and columns (i.e., layers of neurons). Something about the arrangement of the neurons, their signals, and the connections among them has important implications for information processing. For many years, that something has had only minimal influence on the design of artificial networks. If the collective weight of the signals received by a neuron is large enough, for example, the receiving neuron will send its own signal to other neurons. The weighted sum of inputs brings the target neuron to a threshold for its own signal to travel on. These features of neurons and their connections are, in general, common to most regions of the brain. They are necessary but not at all sufficient to describe how brain networks function. Incorporation of such features into computer-based systems endowed them with some interesting properties, but their functions were still extremely limited.

In the 1960s, it became apparent to some of the pioneers of computer-brain comparisons that much more would be needed. For example, there would have to be certain rules to govern the operations of the artificial networks. It was already well known that some rules were imposed by the precise organization of connections among neurons in such structures as the mammalian retina, cerebellum and hippocampus. But these networks were often not understood well enough to inspire architects of artificial networks, particularly networks with the capacity to learn to recognize patterns. A number of early thinkers in the field understandably derived their inspiration from intuitive impressions of animal learning behavior, analogies to functions of molecular arrays in purely chemical or physical contexts, or mathematical theories about systems in general. With few exceptions, the rules for signal processing in these initial artificial networks were ad hoc. However they were inspired, they were, for the most part, not rooted in concrete observations of neuronal systems. Some of these first attempts did simulate a few aspects of brain processing and so caught the imagination of a generation of neuroscientists and mathematicians. These were the brain children, so to speak, of such pioneers as James Anderson, David Rumelhart, James McClelland, and Tuve Kehonen. One pioneer,

Steven Grossberg, was particularly attentive to actual features of behaving animals and their brain systems.

Back propagation networks, brilliantly conceived by Rumelhart and McClelland, are popular examples of ad hoc designs. One "back-prop" network, "NET-talk," designed by Terrence Sejnowski and Charles Rosenberg, illustrates what such networks can and cannot do. Many listeners at a NET-talk demonstration walk away believing that this machine learns and remembers in the same way we do. In fact, its designers originally described it as "a parallel network that learns to read aloud." A tape recording is played to produce the sounds made by a computer as it responds to the visual forms of consonants, vowels, syllables and words. At first the computer sounds are simply unpleasant noise sounding somewhat like gibberish. Over a period of many minutes we recognize a sound reminiscent of an English vowel or consonant. Gradually, the recognizable sounds become more and more frequent. Soon the computer begins to sound strangely familiar. It is no longer the alien tinniness of machine sounds we hear. It is the voice of a child, of our child, of ourselves learning to speak. Miraculously, the halting, clumsy attempts at spoken language begin to succeed. Eventually, riveted by the stunning climactic speech of the computer, we sit dumbfounded as if we had been witness to divine creation. Could anyone not be moved by this experience? The lecture hall has become a cathedral and the lecturer our priest. But is our new faith justified? Or has it been at least misplaced? Let us reconstruct what actually happened.

In one corner of the computer called the "teacher," somewhere in its program the correct relationships between sounds and visual images of letters and words have already been entered and stored. In another corner of the same computer is the student, childlike in its ignorance and its apparent ability to learn. Entry of a letter or word into the teacher corner of the computer, always elicits the correct sound, which the computer has been programmed to make. The same letters or words entered into the student corner at first elicit only unrecognizable sounds from the computer. Within the computer, a series of electrical paths connect the student to the teacher. Signals travel to the teacher from the student as the computer emits a sound in response to a letter. By comparing the student's incorrect sound to the correct sound from the teacher's corner, the computer calculates a difference value, or error. From the calculated difference, the computer then slightly adjusts the weights of the artificial network to reduce the difference between the student's and the teacher's signals. This sequence of signal comparisons between the two corners of the computer may be repeated hundreds of thousands of times. Ever so slowly, the difference, the error, is minimized until the student's response is close to the teacher's. This is how a back-prop network works, through the principle of "error minimization."

Isn't this exactly what happens when a human student learns from a human teacher? Don't students compare their attempts with the standards provided by a teacher? Of course. In this particular aspect of a child's learning, back-prop does a lovely job of simulation. It also simulates the unavoidably tedious process of improvement with practice. The child learns by trial and error. Any artificially intelligent network should possess these necessary features. However, improvement with practice and error minimization do not a learning machine make.

First, who teaches the teacher in the computer? The teacher's knowledge has to be acquired in some way, but it is not by learning. That knowledge is programmed into the computer. The computer does not learn the information based on its experience. Here we have a fundamental difference between the NET-talk network and the child. Before making its first attempt to link a sound with the visual form of a letter, the child first learns the correct linkage from its teacher or parent. The linkage enters the child's brain through sensory pathways, and is usually not between exactly the same sounds and letters. A child from Maine and a child from Georgia will pronounce the letter *a* differently. Each teacher will write the letter *a* with variations of size, shape, and proportion. There will, however, be enough similarities among the sounds and the shapes of the letter for the essential letter-sound relationship to be repeated. With repetition, the child learns a sound-form prototype, a standard with which to compare the sound it makes when it sees the visual form of the letter. The child *learns* its standard, while the back-prop network is fed or programmed with its standard. Even if the child learns its standard quickly, with only a few examples from its teacher, it still must acquire and hold the standard in its short-term memory, based on the frequency with which that standard is sensed. In the child's case, knowledge or information was transferred from a constantly changing environment to the child's brain. NET-talk, however, acquires its information from the programmer's brain instead of directly from a changing outside world.

The crucial difference between learning and being programmed with information might become more apparent from the following hypothetical situation. Scientists on earth discover aliens on a distant planet. They send a rocket to the planet with a machine on board designed to learn the language of this extraterrestrial race. Since the scientists have no knowledge of the written or verbal forms of this foreign language, the machine will have to learn its own standards. A machine designed like a child's brain will sense the sounds and forms of letters, words, etc. Those sound-form combinations that occur with sufficient frequency will teach the machine the "correct" or accepted links of sounds and forms. The back-prop machine, however, is not designed to extract the varied and essential sound-form combinations used by the aliens. Back-prop networks can tolerate some variation in either the sound or the form, but not both, and they cannot generate the standard prototype without a human programmer.

Today, artificial networks can learn a few patterns, but they use up their capacity very quickly and require enormous computing power. Today, there are no artificial networks that could in fact learn a language spoken on earth or any other planet.

What approach is most likely to reveal the network design(s) that would make true learning possible? How can we arrive at the key principles by which to organize the elements in the network? Should we continue to extrapolate from physics and mathematics into a theory of networks that only superficially resemble the collections of neurons and their connections found in the brain? Must we develop a new physics, as suggested by Roger Penrose, in order to derive networks from the brain? Do we need this new physics to also understand how the networks of the brain accomplish such tasks? My own research has been based on an opposite strategy.

Why not look to the brain to reveal its networks, which in turn might explicate physics? This, of course, assumes an intimate knowledge of brain functioning, which has only recently begun to become available. As of a few years ago, however, enough was already known about the snail's learning network and mammalian networks to offer some guidance. Features of biological networks might be described in abstract mathematical terms and then incorporated into a computer-based network.

There has been ample precedent for such a strategy. In the 1920s von Békésy derived equations to describe how the responses of cochlear neurons were tuned to represent different frequencies of sound waves. Later, Hartline and his colleague Floyd Ratliff quantitatively described synaptic inhibition between neurons within the eye of the horseshoe crab *Limulus*. Mathematical representation of the neurons and their connections provided the basis for a model of the eye's function. Hartline's equations constituted probably the first and still one of the most elegant models of a biological network. Based on the properties of the actual network, it accurately predicted the crab eye's ability to enhance response differences of cells that sensed the transition from darkness to light. Today, models are being constructed to simulate the functions of much more sophisticated sensory networks, such as those of the mammalian retina and cochlea.

Hartline's equations concisely formulated principles of contrast enhancement within a network. Could mathematical learning principles be extracted from the visual-vestibular network of our snail? Hartline and I planned to begin asking these questions together, but it was not to be. As the time approached for our collaboration, his failing eyesight deteriorated rapidly, soon making it impossible for him to do experiments.

From the little contact we had, I saw Hartline as a patient man of gentle disposition. Although a determined scientist, he was not assertive. His more passive style was in many ways the opposite of mine. He was not interested in changing networks. Rather he held them in reverence. He concentrated not on how experience changed networks, but on why and how nature had formed them. Yet somehow, in spite of our differences, we seemed joined by an intellectual bond. Following different conceptual and experimental routes, we had arrived at a common path with a shared pleasure in the economy and conservation of nature's network designs. He was interested in network codes for the present, I for the past. Had he been able, we might have joined forces to study the emergence of one from the other as the codes interact to predict the future. I would instead have to find other colleagues with whom to venture into this strange, nonbiological realm of artificial networks and computer science.

LINKS IN TIME

Since the time of Golgi and Ramon y Cajal we have been able to picture in our minds what networks of neurons look like. Under the microscope, they appear in sections of brain as a sheet of egglike cells, which are often aligned in rows. Wirelike extensions of tissue crisscross through the sheets to form a fine meshwork of connections between the cells. Artificial networks can, if we wish them to, look like biological networks. The properties of artificial networks, however, are usually vastly less complex than those of real brains. Real neurons have all sorts of idiosyncrasies tucked away in the corners of their structures. The electrical signals, channels, and chemical messages are by no means uniform throughout the neuron. States of excitability and responsiveness to chemical messages vary widely even for sites distributed across the surface of the same neuron. Nor are neuronal responses the same from one instant to the next. The artificial networks of today are gross oversimplifications, even when closely modeled after actual biological networks, and this will probably be true for a long time to come.

Artificial networks usually provide paths for the flow of signals through their elements and connections. Most commonly, signal flow through networks is represented as current flow through electrical circuits. And, in fact, probably the most outstanding functional feature of

179

neuronal networks is the flow of electrical signals through anatomically defined wiring. It is therefore not surprising that neurons and neuron fibers have for decades been pictured as electrical circuits. Individual neurons have been conceived of as electrical circuits connected in series and parallel with each other. Circuits in the receiving branches of the dendritic tree are connected to circuits of the main dendritic trunk, the cell body, the axon, and the terminal branches that release chemical messages onto other neurons.

Neurons, to be sure, are not simply electrical circuits wired together. They live and breathe, requiring energy, giving off waste, moving, and even dying. Yet many of their essential functions can be described by equations for electrical circuits. Taking the analogy a step further, Carver Mead and his collaborators at the California Institute of Technology have built electrical circuits onto chips to simulate the neuronal networks within layers of the retina. Despite the unavoidable simplification of the biological circuits, the chip reproduces to a remarkable degree a number of the information-processing functions of the living retina. Still another direction emerges from the electrical-biological hybrid technology now becoming available. Workers have begun to grow cultured neurons on chiplike matrix structures. As the neurons grow, they begin to form synaptic connections with each other, in effect creating the wiring. Electrical currents injected into the matrix help determine what connections form. Albeit still primitive and difficult to control, these growing circuits may be common artificial networks in the future.

Key features of the artificial networks of today can nevertheless still be represented within a computer program. In reality, the artificial neurons are locations within a complex circuit of the computer. Rules are entered into the computer to govern the way the current flows and to simulate what occurs at the location of a simulated neuronal element and/or its connections with other elements.

Pavlovian conditioning and its effects on our snail networks suggested some interesting rules for an artificial learning network. One rule concerns the coming together of learned events, which so impressed me during my clinical experience. A father's love for one patient became linked with sexual abuse. A mother's love for another was linked in time with her oppressive domination. Michelle's need for her father was linked to his verbal and physical pummeling. Biological networks in the snail and the rabbit changed according to the same rule. There were connections between neurons in the networks, which increased in weight[1] when the events occurred together and decreased in weight when the events alternated. As well as I thought I understood the arrangement of the neurons and their connections, however, it was not clear how all the rules were implemented by the network. The rules required something more. For example, critical properties controlled conditions under which the neurons were activated by the flow of signals through the network: one neuron should be entirely inactive unless stimulated; another should fire signals spontaneously; some neurons should fire signals briefly when stimulated; others should continue firing long after stimulation has stopped.

In fact a logic was built into the biological network through the detailed properties of neuronal elements and their connections. It became my task to abstract those properties with enough precision to allow Tom Vogl, a physicist and my principal collaborator in this work, to build the properties into our artificial network, later named Dystal. We made many false starts. First I had to identify the key properties. We knew enough details about the snail networks to fill a book, but which ones were essential to capture the essence of their function? Even when I thought I had the right level of detail, it seemed impossible to include all the properties and all the rules. It was a bit like juggling. A juggler follows just the right sequence of movements to keep all the balls in the air without hitting each other. One rule cannot knock another rule out of the network.

Some rules, for instance, allow the networks to sense and represent separate events as they are happening, independently of other events. These networks monitor events as they occur in real time along pathways whose connections don't change their weights. The real time network can be compared to an unusually sophisticated television camera. The camera senses images continuously as they occur, but like the brain's real time sensing network, it only monitors the events—it doesn't record them. Visual information is monitored, for example, by electric signals flowing along pathways from the sensory cells in our eyes to subsequent brain stations. However, such fixed-weight or hardwired pathways must also communicate with other pathways whose connections do adjust to record the pattern of events (i.e., how the events are linked in time). For recording, we need other rules, also suggested by Pavlovian conditioning.

In Pavlovian conditioning, the smell of meat is unambiguous for the dog—it causes reflex salivation. Turbulence caused the snail's clinging reflex. Abuse causes pain, fear, and anger. Reflex responses to unambiguous stimuli involve hard-wired, or fixed-weight, network pathways. Our artificial network, therefore, should have fixed-weight pathways responsive to unambiguous stimuli. Ambiguous stimuli, on the other hand, such as the sound of a bell, the color of a flower, or the image of a face, could acquire responses learned by adjustable-weight pathways. The timing of ambiguous stimuli in relation to unambiguous stimuli could govern the weight adjustments.[2]

For months, I continued my mental juggling act, repeatedly frustrated as one rule conflicted with another. One day, juggling and walking along Bell Tower Road, which hugs tranquil Eel Pond in Woods Hole, I was finally able to picture all at once the key properties of the snail networks and the minimum number of rules we needed to include both the real time and remembered time functions. Within the neurons' signals to each other was just the necessary combination to represent clearly valued events and to learn and store their relationships with ambiguous events. I hurried home to sketch my picture. The picture, consisted of rows of neurons with an array of interacting pathways and a key with which to locate excitatory and inhibitory connections. There were also rules governing how the neurons and connections responded to signals from images sensed by the computer.

In Washington, Tom Vogl saw something in my faxed picture that in Woods Hole, up close, I could not. The network's sensing pathways seemed to converge into collections of endings on each artificial neuron. These collections were reminiscent of the way incoming signals group on branches of brain neurons. For example, each hippocampal neuron receives 100,000 to 200,000 signals on its elaborately branching dendritic tree. Thus there would be ample room for inputs to group together on one branch separate from another. Tom and I decided to call these collections "patches" since each represented a patch of experience—a combination of sensory signals at a point in time. If that particular combination occurred again and again, its patch gained weight. With sufficient weight, the patch of experience could be stored and later recognized.

This picture, which was the true beginning of our artificial learning network, had real neuronal properties that would prove crucial for pattern recognition. Neurons on later rows, for example, do not just fire briefly when they receive input signals. Like certain neurons in real brains, they continue to fire their signals until the next image is sensed by the network. In this way an image relates not only to other images that occur at one time, but also to later images. Such rules can allow the network to sense and eventually store a sequence of images.

When my Woods Hole picture had been translated into computer language, it showed immediate promise for representing and storing the relationships of events. But there was one network feature with no direct biological analogy: the connection between the fixed-weight, or hard-wired, pathways and the adjustable-weight pathways. These particular connections required a most unusual property to complete the learning function of the network. They should be excitatory when the two pathways were active at the same time and inhibitory when activity alternated in time. I knew that this property was approximated by the collective function of several synaptic connections among the snail neurons but not by any single synapse.[3] Yet the most efficient learning network would require such a synapse. I returned to the real synapses of the snail to see if it was possible to fill this gap, but now I looked at the synapse with different eyes to view its fit within our emerging picture of an artificial learning network. Mental pictures of what we are looking for exert surprising control over what we can see. This had been amusingly demonstrated for me several years earlier.

Returning from a trip to Europe, I went to the long-term parking garage. I knew my car was on the second floor but didn't have the exact number of the space or its row. The level was small enough so that I could walk by a few rows to scan all of the cars. For some reason, however, I couldn't find my car. I walked back and forth repeatedly without success. Could it have been stolen, I wondered. Perhaps I was mistaken and had actually parked it on a different level. I repeated my scanning on the first and third levels, now reaching a mood of quiet desperation. At this point, I thought, let's get a bit of perspective. I am in Boston's Logan Airport, not Washington. Since my own car is in Washington, I had to rent a car to get to Logan, and this rented car is a white compact, not the big old golden crate I am used to driving. I returned to the second level and immediately located the white rental car, the same car that I had repeatedly stared at without seeing it since I wasn't looking for a white compact. Expectations can exert the same influence over experimental observations.

For eighteen years, every time we stimulated the snail's vestibular sensory cell, we only noticed that it inhibited the type B visual cell by releasing a chemical messenger that we recently identified as GABA (short for gamma-amino-butyric acid). We knew, however, that training the snail requires stimulating both the vestibular cell and the visual cell together. Our computer-based network model suggested that the inhibitory effect of GABA might become excitatory when the visual and vestibular stimuli occurred together in time. This time we looked at the GABA synapse both before and after stimulating the visual and vestibular cells together. We could hardly believe what happened next. Now GABA excited the visual cell, something we had never observed before. We saw this metamorphosis, an entirely new synaptic function, because we were looking through glasses that filtered out real time in favor of remembered time. The GABA synapse remembered that two stimuli occurred together, linked in time, and as long as it did, it was excitatory, not inhibitory.

In the history of neuroscience, the sign of a synapse had never been known to undergo long-term change as a result of experience. Yet GABA synapses are the most ubiquitous of all synapses in the cerebral cortex. GABA has always been thought of as a major inhibitory synaptic messenger in the cortex. Perhaps many of the inhibitory GABA synapses in the cortex change when the necessary inputs occur together. Perhaps there are billions of opportunities for associated stimuli within images and image sequences to alter GABA synapses and thereby to link unit networks together. As part of an elementary code, the GABA synapse seems ideally located in the cortex. Now, it would be even more interesting to construct brain network models based on unit networks that included the GABA synapses we had uncovered, and to look for such transformable synapses in the kingdom of real brains.

BRAIN BUILDING

To be more like a brain, an artificial network should have a very large capacity to learn, store, and later recognize patterns of stimuli. An almost infinite number of light and sound patterns, for example, would have equal access to the network's memory. The network would not predict, nor would a computer programmer choose, which patterns were presented and then stored. Patterns, once learned, would be recognized, even if incomplete. The network should complete patterns as it recognizes them. Presented with lines connecting only a few dots, the memory network would, for instance, connect the other dots to fill in the missing lines and thereby produce an image. Alternatively, a portion of one pattern should be enough to elicit from the network an entirely different pattern to which the first had been linked in time. A sound sequence, say that for a name, may have been linked to a visual image, such as that of a face. On hearing the name, or even a portion of it, the network would produce the face. It would fill in the visual pattern that it expected to accompany the auditory pattern.

This is a continual process in our own experience. Playing the game of connecting numbered dots, we compete to be first to recognize a form after a minimum number of dots have been connected. All of the necessary lines have not been drawn, but we mentally complete the form from memory. The hangman game or a crossword puzzle involves a similar process. A similar phenomenon is exploited by the caricaturist portraying a face, whose art is such that we see just enough on the paper to fill in the rest of the face.

These last few examples illustrate completion of *visual* patterns. The same phenomenon occurs with other sensory patterns as well. Hearing a few notes of a refrain may bring back an entire melody or symphonic movement. We fill in emotional patterns every day. We arrive at work with expectations of achievement, of mastery, or, alternatively, expectations of anxiety, frustration, or anger at the boss. The context of work triggers completion of the emotional patterns before the experience actually unfolds. To some of us, Christmas means warm family gatherings, acceptance, celebration, and giving. To others it is loneliness, pressure, guilt, inevitably hurt feelings. And for some of us it is another people's holiday. We fill in the patterns as we know them from our own remembered past experience.

The flow of seamlessly interwoven patterns becomes more analyzable in the behavior of animals, particularly those we get to know well. My daughter's dwarf rabbit, for example, about half the size of the more familiar fully grown species, has darkly colored ears and paws set off against an otherwise white coat. The rabbit's long white whiskers project to either side a distance about the length of its head, using touch to measure the nearness of surrounding objects. A small black nose the size of a penny is at the hub of the large whisker wheel. The nose constantly moves in a regular up and down motion. It reminds me of the constant movement of our own eyes, movements that allow us to sample differences of light intensity and color in the space of our visual world. As it sniffs the air, the rabbit is constructing a similar three-dimensional map or pattern of odor locations. A few minutes' observation reveals the animal's reliance on its senses of smell and hearing rather than vision. For creatures that spend much of their time burrowing and moving within dark underbrush, this is not surprising. The rabbit's hearing is amazingly sensitive. The slightest vibration—a door shutting in a distant room, an airplane passing overhead—rivets its attention. Its vision, though not as important, still allows it to detect movement with exquisite sensitivity. A slight shift of my position immediately attracts its notice even when the rabbit is across the room.

When we first purchased our rabbit, we placed its cage in a corner of our family room. In the midst of so much everyday activity, the rabbit was constantly stimulated. Aware of other living creatures, it did not feel alone. Each day, in the morning and the evening, my daughter would take the rabbit out of the cage and allow it to run free within the family room. It was exciting to watch the rabbit first tentatively explore the area, then gain confidence, racing about in bursts of speed. It loved to go under the sofas, as if burrowing, eventually peeking out from under slipcovers. It would often stand on its hind legs, extending its head to the top of a coffee table, where it could smell new smells, touch new objects, and perhaps, gingerly nip new foods. All the time it would be constantly sniffing, continually mapping out the space. Occasionally it would find something of the right consistency and texture to encourage it to chew. It kept returning to this object—a pant cuff or a pillow's seam—once having established it within a certain pattern of smell in a spatially arranged world.

Returning the rabbit, whom we call Hannah, to its cage was always difficult. My daughter Ava would pick it up, one arm under its legs, containing its movement from above with her other arm. The rabbit would resist, squirming, attempting to jump, often scratching my daughter in the process. The longer we continued this routine, the more the rabbit hated its return trip, and the more clever it became in anticipating it. Soon it refused to hold still whenever either I or my daughter approached. As if to avoid the possibility of being forced back into its cage, it would race away when we drew too near. It had learned to fill in imminent confinement upon seeing us approach—or even try to touch or hold it. If this were not enough to upset my daughter, who treated the animal more as her child than a pet, the rabbit's other new behavior was equally disturbing. It began to spend long periods of time chewing on the cage door. Now this cage was about four times as long and two times as wide as the animal's body length. Food and water were located away from the door. Yet the rabbit chewed only on the door. It seemed to both my daughter and myself that the rabbit was simply trying to escape. It knew enough to link this door and its closed state with confinement, and thus its natural response was to chew a way out.

Having decided the situation was untenable, I came up with a new arrangement. One of the spare rooms in the basement would become the rabbit's home. I emptied the room of most of its furniture and put the cage, now permanently open, in a large closet. The direct entrance to the room was blocked by a suitcase, too high for the rabbit to jump over. The floor was covered by a soft but durable rug, which the rabbit never soiled since it had learned to restrict its droppings to the cage and its immediate surroundings. An old bed was left in one corner of the room, and a few colorful toys were scattered on the rug. We also left a large piece of unfinished wood for it to chew. The animal joyfully scampered around the room sniffing out its new environment.

Over the next few days we were amazed by the obvious contentment it displayed. It liked to jump on and off the bed, to chew and sniff, and within a few days it showed a totally new response to our approach. Instead of racing away as it had done in the family room, it raced to greet us joyfully when we arrived. It seemed now more like an affectionate dog. I would come to its room and sit down, quiet and immobile. The rabbit, having raced to my side as I entered the room, now circled me in my sitting position. It sniffed me up and down, occasionally tugging at a sleeve or pantleg. I gently stroked it, reaching over its forehead, moving my hand across its ears, which flattened down over its back. When I did this repeatedly for the first few days, its ears would return to an erect, presumably alert position after each stroke. With more strokes, the ears gradually remained flattened, and the rabbit curled up into a little egglike mass, its eyes now only half open. It let me continue to stroke until I tired of it. Now, in response to stroking by either my daughter or me, the rabbit would often enter what seemed to be an extended state of relaxation and perhaps a light stage of sleep. Its eyes closed, ears laid back, it slowly stretched out its body to full length and pushed its hind jumping legs to the side, allowing its stomach to rest on the floor. A few days later, it did something quite remarkable. In a quiet, sitting position, I slowly raised my hand over its forehead about to begin stroking. Before I actually touched the animal, it flattened its ears. Our rabbit had learned to link hand movement in its vicinity to stroking. The rabbit filled in the stroking, completing the pattern of sensations it had learned to expect after seeing my hand in position above its head.

Through its senses, and the frequency with which those senses are stimulated by patterns of odor, touch, and light, the rabbit's brain creates an equilibrium. Sensations at any one moment are in equilibrium with expectations of sensations at the next moment. If an unexpected pattern repeatedly disturbs the equilibrium, expectations may be revised. Ava and I decided, for example, to move a desk out of the room to prevent its further destruction by the rabbit's chewing. This caused the rabbit great worry. Repeatedly circling the now vacant spot, it sniffed frenetically, arching its head, standing on its hind legs. It seemed to be looking over and around where the desk had been to see where it had gone. The boundaries of its search approximated the desk's old space. It was as if the rabbit were tracing the outline of the desk, which it had remembered. To achieve a new equilibrium, it was learning that where the hard, yellow, piney-smelling desk used to be was now empty space. This would be the new pattern, which, once appreciated and confirmed by repeated sensing, would be accepted into the memory banks. Now Hannah could rest, confident in the certain probability that the desk was no longer to be expected. This process of reequilibration has now become familiar to us. We see it if we bring a new food or object for chewing, if an unfamiliar face appears, or if moldings are covered. Ava and I have learned to expect Hannah's reactions, as the rabbit has learned to expect certain sensory patterns in its bedroom home.

Familiar with us, the rabbit delights in our presence. It may lick my hands or forearms or raise itself on its hind legs to put its face next to mine when I am semireclined. At night, when it is tired, I notice an occasional response of fear to a sudden movement or the sound of my foot on the carpet. Is the rabbit recalling a long-buried memory of being lifted and put back into the cage? Or is this a reflexive response to sudden sound or movement breaking through the dominance of its learned expectations? Apart from curiosity, I also feel a genuine affection for the animal and some identification with its emotional and cognitive capacities. At the same time, I cannot help but be struck by the animal's intrinsic predictability. Exposed to one set of experiences, a caged existence in the family room, it responds in one way. In response to a different set, it responds with predictable differences. The behavior of my daughter and myself, together with the context of that behavior, are the patterns the rabbit stores, which shape its behavior just as if an invisible hand were to reach inside its brain to rewire the networks. This realization doesn't reduce my affection for the animal or my pleasure in its complexity. It does inevitably direct my thoughts to my own biological design and that of my daughter. I cannot look away from the similar emotions my daughter and I share in our responses to the rabbit. Nor can I help being conscious of how I shape my daughter's responses. She knows explicitly and intuitively what I feel and experience about the rabbit and herself, and she is formed by the patterns she has learned. To truly learn, a computer-based network also must be formed by sensory patterns.

In the rabbit's brain, as in our own brains, there are neuronal electrical signals that correspond to the experience of seeing an image pattern in the present. When the pattern is remembered some years later, the pattern itself, let us say a familiar face, need not have actually reappeared. It may be that only a voice is heard, which triggers a memory of the face. As the face is remembered, however, it does seem to reappear, albeit in a somewhat fuzzy version of the original image. The experience of recognition, it seems, involves some of the original sensing experience.

In a computer-based artificial network there might be elements whose signals represent a voice and others that represent a visual image. There would then have to be pathways—circuits—connecting locations that sense sounds to those that represent a visual image. In an artificial network, auditory and visual stimuli could be distributed over a spatial array of elements whose signals varied with the pitch and amplitude of sound as well as the color and brightness of light. Wherever these variations occurred in their respective layers, there would be opportunities for them to be related in time to each other, so that light variations were related to sound variations. Temporal relations of these spatially distributed stimuli might alter connections among the artificial elements according to the same rules by which our rabbit learned to locate the pine desk in its basement home. Like some connections in the snail, the strengths of many junctions connecting the artificial visual and sound pathways will not be predetermined, or fixed, but instead be determined only by the relations in time of sounds and light stimuli. Connection strengths will not, then, be affected by the output of the artificial networks but only by the patterns of sound and light sensed by the computer. This is one of the fundamental differences between our link-forming network, called Dystal, and networks that require a prechosen, or "teacher," standard. In these other networks, the differences between the output and the standard were fed back into the network to minimize the error. Such feedback requires additional computation, which often unnecessarily burdens optimal pattern recognition.

Recognition of a complex visual pattern is not something a snail can do. There are simply not enough cells able to sense the differences. Unable to sense a visual image, the snail certainly cannot store or recall it. As species evolved, the number of neurons and synapses in their sense organs and their brains increased. With increased number came increased capacity to sense and remember patterns, and, of course, with these came increased subtlety and complexity of movements. More neurons mean more capacity to process and respond to the information of stimulus patterns, be they visual, auditory, olfactory, or touch.

To build a model of human pattern recognition, therefore, we turned to mammalian brain cells and organization to expand the more limited functions of the snail learning units. All of our laboratory's evidence for memory storage in the mammalian brain localizes it on dendrites—those regions of neuronal arrays where the synaptic connections occur. Among scientists who use a variety of models to study memory mechanisms, there is considerable controversy as to what precise sites on the synapses are modified during memory storage. There is general agreement, however, that when links between stimulus events are initially learned, mixing of electrical and chemical signals within the dendrites must be involved. The dendritic branches are wondrously adapted to permit this mixing in privacy. Signals mixing in one dendritic compartment need not know or be known by signals mixing in other compartments. If the mixing is repeated enough times, according to our current understanding, a bond between signals is formed.

To construct an artificial network that recognizes images, Tom Vogl and I, and later Kim Blackwell, used the patch concept that we developed from the snail networks. Combinations of signals within an image would activate patches within compartments of many dendritic trees. Each neuronlike element in the memory layer of our artificial network would have input wiring on a structure designed like a dendritic tree. Stimuli received by a distinct combination of elements in the sensing layer would collectively activate one patch of this dendrite-like wiring in each of many elements of the memory layer. When an image activated a distinct combination of elements in the sensing layer with sufficient frequency, those memory layer patches originally responsive to the combination would become permanently more excitable. Because the patch was more excitable, it would be activated even if only a portion of the original sensed combination reappeared. The increased excitability of the compartment would fill in the inputs missing from the original combination. Now the artificial network would see in the memory layer, in its "mind's eye," so to speak, a complete image of a familiar face, even though it sensed only a portion of that face.

To summarize, there are effectively two layers in our artificial network. The sensory, or real time, layer has elements that are excited by environmental stimuli as they occur. The memory layer has elements that are excited by combinations of signals received from the sensory elements. When combinations of real time signals are repeated with sufficient frequency, patches of the memory-layer inputs become more excitable. Later, when only a portion of the real time signals in a combination occurs, the missing part will be filled in by the compartments that have become more excitable during learning. The dendritic architecture, then, provides a framework for correlating many signals in a collection rather than just two or three. Whether for two signals in the snail, thousands in a mammal, or for those entering a computer, the networks would function according to similar rules.

An ideal memory network should see an image, store it, and later be able to generate it from a piece of its original complete form. Still, this network would only model one aspect of the brain's function—learning and memory. The full potential of a memory network can only be realized when other sensing networks are integrated with it. Seeing in real time, for example, does not occur in one layer but many. The visual information is decomposed and analyzed by successive layers, which also extract and enhance features and reconstruct images. The information in the image is processed before it reaches brain centers where temporal relationships among images can be learned.

A number of creative scientists have successfully modeled and incorporated some of this processing into networks to prepare the signals which are sensed before they flow in various combinations to an artificial memory network. Such preprocessing not only helps extract essential information from background or noise, it also vastly compresses the number of signal combinations necessary to recreate the original image. To remember a face, we don't have to remember the variety of colors in the cloud formations behind the face on the last day we saw it. The shape of a car can be recalled in the absence of a showroom setting, although sometimes some of this information is retained. Our rabbit, Hannah, might represent the desk with a few distinctive shape features linked to an odor pattern. By extracting the identifying components of an image, preprocessing also allows those components to move and vary in size and still be recognized. The gestalt of a face, then, becomes somewhat independent of lateral or vertical movement, rotation, and magnification. Successful preprocessing would allow a small letter T standing on its side in a corner to be equated with a large upright T that fills the entire area of visualization.[1]

After we had constructed the basic memory network, which I have described, we added a minimal preprocessing network. Then, even though the network was still in an early stage of development, we wanted to test its performance. We had already demonstrated that our memory network, Dystal,[2] could quickly learn to recognize letters and letter sequences even though they might appear with distorted shapes and against noisy backgrounds. If a letter stimulates the learning network with sufficient frequency, the network adjusts its weights to store the letter. The network is at first dynamic in its response to new letters, but once the letters are stored they achieve a stable representation within the weights of network connections. These dynamic and stable properties are represented in the name Dystal, which stands for Dynamically Stable Associative Learning.

Letter recognition suggested a potential for more challenging tasks, one of which is known as "the post office problem." The post office has invested large sums to develop an artificial means of recognizing handwritten zip codes on mail. It has proven inordinately expensive and difficult for artificial devices to recognize individually written number sequences in a zip code. The think tank for which Vogl and Blackwell worked had recently made progress on the problem using back-propagation networks, but their networks required many hours and many times the computing power needed by Dystal, which recognized even poorly written zip codes on a single computer work station in about one minute.

Dystal appeared ideal for applications requiring a device to learn patterns rapidly and remain available to learn new patterns and/or unlearn the old patterns. Dystal not only acquired the patterns rapidly, it did so using surprisingly little computing power.

To further test the utility of Dystal we sought a task few existing networks could approach. This was provided by recognition of Kanji letters, a Japanese alphabet. Kanji characters are extraordinarily complex, each being almost an image unto itself, but with a minimum of further modification, Dystal quickly learned 160 Kanji characters from handwritten samples. Dystal learned printed characters in far greater numbers. This surprising performance suggests that with design improvements and better preprocessing, Dystal-like networks can be adapted for innumerable pattern recognition applications, from automated recognition of handwriting on credit card slips to analysis of cell shapes in blood smears to face identification for security checks.

Greater resolution of pattern recognition requires more elements in the network, just as better photographic resolution is provided by photographic paper with more silver grains. For an artificial network to recognize a face, for example, it would be helpful to have a network array with 10,000 elements in a layer instead of the 100 that suffice for recognition of simple digits or characters. This will be possible with Dystal since the number of learning trials does not increase prohibitively as the number of elements in the network increases. Furthermore, although the potential for an astronomical number of connection combinations exists within the network, a great number of the connections do not have to be hard-wired. The rules by which the network responds to the patterns do the wiring. The computer has been programmed, in effect, to program itself. This biological design is analogous to the way DNA, with a limited amount of information storage capacity, can determine the organization of an incredibly information-intense nervous system during development. The DNA provides rules, or algorithms, by which a host of physical and chemical conditions encountered by neurons work together to allow the neurons to organize themselves into final networks. Algorithmic designs allow the hard-wired biological material, the DNA, to be packaged on quite small biological chips, namely developing cells. Similarly, a Dystal artificial network can be implemented on chips without impossibly intricate wiring.

The Dystal network creates itself as it goes along. Networks that share this feature but are far more limited in storage capacity and other properties had been constructed by such pioneers as Steven Grossberg, Tuve Kehonen, and James Anderson. Unlike most of its predecessors, however, Dystal was designed to associate entirely different images with each other. The visual image of a face, which Dystal learns to recognize, can be related to the visual image of a name or even the auditory image of the sounds within the name. The rules of function of the Dystal elements, the interaction of the elements, their very architecture, is borrowed from nature. The computational efficiency of Dystal suggests that nature has already arrived at principles of network organization that engineers have been trying to create in artificial networks. The Dystal performance, as well as the performance of a few other promising biologically motivated networks, suggests that nature's neural organizations, largely either unavailable to or neglected by computer scientists until the last few years, hold the greatest promise for building better artificially intelligent devices.

Pattern recognition by brain children, conceived within human brains but developed on computers, will transform everyday life in the coming century as dramatically as has the technology of the twentieth century. Instead of flying, broadcasting, and curing pneumonia, it will link our identities with computer-based images of faces, voices, fingerprints, and handwriting. Pattern recognition will revolutionize the way we communicate with each other, conduct transactions, manufacture goods, deliver services, entertain, do science, and maybe even create art. It will open undreamed-of possibilities for diagnosing disease, providing treatment, engineering health, and constructing prostheses for sensing movement, and controlling a host of natural functions. It will animate machines built from inanimate parts. But most of all, pattern recognition will transform the way we think about ourselves.

Just as biology can guide computer engineering, the converse is also true. Successful network engineering may confirm hypotheses about the brain. We do not and will not in the foreseeable future fully understand the detailed circuitry of the millions of neurons and synapses in brain structures such as the hippocampus or sensory cortex. We do know the organization of the elementary such as the associative learning network of our snail, as well as rules of organization among cell types in brain structures. From these, it is still possible to glean principles of organization to serve as a basis for extrapolation into hypothetical neuronal arrays, whose plausibility can be exhaustively tested.

In the absence of conclusions, I find myself going back and forth between the worlds of biology and computation. It's a bit like cross-referencing in different languages. How, for instance, does a serif on the letter M translate into synaptic weights and then mathematical description of those weights? What network structures allow those weights to represent a sequence of letters, and how can that structure be described concisely with mathematical formulas? Each of these languages and the transformations that make them equivalent reflect the internal structure of our own brains as well as the external world. Although they may inspire the construction of artificial networks, the structures of our own brain's networks, as Mach emphasized, limit what we can sense and perceive. Eventually, we may be able to construct networks without some of those limitations. Perhaps in this way we will expand our ability to sense and perceive by compensating for the limitations we uncover. Biology would still be our guide, but it may lead us into quite unbiological dimensions of experience.

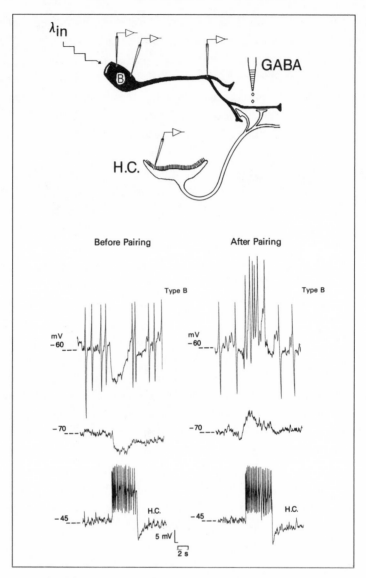

Fig. 31 Stimuli linked in time transform an inhibitory synapse into an excitatory synapse. The neurotransmitter, GABA, mediates both synaptic effects. Microelectrodes are positioned to record the photoreceptor signals and hair cell signals as depicted in the cartoon above. Before the stimuli occur linked in time, the hair cell signals (H.C.) cause downward change (inhibition) in the trace recording the photoreceptor signals (–60, –70). After stimuli occur linked in time (on the right) the same hair cell signals cause an upward change (excitation) in the trace. (Recorded by the author and Dr. Carlos Collin in 1991)

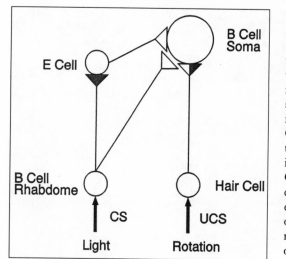

Fig. 32 A model of the elementary snail network that learns to associate a light stimulus with a gravitational stimulus, rotation. This schematic model can also be represented as equations that, in turn, are implemented on a computer. Open triangles indicate synaptic excitation, closed triangles indicate inhibition. The GABA synapse of Fig. 31 that can be either inhibitory or excitatory is indicated as half-open. (Courtesy of the Environmental Research Institute of Michigan)

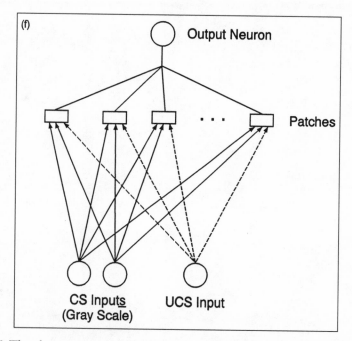

Fig. 33 The elementary model of Fig. 32 is repeated and distributed across a visual space to represent an image. The connections, marked by arrowheads, appear to distribute in dendrite-like branches of output neurons. (Courtesy of the Environmental Research Institute of Michigan)

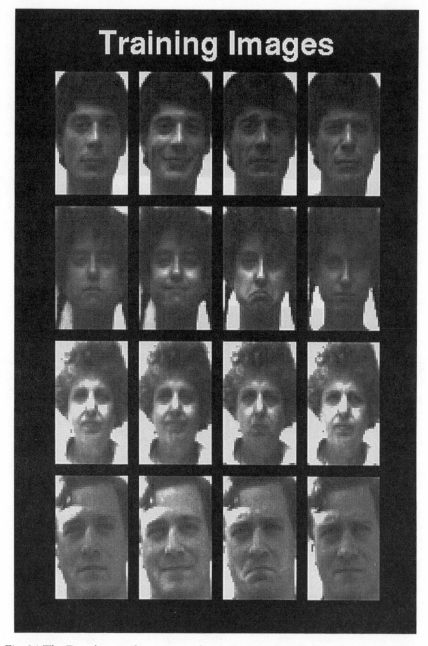

Fig. 34 The Dystal network, constructed on principles described in the text, learns to recognize individuals, regardless of their facial expressions. Here, the sixteen images shown were presented during training. Images of the same face but different expressions were associated with each other four times for each of four different faces. Subsequently, as shown in Fig. 35, the computer recognizes even very fuzzy images. (Courtesy of Mont Blackwell of KMR Photography, Inc., and the Environmental Research Institute of Michigan)

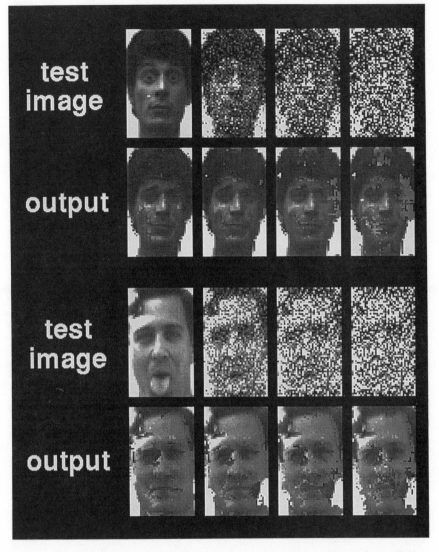

Fig. 35 The Dystal network recognizes even fuzzy images of faces with different expressions. New images of the faces with expressions different from those used for training are used to test the network's recognition ability. Two of these test images are shown on the left on the first and third rows. The outputs of the computer network that correspond to these two test input images are shown immediately below each of them. Note that the output is a representation of the facial expression learned from the training set. Notice also the difference in the eyes of the upper test image and in the mouth of the lower test image. To increase the difficulty of the task, the two test images were made fuzzy by the addition of noise. The amount of noise added increases from left to right across the figure. Despite the large amount of noise in the fuzzy test images on the right, Dystal is still able to print out a recognizable image of the correct individual. (Courtesy of Mont Blackwell of KMR Photography, Inc., and the Environmental Research Institute of Michigan)

MICHELLE REMEMBERED

Traumatic conditioning depends on a special kind of pattern recognition and completion. An adult, traumatized in childhood, repeatedly completes the familiar pattern of abuse. Traumatized individuals in fact seek out patterns they can complete and recognize. In this way, the traumatic experience, like any familiar sensory pattern, uses the brain to complete and thus, in a sense, reproduce itself. This, then, is the awesome conservatism of the brain in action. This was where my search had led me.

Years earlier, I did not think of my childhood friend Michelle's suffering in these terms. I sensed only intuitively a pattern that was perpetuated not only for Michelle, but for her father and his father, and for her children, the fathers, and mothers-to-be. The entrenchment of the patterns was not deterred by the mortality of the brains in which they resided. Like deadly viruses, they need only inhabit their host for a limited time to infect the next generation, which becomes the instrument of their reproduction and their survival.

"You never really understand a person . . . until you climb into his skin and walk around in it," said Atticus in Harper Lee's *To Kill a Mockingbird.* Inside Michelle's skin, oppressed by her pain, would I have had other choices? There were a few moments in my life, particularly during late adolescence, when I felt a panic born of loneliness and feelings of undesirability. In these moments, I was seized by hopelessness, by the conviction that nothing I could do would change my lot for the better. Those moments, mercifully few, were the only times I understood how mental suffering can be so great that life loses its purpose; how ending the pain can be the most reasonable choice.

Humans are purposeful beings. We don't have to be conscious of our everyday pattern of doing things to achieve pleasure. We don't choose to seek pleasure—we are programmed to do so, we do it automatically. In this respect, like biological robots, our brains are wired to move us toward obtaining satisfaction of particular drives. There is no free will in these aspects of our lives. We need to eat, sleep, and make love. It is also intrinsic to our design that when satisfaction of our drives is denied, they become a source of pain. None of us can tolerate unending hunger or loneliness. When this is unavoidable, the functions of the nervous system change. As long as we are seeking pleasure, our sensory pathways are fully tuned, uninhibited, with complete access to our brains. Information is collected by the brain to achieve pleasure in the present and to maximize the probability of pleasure in the future. By sensing and recording the relationships of events in time, our brains have a wondrous capacity to recognize those patterns of sensory stimuli that will lead to pleasure. Patterns of movements enabling us to obtain pleasure are linked to patterns of pleasurable sensation. Similarly, the brain collects information to recognize patterns that precede pain and to execute the behavior necessary to avoid it.

Confronted with chronic frustration or unavoidable pain, it becomes adaptive to inhibit sensory pathways, thereby reducing their access to the brain. Now the adaptiveness of predicting events in the future and recognizing stimulus patterns, pleasurable or painful, is called into question. Now learning the relationships of events in time may not be helpful. The very meaning of *adaptive* is transformed in a context of unavoidable pain. While it is adaptive to sense and predict events in a pleasure-seeking, pain-avoiding mode, it is also adaptive to shut out and forget events in a survival mode. A soldier at war, starved and brutalized, finds comfort in thoughts of his girlfriend, a turkey dinner, and Christmas. Lost in the desert, a wanderer dreams of water, shade, and a cool breeze to the extent that a mirage miraculously appears before him. Michelle had been so brutalized that to live at all, she had to reduce her sensation of pain and the memory of her learned hopelessness. To live, she had to cause part of herself progressively to die. A limb is amputated to prevent gangrene from spreading to the rest of the body. The person survives, but at great cost. So, too, with Michelle's survival. In effect, part of her died so that the rest of her might survive, at least for a time. She first cut off the memory of her pain and hopelessness with fantasies and obsessions, and then gradually she cut off all sensation.

Consider, however, the evolution of her handicap. Brutalization at the hands of her father was associated in her mind with any wish on her part to feel protected, to gain approval, and have self-respect. Her self-concept, her entire collection of memory links about her own person, was associated with the misery of her relations with her father. Her lack of self-esteem became linked to a myriad of attempts she made to win his approval: attempts to be a ballet dancer, to be an outstanding student, to write poetry, to swim well, to be an intellectual. Her feeling of failure, already imprinted by her father, conditioned her expectation to fail in every other endeavor. The expectations of failure in specific contexts multiplied and ultimately coalesced into a generalized expectation for any context. Furthermore, the imprinted feeling vastly increased the probability that the feeling was justified. This again is the sad conservatism of memory in the brain. Novel experience becomes linked to what is already in the memory banks.

Invited to a family wedding, Michelle was seated at a table of honor with other family members, many of whom were delayed by traffic en route. She sat for some time with almost no one near her. Painfully sensitive, she perceived that the seating arrangement was chosen to isolate her and experienced the temporary isolation as intentional.

Nor did the nurturing, protective attention of Michelle's mother teach different expectations. Passive in the face of her husband's brutality, her mother tried to compensate for her daughter's deprivation, but often that compensation led to aggravation. Every attempt Michelle made to succeed, to gain approval, was associated with her mother's unconditional acceptance of failure. Her mother's message was clear and constant: for me, you don't have to succeed at all, and you probably won't. The love of her mother was linked in Michelle's mind to the absence of achievement or any positive attribute.

While it is true that her mother's love was a vital refuge for Michelle, it was also a reinforcement of the imprinting linked to her father. Her image of herself was a portrait of ineptitude, weakness, and handicaps. Her confidence was so crippled that even to choose appropriate clothing became a time of crisis. Any choice, any moment when direction of her own or anyone else's life had to come from herself became overwhelming.

As a refuge or an escape, her mother's love had only limited reality. It could not solve the problem of her father's abuse, let alone the myriad problems, the challenges, that defined her existence. To a significant degree, Michelle believed her mother's reassuring "I'll protect you," and to that degree she was disarmed, she withdrew and chose death over life. Such was the fatal mismatch of the patterns she learned from the patterns she sensed but could not perceive.

This stream of failed efforts, of connected and confirming losses, became the *I* of Michelle. No wonder it was blessed relief for her to lose herself in music or to dream of her knight in shining armor. But while she dreamed, time passed. She developed, passed through different stages, grew older. All the events we link to the seasons of our lives have their own meaning and importance for anticipating the future and behaving accordingly. To survive, Michelle tuned out these events. So the preponderance of her collections of memories arose in earlier periods. Her orientation with respect to the world was derived from places, times, and needs that became increasingly less relevant to her present. Because she was forced by the extremity of her life to censor her awareness, she remained trapped in the time of her traumatic past.

What was happening inside Michelle's brain during this process? As set forth in earlier chapters, memory banks are built up over years by learning associations between events that occur together. The associations become sufficiently numerous that they form whole classes or collections, and the collections, too, become linked. Based on these links, Michelle had recorded in her brain expectations of future events. To form links and to recall them, the brain must pay attention to particular events, presumably those of greatest emotional value. We don't know how the brain selectively attends to the events with greatest emotional linkage, but the available evidence suggests involvement of two general processes—one excitatory, the other inhibitory. It is known that certain brain regions are active during the awake state of mammals and that at least one other region is particularly active during arousal. This arousal center, in turn, excites many other brain regions, some of which are stimulated when an animal is paying attention to events in its environment. It is also known that some brain regions become less responsive to sensory stimulation while an animal is paying attention to other stimuli. It is as if neurons activated by one group of stimuli are inhibiting neurons activated by others. Observations suggest that such inhibition occurs not only in the most central brain regions, such as the sensory cortex, but also at more peripheral neuronal stations along pathways that sensory signals travel to reach the brain. Neurons representing events at the center of attention, therefore, might send electrical signals releasing inhibitory chemical messages onto other neurons, whose signals are less important at the time. Inhibition would then help the waking brain to focus its attention, perception, and memories. With inhibition and attention, the brain integrates information received from the outside world. With inhibition, the brain maintains a control of stimulus input, channels the resulting signal flow through neuronal networks, and accesses memories relevant to the real time stimuli.

An experience familiar to most of us illustrates how excitation and inhibition could interact during moments of consciousness. During the day we engage in some form of vigorous, repetitive physical exercise for an extended period of time. It may be climbing a mountain, a bicycle trip, ice skating, or rowing. Although vigorous and prolonged, we soon forget the exercise as we go on about our business. Much later, as we drift off to sleep but are still awake, memories of those repetitive exercise movements may momentarily return. It's as if we have briefly resumed the activity. I would speculate that during the exercise some of the movement is being learned or improved. While we move, our senses convey information to our brains about the sequences of our limb positions in space and the muscle movements necessary to achieve the positions. Actively engaged, we pay close attention to what we are doing and to our success or failure in achieving the movements sought. Our attention can be so intensely focused, sometimes to the extent, as in competitive sports, that we may not be conscious of a painful injury or muscle spasm. Paying attention to the activity reduces or inhibits attention to other sensations, even painful ones, which may be occurring at the same time. When the exercise is over, attention to new sensations now inhibits attention to the vivid recent memories of the activity. This inhibition would not eliminate the increased excitability and perhaps increased firing of signals from the neurons involved in learning the movements. A lack of attention would simply deny those signals access to many other brain regions that might be recruited into a total or conscious experience. We are temporarily unaware of the experience only in order to be aware of and participate in what comes next. When we are drifting off to sleep, sensations stimulated by the outside world disappear. Now attention to new sensations no longer effectively inhibits access to those neurons most excited during the day, which, relative to other neuronal populations, are still the most excited. So the activity that occupied us most intensely during the day returns just before sleep. Presumably due to enhanced firing of electrical signals from the relevant neurons, we "feel" the movements of rowing, hiking, or skating, as we drift off to sleep.

These thoughts suggest that to be conscious of an event we first receive a barrage of sensory information about that event as it is actually happening. That event, then, must be sufficiently important or interesting to draw our attention while inhibiting attention to other events occurring at the same time or in the recent past. Once attended to, the sensed event triggers a host of memories that begin to provide context and meaning. I would expect the memories to involve many different senses and many different times in the past, classes of past events, and a constellation of emotions. While the sensed event is still commanding our attention, the memories may be arising in the most distant corners of our brain, together providing a massive chorus of electrical responses related to the sensations elicited in the present. The memories themselves may feed back enhancing or inhibiting signals onto the neurons doing the sensing. In this way the triggered memories may help choose what continues to be sensed.

In the awake and conscious state, events in the present trigger memories of the past. During sleep, events in the external world are no longer sensed by the brain. There is no longer a need for selective attention or inhibition. Within the sleeping brain, neurons are still firing impulses, albeit with different levels and patterns of activity. Which neurons and patterns are active might be partly determined by the most recent and most intense experiences of the day. A romantic tryst during the day might be followed by a dream of future encounters. A mugging could lead to a nightmare of further physical trauma. Concern about an upcoming examination in school might find expression during sleep in scenarios of wished-for success or dreaded failure.

There is some direct evidence that increased activity of neurons in sleep states corresponds to increased activity during the preceding waking period. Jonathan Winsom and his colleagues found that a hippocampal neuron signaling a particular spatial location when an animal is awake shows enhanced signaling during sleep. A reasonable hypothesis to explain enhanced signaling due to experience preceding sleep is suggested by the electrophysiological changes observed with associative learning. It may be recalled that early during the acquisition of a learned association, certain snail neurons have persistently increased levels of firing and excitability. The increased level of firing diminishes after the training period, but the increased excitability remains. We can imagine that neurons most recently involved in remembering could be either still firing or at least remain more excitable in comparison to their neighbors. During sleep, in the absence of external stimulation and inhibition, those collections of neurons with the greatest impulse activity and excitability might generate the images of dreams.

The most excitable neurons may be determined not only by the most recent experience. Particularly important memories, such as Michelle's links to her father, might be represented by chronically more excitable collections of neurons. During sleep, the chronically overactive neurons may fire and generate nightmares based on memories from the past. These in turn might mix with memories of the day's experience giving rise to strange, seemingly unrelated combinations of images. In the realm of sleep, the memory principle based on proximity in time is suspended. Events of the day may not have occurred together in time with a destructive interaction of Michelle and her father, but in sleep, recurring dreams of the interaction may be juxtaposed with dreams arising from recent experience. This kind of juxtaposition is created within the brain rather than as a result of events that are sensed together within the external world. These dreamed relationships in time therefore have less to do with reality and less predictive power. In waking moments, they would be considered bizarre, irrational, or crazy.

Memories triggered during the day can also be kept unconscious by learned shifts of attention to other thoughts. Michelle's fantasy of a savior-boyfriend helped her to ignore painful events and memories during her teen years. By focusing on her fantasy, she inhibited and ignored other painful thoughts. During sleep, with the inhibition gone, the painful thoughts, and fears linked to them, enter her dreams. The underlying increased impulse activity and excitability of neurons storing the painful memories would persist and find expression during the sleep cycle. Fears linked to painful memories may be so terrifying that we are seldom aware of them during wakeful moments. Michelle's fear of killing her father or being killed by him probably only took the form of uninhibited neuronal activity when she was not fully conscious.

Events are linked together in our minds from an unending stream of sensory experience beginning with birth. Some events, though in fact brief, may seem prolonged. Others, though longer and perhaps particularly pleasurable, may seem all too brief. The stream averages out these distortions and generates, in its long progress, our sense of time passing. We learn that a variety of novel stimuli precede clearly valued stimuli. New events are linked to and thereby classified in relation to older events. The physical representation of such links might be analogous to the concentric rings of a redwood tree trunk. Over thousands of years, the redwood rebuilds and loses one layer of bark after another. The layers leave traces behind so that the lifetime of the tree can be tracked from its center to its periphery. A similar correspondence of time to structure might be expected in the brain.

All of our observations indicate that memory storage occurs at numerous sites along branches of dendritic trees. Links between events would be formed when signals elicited by the events meet at such sites. Early in the development of central brain neurons, the branches on the dendritic tree are sparse. With time the branches become more dense, and the sites where the branches of other neurons make synaptic contacts become more numerous. After the early developmental stages have been completed, it is uncertain whether the number of synaptic contacts changes, but their strengths or weights almost certainly do. We can only speculate how time is actually represented in the distribution of synaptic contacts throughout the branches of a dendritic tree. A common notion holds that the earlier in life a memory is stored, the closer are the involved synaptic sites to the trunk of the tree. Memories stored later in life, according to this scenario, would be stored at progressively more peripheral locations on progressively finer branches of the dendritic tree. Undoubtedly it is more complicated than this. Nevertheless, as one hypothetical means of encoding the time of memory storage, which for us is time itself, the center-peripheral tree distribution seems reasonable. At least such a framework for human memory highlights the complex, layered, and irreversible processes that are probably involved.

During her childhood years, Michelle accumuled layers of memory that solidified her concept of herself in relationship to others. People who might intervene to help her later would be confined to the periphery of the dendritic trees. They would have to work through the branches on which the intricately complex layers of weighted synaptic sites had become ingrained over time. Since it is not likely that such layers can change, those who would guide Michelle to new expectations must work in a limited space, be it of Michelle's thoughts or the dendrite's branches. A signal that arises from a new link between events runs a gauntlet of many other incoming signals, as well as many stored links from the past. New information is filtered through the perspective of the old. In addition to the layered complexity of memory acquisition, the permanence of the memory records themselves stands in the way of learning new expectations and new behavior.

Earlier I discussed physical and chemical mechanisms that could underlie the storage of memory. Memory-specific changes affect membrane channels, the synthesis of particular proteins, the flow of such proteins within neuronal branches, and the structural geometry of the branches themselves. Some of these changes are not readily reversible. Once a memory link is formed, there is a short period of perhaps hours to days during which the responsible cellular changes can reverse. Then the cellular changes become permanent. Given such permanence, the limited access of signals from new events linked in time, and the complexity of the innumerable memory layers, it is not surprising that memory records can persist for the lifetime of the neurons involved. Learning a new expectation, then, may require learning that an older, permanently stored expectation is no longer true. The old memory cannot be erased. Instead, to modify the meaning of the older memory, new memories must be added.

Memory of an acquaintance, for example, includes entire sets of interconnected associations. These include the visual pattern of his face, the auditory pattern of his name, the visual patterns of his most familiar activities and the places he was usually encountered, the emotional patterns he elicited. All of these patterns together make up the remembered characteristics of the individual. When the acquaintance dies, none of these identifying memory patterns are forgotten, but now a new set of events is linked to the older events. These might include hearing the news of his death, seeing him in his coffin, sharing the grief of his loved ones. The net effect of these new associations is to modify our expectation, to change what can now be anticipated with respect to this friend. He is first remembered together with some expectation of meeting him again, and then, through the events more recently linked to him in time, he is remembered with the new expectation of never seeing him again. The sequence of memories linked to this individual takes time to develop. The longer the sequence, the more time it takes to recall him. There is a greater delay now before the brain decides what final expectation applies. But the more times the entire sequence is remembered, the less time is necessary to complete the sequence, and the shorter is the delay to arrive at a new expectation. This process of learning a new expectation is the essence of mourning.

Adding new links to old memory chains could involve some form of inhibition at the physiological level. Memory sites of new associations might have some pathway by which to inhibit and thereby contradict the no longer appropriate information of older sites. In this case, the inhibition may not be effected within the dendritic trees of individual neurons but between neurons. Entirely different neurons, for example, may be activated by signals arising from the acquaintance's death than by those arising from his life. The neurons representing the individual—for example, the image of his face, patterns of his behavior, and context of his location—might be connected to other neurons representing that he is alive. Information conveying his death, with new learning, may then become connected with the neurons representing the individual and inhibit the neurons representing that he is alive. Every time the now-dead individual is recalled, this inhibition would increase. After mourning is completed, the lost friend is recalled as dead with minimal awareness of the original memory that he is alive. Learning new information in this way can involve inhibition and "forgetting" of old, no longer accurate information. I suspect that this inhibition bears some functional resemblance to selective attention in general since they are both suspended or relaxed during sleep: people often dream that a dead friend or loved one is alive, or in a particularly nostalgic context may momentarily recall a dead individual as if he were alive. These fleeting thoughts indicate that the original memories associated with the life of the friend are still present, still recorded in the brain. When they are forgotten, the records are not erased but inhibited.

During the learning of the original memories, as mentioned above, there is a period when the memories are reversible, when they can be erased. This is consistent with the sequence of cellular changes observed in our model learning preparations. Once completely formed, however, the memories can be suppressed but not eliminated. This would also explain why inaccessible memories can be recalled under hypnosis, when the hypnotist's command presumably suspends inhibition. It may also explain the effect of free association used in a psychotherapeutic setting. The patient is encouraged to be uninhibited, to say anything that comes into his head. In a physically and mentally relaxed state, the patient tries not to focus his thinking but to allow apparently nonsensical combinations of thoughts into his consciousness. Under these circumstances, he is reducing the selective attention essential to directed, purposeful thinking. He could also be reducing inhibitory mechanisms common to both selective attention and forgetting.

Forgetting can offer solace. As the full significance of losing a friend is learned, the memory that he is alive is forgotten, but not the memory of his life. When this sequence is learned, the expectation that someone is still there for us is suppressed. The shock of seeking but not finding that person dissipates. If the grief is too great, however, the sequence of relearning and forgetting may be short-circuited. If the awareness of a loss is too excruciating, we may not be able to bear it long enough to learn new expectations and thereby forget. Instead, as was necessary for Michelle, the awareness itself must be inhibited. Michelle did not want to remember her father or her need for him. Yet she had no other father with whom to learn a new relationship. So she sought to redirect her attention with obsessions and fantasies.

Just as the loss of a parent may be unbearable for a young child, the loss of a child may be unbearable for a parent. A parent can never totally forget a dead child or the occasional thoughts that the child is alive. Years of learning the new expectation of permanent separation softens the shock. The parent settles into new patterns of thoughts without the child. Forgetting is essential for the parent's survival. Yet from time to time the old expectation of being together again will suddenly reappear and bring back the unbearable pain. As a phantom limb plagues an amputee, the memory of a beloved departed child haunts the parent. When forgetting fails, it becomes necessary to fool the senses altogether.

For many of her childhood years, Michelle adapted to her losses with strategies of forgetting and distraction. The irony was that during those years, they were adaptive; the strategies helped her survive. They also guaranteed that Michelle would know little else in her life than the deprivation that she fled. They prevented her from learning that there were other men who would not abuse but instead cherish her. Here seems to be an essence of our inherently flawed human condition: our extraordinary capacity to learn relationships from and make predictions about our world endows us with more adaptability than any other species. Once learned, however, the relationships and predictions may trap us in an earlier time of life, forcing allegiance to a belief system that later in life often no longer applies.

At twenty, the intelligent, sensitive, beautiful Michelle no longer needed her father as she did when she was ten. She did not need his financial support, his guidance, or his approval. She could have been free to make choices. Michelle, of course, was anything but free. The degree to which she adapted in her childhood was also the degree to which she was rigidly confined later in life. The only compromise compatible with an earlier time becomes incompatible with a later time.

Optimal learning allows for relearning and forgetting, for adaptation to new circumstances, for revising the links learned during life's progress. In childhood, Michelle optimally would have linked her father with nurturance, support, a focus for her dependence. With maturity, she would have linked men to mutually supportive and mutually gratifying experiences. In old age, she might have linked her sons to new expectations of giving and receiving. A certain amount of resistance to change, of clinging to the old, is inevitable. Those of us who have had a healthy upbringing remain more flexible, however. By not being forced to distract ourselves from traumatic memories, we remain more open to forming new memories. This is not absolute free will, but it is relatively free. It's the best we can do with what we have been given.

EXPLORING THE POSSIBLE

A GOOD PART OF THE TRIBULATIONS OF PATIENTS (AND THEIR PHYSI-
CIANS) COMES FROM UNREAL ATTEMPTS TO TRANSCEND THE POSSI-
BLE, TO DENY ITS LIMITS, AND TO SEEK THE IMPOSSIBLE: ACCOMMO-
DATION IS MORE LABORIOUS AND LESS EXALTED, AND CONSISTS, IN
EFFECT, OF A PAINSTAKING EXPLORATION OF THE FULL RANGE OF
THE REAL AND THE POSSIBLE.

—Oliver Sacks,
Awakenings

A man called a "lousy Jew" flies into a rage. A veteran dives for cover
when a truck backfires. Hearing the strains of his national anthem,
an immigrant bursts into tears. In each case, an emotional, conditioned
response is triggered by a particular pattern of stimuli. There is very
little delay before the responses. They are somewhat like reflexes in
that the brain devotes minimal time to evaluating reflexive stimuli or
conditioned emotional responses. Forming new associations, new
links, that inhibit conditioned responses is a slow and often discouraging process. However, learning to inhibit conditioned emotional
responses forms the basis of a number of treatment strategies that focus

on the relationships formed between patient and therapist or between patients.

Therapists use their relationship with the patient as a model for teaching new expectations and ways of relating. Many of the principles of this treatment, often called the psychodynamic approach, have roots in the late nineteenth-century school led by Freud. Parts of Freudian theory and treatment can be readily translated into terms of associative learning, learned expectations, extinction, and conditioned emotional responses. Early childhood experiences, if traumatic, are repressed. Repression corresponds to mechanisms mentioned in preceding chapters for minimizing attention, or distracting. Painful memories are avoided by compulsive behavior, fantasizing, or dulling the senses.

The repressed memories may become more accessible during classical Freudian or psychoanalytic treatment when the patient free associates and inhibitions are weakened or suspended. The therapist attempts to reveal what learned expectations the patient brings to the therapeutic setting, as the patient transfers memories about relationships in the past to the relationship with the therapist. Through transference and free association, the patient is gradually guided to shift attention onto long-buried memories. With sufficient attention, an awareness emerges that endows patients with consciousness of how they are behaving and why. The aim is to offer patients more choices about future behavior, to alter conditioned responses.

It is the nature of conditioned responding that it is unconscious. No attention is paid, no thinking occurs. Memories are recalled, but they trigger an emotional response so quickly that an individual may be hardly aware of them. The minimal delay between the stimuli, the memories, and the response poses a challenge to therapists. Like classical Freudian approaches, psychodynamic approaches sometimes, but not always, aim, to "catch the memories." The repressed memories at first surface in an apparently meaningless context. A less emotionally charged atmosphere may encourage an individual to look under the bed, so to speak. Slowly, the buried memories are recalled together in time with situations, people, or feelings that tend to elicit them. After a while, memories may also be recalled together with the emotional responses they trigger. With time and perseverance, a patient may be able to recall a sequence of stimuli, memories, and responses. The stimuli, of course, may be whole classes of stimulus patterns, as the memories may be entire collections of certain kinds of memory patterns.

Michelle was conditioned to panic and later attack in response to any situation in which she was evaluated or seeking approval. If she could have been aware of even a small number of such situations in relation to her responses, she might have gained insight into a fundamental principle of her life. To gain such insight, however, Michelle needed incentive, opportunities to sense the possibility of new expectations. A supportive male therapist for one or two hours a week would have been no competition for Michelle's father, to whom she was bound for the rest of the week. Michelle would have needed to generalize her new association of the therapist with kindness to the other relationships in her life. To become aware of the sequence in which she was trapped, and to maintain this awareness, she would have had to learn that the new learned correlation between a father figure and kindness might become valid, and that the correlation resonating through her childhood could become invalid. If Michelle could have sensed this new correlation of a father figure and love enough times during her daily life, it might have begun to inhibit the old correlation. This might involve an increased delay in her conditioned fear and mobilization. A little more time would be required for the conflict of the opposing correlations to be resolved. New memories would be recruited, consciousness would be raised. The longer the delay, the more she might have been able to scan her newest, less ingrained memory links to benefit from her most recently acquired memories. The most recent memories would be the least familiar, the least potent at connecting with her memory collections from the past, but possibly the most promising for finding undestructive, gratifying relationships. Given the opportunity, Michelle might then have had a number of positive meetings with a therapist. These encounters would have offered enough new correlations and expectations to delay slightly her conditioned emotional responses. The initial delay would lead to increased consciousness of the memories that triggered her responses, resulting in a greater ability to delay her response and thereby open her mind to new associations and expectations.

There was, however, a major problem for Michelle. A therapist's efforts during the years before she could be truly independent had very little chance of success. Her situation did not change. There were effectively no new opportunities for forming major new relationships. For the first eighteen years of her life, Michelle lived in the same environment in which she had been traumatically conditioned. The original traumatic links she learned early in childhood were continually reoccurring—they were reinforced into young adulthood. Psychodynamic therapy depends for its efficacy on learning new links that contradict, inhibit, and eventually overwhelm old links.

To succeed, psychodynamic therapy must be used with people who first of all are reachable—they must have problems that are neither organic nor so severe that they preclude meaningful communication between doctor and patient. Later in Michelle's life, her blunting of her senses had become so rigid that her imagined world was no longer distinct from the real world. Her ability even to hear, let alone understand, the voice of a therapist had become minimal. Earlier in her progression, when she was still compulsively seeking approval, or at a subsequent stage, when she knowingly fantasized, Michelle was still able to learn new associations. At these earlier stages, a psychodynamic approach might have been effective. For an even higher likelihood that the therapy would work, however, something else was necessary. Michelle would have had to be able to form new links not only in the therapeutic setting but in the rest of her life. This would have required a changed family environment, changes in the behavior of Michelle's father and, perhaps to a lesser extent, her mother and siblings.

Working in this direction, a school of clinicians called family therapists focuses on changing the pattern of relationships within a family. Alternatively, Michelle might have had to move to a new community. This is sometimes, but rarely, approximated by psychiatric residences. The problem with these is that so many members of such a community are themselves in trouble. New positive links with staff therapists can be offset by negative encounters with other patients. A few experimental programs, for instance in Israel, do attempt to provide a new community not just made up of patients and therapists. The Kibbutz model, in which parenting is shared by different adults, may also serve to ameliorate negative interactions between parent and child.

Probably the best opportunity for Michelle to learn whole new sets of associations and expectations would have been provided if she had been well enough to leave her home entirely, to attend college, for example. There, working together with a therapist, she might have tried out new relationships, and, perhaps facilitated by visits home, modified old relationships. The practical obstacles to establishing a new outlook and significantly changing behavioral patterns are difficult to overcome, however. Even a gifted therapist who works with a patient at the right stage of life and in a new, less destructive setting is sorely tested. Had I felt that a great many such patients could be reached, I might have devoted myself more to clinical work. Even minor victories of positive growth justify the treatment, and can be immensely moving for patient and therapist. Yet available treatment strategies seem woefully inadequate considering the untold numbers of abused children, battered wives, and victims of so many other types of addiction. It also seems likely that more chemical adjuvants will need to be developed to change age-old traditions of behavior and learned interactions for many people.

An individual's expectations are learned from ever larger circles of people. The circle of the family dominates but falls within a group of friends and neighbors, which in turn is circumscribed by a local community and then a nation. Rarely do these larger circles have enough impact to alter the relations within a family. There is simply no available mechanism in most of today's societies to intervene effectively. Society cannot delay or halt the breakdown of family relationships, and this leaves the hapless apprentices to misery—the children—on their own.

About fifteen years ago I happened on what a society might be. Almost as in a dream, I walked with a scientist colleague through the marketplace of a small Italian village. Located among a coastal chain of villages, the village was tucked into a verdant countryside of vineyards. It was a self-contained niche for a community of families that had lived together for many generations. My colleague and I were accompanying friends on a walk with their six-year-old son, Luigi. Diagnosed as autistic, the child was unable to walk on his own. He stared straight ahead, his chin almost buried in his chest. But as his parents guided his wheelchair along the narrow cobblestone streets, I could see that his eyes were not totally vacant. They seemed to show some awareness, particularly of people when they approached him closely. This happened continually. Throughout the village, passersby, shopkeepers, and family friends would always stop to greet his parents and then Luigi. Each knew that to make contact with Luigi, one had to come within Luigi's visual focus, which only extended about a foot in front of him. All expressed their pleasure at seeing him, their care for him, and their unconditional acceptance. These townspeople knew nothing of psychiatry, Luigi's diagnosis, or his prognosis. They knew nothing of why he was the way he was or what might change. They did know the infinite pain of his parents and they unhesitatingly shared it.

To involve themselves with such intimate greetings meant sharing the pain. The community was an organic whole, which did not cut off an alien member or disown one who was different. Instead they made their strength his strength. From what I could tell, Luigi's problems had not arisen from deprivation. If they had, his community would have helped make change possible. With sickness that was not likely to be forgotten, the suffering was absorbed by the group. Watching these people functioning as an organic whole was a religious experience for me. Wasn't this what is meant by God creating man in his own image? Wasn't this the potential that we, in our best moments, hope to realize? This idyllic village by the sea is not the norm, but as the exception, it humbles the rule. Societies often don't know their handicapped, let alone reach out to them. When provision is made, it is so artificial and isolating that the dysfunctional member is made to feel even more alien and less hopeful of charting a new course in the community.

Luigi's acceptance illustrates what can and what can't be done. His troubles, being of an organic nature, were not amenable to psychodynamic treatment. Memories, to be sure, have their organic qualities, as described in earlier chapters. Mental disease is thought of as organic, however, when it involves more than the physical-chemical process of memory storage; when it involves the neurological apparatus independent of experience. For example, brain tissue can be altered disastrously by genetic defects, as in Down's syndrome. It can be altered by diffuse degenerative changes, as in metabolic diseases or diseases resulting from neurons losing their normal insulation, called myelin. And it can be altered by a space-occupying lesion such as a tumor, hemorrhage, or excessive secretion of the cerebrospinal fluid in which the nervous system is bathed. An organic lesion can also take the form of a neurochemical imbalance that in one case may produce a major depression, in another, for different neurochemicals, Parkinson's disease. An organic lesion could be a genetic defect that results in malformed or poorly functioning neurons. Organic vs. nonorganic origin for mental disease calls for radically different treatments and investigative strategies. Although organic disorders occur independent of sensory input to the brain, the time when they occur during an individual's life has a lot to do with their impact. A tumor in middle age may cause deficits of sensation, integration, or movement, but many memories will already have been formed without the deficit. The same tumor could be much more devastating in a child, who needs the affected region to develop motor and conceptual abilities.

It is intuitively reasonable that a patient who is hallucinating, who talks to himself, or who is frozen in silence has some organic problem. The patient's symptoms are so severe that we expect something important to be wrong with the brain. Similarly, a chronically depressed patient seems to be governed by a process so global that we might expect a hormonal or neurochemical imbalance. On the other hand, an individual who lacks confidence, works compulsively, and has difficulty sustaining relationships would seem to have learned "maladaptive" habits. It is not that such learned habits don't correspond to physiological records in the nervous stem. It's just that there seems to be some possibility for changing those habits during future experience. Maladaptive habits intuitively seem to be more reversible than a so-called organic disease. Closer consideration of the causes suggests that here, again, the time when the disease occurs may critically determine its reversibility.

Let us take schizophrenia as an example. Schizophrenia is a general class of mental illness encompassing a variety of different syndromes. Common to most of the syndromes are hallucinations. Patients believe they are hearing voices or seeing visions and think these voices or visions are actually occurring, not just remembered or fantasized. Schizophrenics tend to show a "dulling of affect" (i.e., they don't express their emotions). They also frequently show a "loosening of associations," shifting from one thought to another without any apparent logic or direction. They seem not to maintain a focus in their thoughts. Their purposeful behavior, as a result, becomes limited. Bizarre behavior, such as undressing in public, can sometimes occur. Other forms of behavior and thinking are unique to particular forms of schizophrenia. Paranoid schizophrenics may have an elaborate delusional system in which they are chronically persecuted and are the victims of complicated plots. Catatonic schizophrenics may become immobile for long periods, apparently sensing nothing and expressing nothing. Many clinicians believe that schizophrenia encompasses too many different and distinct syndromes to constitute a single category of mental illness. The variety of symptoms suggests that this is possible, but enough characteristics are shared to make it possible to study large groups of patients who, by accepted criteria, are schizophrenic as opposed to normal, neurotic, manic-depressive, or psychotically depressed individuals.

The organic nature of schizophrenia is suggested by a number of observations. A brain scanning technique that uses harmless radioactive sugar as an imaging agent shows that brain areas of schizophrenics appear to be somewhat misshapen or reduced compared to those of normal individuals. It is impossible to determine, of course, whether these abnormalities are related to the cause of the schizophrenia or are disastrous consequences in a brain occupied with hallucinations and unable to pay attention to much of the stimulation received by its sensory apparatus.

Another indication of organic causes comes from studies of twin siblings raised in different families and circumstances. An individual has a greater chance of becoming a schizophrenic if an identical twin sibling has been diagnosed as schizophrenic. Since the identical twins were separated at birth and raised apart, they could not have been exposed to the same environment. Therefore, they were considered unlikely to have derived their symptoms from learned interactions with relationships and friends. The greater incidence of schizophrenia shared by groups of separated identical, but not fraternal, twins strongly points to some genetic contribution to the disease, since only identical twins have exactly the same genetic material. A genetic defect present at birth would be far more likely to play a role in the development of the disease than anatomical abnormalities observed later in life. That a genetic defect causes schizophrenia is, however, far from conclusively demonstrated.

Take Michelle, for example. In adolescence, her behavior was typically neurotic. She compulsively sought her father's approval. As a perfectionist, she was both highly mobilized and chronically anxious. Her neurotic symptoms took on a different appearance in late adolescence when she spent increasingly more time daydreaming, having fantasies about recurrent themes. She also started reacting against her father, challenging and confronting him rather than seeking his approval. Her sense of rejection metamorphosed into aggression toward the source of rejection. This, too, might be considered neurotic behavior, but with a paranoid tone to it. Throughout this period, there was almost no hint of classically schizophrenic or psychotic behavior. No hallucinations, delusions, or bizarre behavior. No loosening of associations or dulling of affect. If there were an organic basis to Michelle's later schizophrenia, it had not shown itself even well into her adult years. Does this mean that an organic process was latent until her middle thirties when she finally became severely ill? Or does it mean that whatever organic lesions were present interacted with Michelle's memories over the years, including those confirming a keen sense of her own inadequacy? Perhaps organic factors in her disease had nothing to do with schizophrenia itself but negatively influenced her learning experience. The complexity with which organic factors and learned behavior might interact to result in later psychotic symptoms is suggested by an entirely hypothetical but not unreasonable scenario.

Assume in this scenario that Michelle was born with a genetically determined difficulty in controlling her impulses. Constitutionally, that part of her brain responsible for "fight or flight" was more reactive; it had a lower threshold. With less provocation than her siblings, Michelle would become terrified, mobilized, and enraged. Assume also that she and her siblings received the same amount of abusive treatment from their father. Michelle would have more quickly been brought to a point where she was crying and screaming in response to such treatment. The father, already feeling helpless and impotent in the situation, would become more enraged and more abusive. Michelle, in this scenario, would be more likely to receive worse and more prolonged abuse because of her hyper-reactivity. Continue this type of interaction over a period of years, and Michelle would acquire a conviction of helplessness and frustration. Every encounter with her father would bring to mind not only feelings of rejection and expectations of abuse but also rage. Yet Michelle, according to this hypothetical scenario, was constitutionally plagued with hyper-reactivity. As a child in her father's house, she must control the rage. Her thoughts of what might happen were she not able to control her impulses could themselves be a source of terror. Uncontrolled, her rage might drive her to try to kill him or be killed by him. The terror is too great for Michelle to confront so she turns to fantasy. Every time she is threatened by uncontrollable impulses, she reduces the pain of her anxiety by daydreaming—being somewhere else, doing something else, with someone else. To control her impulses, she minimizes her attention to the sensory input and memories that are eliciting the impulses.

Within this scenario, then, Michelle's genetically programmed hyper-reactivity interacts with learned traumatic expectations to force a reliance on fantasy, self-distraction, and finally the onset of schizophrenia. In this scenario, the genetic defect is not responsible for a delayed onset of schizophrenia. Instead, the defect provides an emotional predisposition. Had Michelle not been traumatically conditioned, the predisposition might have colored her personality, perhaps causing her to be more "excitable," the "nervous, creative type." She might have had some of the neurotic perfectionistic tendencies she showed in her early childhood, but nothing worse. This is one scenario. Consider another.

Assume that Michelle was not hyper-reactive, but because she triggered certain memories in her father, he singled her out for worse treatment. Assume also that Michelle's nervous system was genetically designed to more easily inhibit sensory input. Therefore, in response to repeated traumatic experience, Michelle, more than many others, had a capacity for inhibiting her senses and was therefore more able to withdraw into her imagination. The constitutional ease with which she could fantasize would have offered her a route of escape: to retreat into her imagination in response to painful realities. This, too, in the chain of events might have led to schizophrenic symptoms, not because the schizophrenia was genetically programmed, but because of a pro-grammed predisposing feature of brain function. Provoked by child-hood trauma, a genetically determined ease of sensory inhibition would increase Michelle's retreat into fantasy. Prolonged dependence on fan-tasy and withdrawal would be followed by blunting of the sensory apparatus itself. Chronic sensory deprivation would set the stage for loosened associations, dulled affect, and hallucinations.

In each of these two scenarios, a genetic defect, an organic flaw, interacts with memories recorded over many years to produce a pro-gressive derangement of cognitive function. The derangement emerges from a complex, slowly evolving sequence of learning, perhaps analogous to the sequence of learning a child passes through when it learns a language. In the hypothetical scenarios for schizophrenia just mentioned, as in the learning of a language, the pathological personal-ity develops from elementary to increasingly more complex collections of linked information. The patient learns a language of emotions, help-lessness, controlled impulses, fantasies, and imagination run amok. All of these are imbedded in the memory's telephone book of times and places. By the time the personality begins to disintegrate, a whole his-tory of experience has been recorded.

A totally different scenario is also possible, one that I find intu-itively improbable, however. Assume that an individual goes through life in a fairly normal fashion. This person is not different from most others in emotional, sensory, intellectual, or motor apparatus. Assume that an inherited defect for schizophrenia lies dormant until he reaches middle age. Suddenly a schizophrenic flaw in some biochemical path-way causes the excessive secretion of a psychedelic substance that undermines the individual's entire thought process. He loses his ability to focus attention, his thoughts run wild, and hallucinations begin to flourish. This scenario is, of course, an extreme. It could also be that the schizophrenic flaw is expressed much more insidiously. Initially, perhaps in late childhood, the individual shows mild symptoms, which become worse later in life because only then does the biochemical defect become severe. The sudden onset late in life of a genetically specified neurological defect is not without precedent, however. Huntington's chorea, a dreadful breakdown of motor and then other brain function, classically seizes its victims in this way. Furthermore, symptoms of schizophrenia can become flagrant during adolescence as well as in middle age. This may be due to the heterogeneity of schizophrenic disease. Schizophrenia may not be one but many diseases, with different ages of onset as well as different degrees of genetic programming.

Michelle ended her life with classic schizophrenic symptoms. Yet she spent her preceding years without schizophrenic behavior or thoughts. Michelle was diagnosed as schizophrenic only in her late thirties. No doctor would have made such a diagnosis before she had what she called "my breakdown." This woman had never been psychotic, never had hallucinations, never was incoherent, did not have dulled affect. She was obsessive-compulsive, she did spend time daydreaming, she was overly sensitive and easily given to feelings of rejection. She did act out those feelings with aggressive, projective responses. She did become alcoholic. Michelle's schizophrenia, and that of many others like her, had an acute onset, but it was rooted in a personal history of traumatic oppression. There may be other forms of schizophrenia, but Michelle's form did not reasonably emerge like Huntington's chorea. In Michelle's case, if there were a genetic defect that directly expressed schizophrenia, it most likely contributed to her decompensation over a period of many years. What she called her "breakdown" occurred as a culmination of a long history of learned expectations of abuse, learned helplessness, and a learned sense of personal worthlessness. If there were direct mental consequences of a brain programmed for schizophrenia, these would have most likely influenced much of Michelle's learning throughout her life. Always lurking in the background, they would have increased her fragility and undermined her ability to cope. Such genetic consequences might have affected her impulse control, inhibition of sensory stimulation, or tendency for uncontrolled fantasy. Maybe those consequences even affected the function of her neurons and synapses, the secretion of chemical messages of the synapses, or circulation of mood-regulating hormones. Whatever the targets of a genetic flaw in Michelle, they could, according to this scenario, be involved insidiously. A chronic collaboration of constitutional with environmental factors would have conspired in Michelle's demise.

In still another scenario, the environmental factors, namely years of traumatic conditioning, would precede the constitutional influence. Brought to a point of desperation, Michelle would have begun to hallucinate and act bizarrely because she was so constitutionally predisposed. Had she not come to such a point, according to such a scenario, her constitutional predisposition for schizophrenia would never have been expressed.

Whichever scenario of Michelle's odyssey is accurate, all of them include a significant role for her learning experience. Most of them suggest that unlike Huntington's chorea, the schizophrenia did not simply explode onto the scene. Most of them suggest that Michelle's schizophrenia was not inevitable, that optimal learning might have ameliorated, if not precluded, her final nightmare. But this is a matter for conjecture and further research.

What if there were a drug that immediately and specifically eliminated Michelle's worst symptoms? Powerful tranquilizers can help control hallucinations and bizarre behavior. Some of these tranquilizers, particularly one or two recently developed, are quite effective without inducing debilitating side effects. Suppose the next generation of drugs does more than subdue the demons. Suppose they actually remove any future tendency toward schizophrenia? Michelle would have been cured, but what would be left? She had spent her entire life under the weight of progressive decompensation. Were she at once freed from the most drastic form of her debility, would she be ready to live like any other woman of her age in her society? Once cured, Michelle would face what an addict might face once relieved of an addiction. An entire way of life is molded by and around drug dependence. Removing the physiological dependence does not remove the psychological dependence. Michelle, like an addict, had accumulated vast collections of associations conditioned by illness. Almost every aspect of her life was experienced within some context of defeat and withdrawal. These aspects have to be relearned in new contexts.

A sighted man goes through life relating to his world in the richness of visual imagery. The sudden onset of blindness forces him to learn his world over again. Now he has to explore and expand the limits of his auditory perception. He relearns the world in a new context where hearing substitutes for seeing. What is so amazing about perception is that the intricate memory links among the bits of information we hear can approximate what emerges from the links among the bits we see. They are not the same, but one universe can, to a great degree, substitute for the other. So an owl's eye can locate its prey in space, while a bat's sonar targets its food. Michelle cured, and an addict no longer dependent, would be like blind men suddenly given their sight. Relief from their symptoms would open the door, but it would not provide a new mind. A child learns language, mathematics, music, by building ever greater complexity and abstraction from the initial building blocks, be they letters, numbers, or notes. So, too, would Michelle have had to come into her life, once cured, as a child, to experience it anew and learn about it all over again. But she, like the reformed addict, would undertake such learning with a handicap the child does not have.

The untold millions of links of information stored over the years would have to be forgotten. Not truly forgotten in the sense of erasure. All of what is known about memory records indicates that once permanent, they never can be erased unless by physical removal of the brain tissue where they reside. No, they would have to be forgotten by the slow prevailing of new and contradictory information. Newly learned information would have to inhibit and effectively repress the old.

The brain is not like a computer that can be reprogrammed after the deletion of old programs. The new programs have to be reconciled with the old. If vision is lost in adulthood and restored after several years, the visual brain areas may still be largely intact. Relearning in visual terms would not offer the same difficulty that might face Michelle or the reformed addict. The auditory memories need not compete with newly formed visual memories. On the contrary, one modality might facilitate acquisition of information by the other modality. Presumably, memories within the distinct modality could be stored within distinct brain areas. They need not compete for space in the same territory. Not so for Michelle, learning anew about old expectations. Their space in the brain would already be occupied. New memories would have to gain admittance.

Michelle's thoughts, collectively, might be seen as creating an interior milieu replete with traditions and customs. Colonists, upon settling new territory, have often made the mistake of attempting immediately to supplant the traditions of native inhabitants, to impose one culture coercively at the expense of another. In other cases, native cultures have been diluted without substitution. Robert Ruark, in his book *Something of Value*, warned colonists in Africa to consider what they really had to offer in place of the native culture. Cured, Michelle would be asked to accept and learn a new culture, one that must at first be alien and frightening. Welcoming Michelle to a new land would begin with respect for the ways of the old. Like those of any culture, these ways integrate layer after layer of experience. Treating schizophrenia, whatever its causes, like treating addiction, whatever its metabolic derangement, only begins with eliminating the most florid and characteristic symptoms. The awesome tasks of treatment must include restructuring the memory banks, reorienting the mind itself. If most psychodynamic approaches have limited success with neurotic patients, what success can they have with a recovering alcoholic or a schizophrenic in remission?

An anthropologist looks for the roots of a culture by digging through the layers of earth corresponding to the ages of its contributing civilizations. Artifacts, bones, and minerals give clues about how each succeeding civilization grew out of its predecessors. So too does a therapist guide patients through the layers of the remembered past. Sifting for artifacts, elementary links, and reassembling complete forms and conceptual structures in the mind is part of the work. Learning new expectations and new habits is also critical to replace those now archaic and inappropriate. As discussed earlier, precise and specific knowledge of how memories are formed, recalled, and forgotten may lead to drugs that allow us to intervene. The goal would be to assist the therapist-patient collaboration, not to replace it. Molecular manipulations will not create memory links. These have to come from experience—sensed events integrated into new patterns of representation within the brain. Whatever pharmacological tools we can devise to facilitate remembering, forgetting, and learning anew, they will not replace the memory banks themselves, or the steps by which they are acquired. At least not for us. For this is what we are, and how we came to be what we are.

NEURONS GONE AWRY

At Gabriel's birth, an unshakable resolve surged through me, pushing aside every previous commitment in its wake. Never again would I work long hours into the night, losing myself, oblivious to all other concerns, obligations, and passions. At that moment, an invisible channel formed through which a portion of my energies would flow to him alone. Not only was our son physically beautiful, with his round face, wide eyes, button nose, rosy cheeks, and bright smile, he had the mild disposition of my wife whom he so clearly favored. His gentleness, in fact, puzzled and sometimes concerned me. I never saw an aggressive move, a trace of anger. He was cooperative, accommodating, sometimes even docile. In response to anger in playmates, he was patient, always avoiding conflict. Was this normal? Did he lack a necessary minimum of territoriality, willingness to mobilize to protect his own interests? How would he make his way in life without fighting when he had to? More curious than worrisome, Gabriel's unflappability did not change until he was about four years old.

As I was rocking our newborn daughter in my arms one day in our dining room, Gabriel, clearly distressed by the focus of my attention, pointed to a nearby window opening onto our front lawn. "Why don't you throw her out the window?" he suggested. Over the years his anger and jealousy have always been obvious, although he has never harmed her. As he grew older, while he did start to assume a more parental, protective role in her behalf, he often expressed his teasing, mean side with her as a target. This side of him had always been there, but a particular context was necessary to bring it out. He is constitutionally a gentle soul. Even so, he is aggressive, sometimes angry under the right circumstances.

So, too, do many aspects of human behavior seem to depend on a dialogue between an individual's biological design and patterns of stimulation experienced by that individual. Michelle was, I believe, constitutionally hyperexcitable, volatile, quick to react, and easily angered. Yet her tragic denouement seemed not to have been inevitable. It required the interaction of her willful nature and the unprovoked rage of her father. Michelle may have had a genetic predisposition to anxiety, depression, and/or alcoholic addiction. But these might have remained dormant had not Michelle learned to expect hopelessly unavoidable abuse.

What starts this dialogue? Do the hereditary prescriptions for varieties of mental fragility mold the life situations that then elicit the symptoms? Or do the life situations find fertile genetic ground in which to sow the seeds of decompensation? Anorexia nervosa typically afflicts young women obsessed with their weight. Terrified of being overweight, they sometimes literally starve themselves to death. Recently, studies have shown that male jockeys are at risk of suffering from the same syndrome. Presumably, the stress of their job requirements plays a role in precipitating the disease, perhaps in a manner analogous to the stress women feel about fulfilling the stereotype of slim-figured beauty. But why does one woman or one jockey and not others fall victim? There are no experiments, no data currently available that even begin to approach this issue.

But what makes sense? It is not reasonable to me that people become addicts because they are born with cravings that must be satisfied. Their cravings don't dictate that they find substances to abuse. They are not *fated* by their genes to become addicts. More reasonably, they are *predisposed* by their genes. Like anger, jealousy, and competitiveness, addiction may be a universal potential whose actualization emerges from individual proclivity as well as experience.

In response to lower levels of chronic pain, do smoking, eating, or working too much arise any differently than does drug addiction, albeit with fewer self-destructive consequences? During my own teenage years, unable to escape my father's arbitrary disapproval and impossibly demanding standards, I decided to devote myself to the school work he refused to praise. My anger spent itself in the work, which eased my angst and helped me to forget a sense of loss and abandonment. It also prevented me later in life from knowing that others dear to me were not disapproving or abandoning. This is the sad pact we make with the devil. An adaptive strategy at one time becomes maladaptive at another. Why my son's birth shook me loose from my workaholism I don't know. It didn't change my basic style, my strategy for coping. It did soften it, opening me to new possibilities.

My addiction to overwork is not uncommon. It is often even socially acceptable. Yet, like socially unacceptable addictions, it offers escape. Working even harder in the laboratory helps create the illusion that I can do something about an unfair rejection of an article or withdrawal of funding for a favorite project. No amount of work will bring back a lost friend or reverse the alienation of a lover's quarrel, but working does help one to forget and blunt the pain.

I have even experienced a kind of withdrawal when beginning a long trip. There is the initial shock when I suspend my frenetic routine and am forced to accept many passive hours on a plane or train. During the first few days of a vacation, I might experience anxiety, aimlessness, extra energy to burn. Almost inevitably, withdrawal is followed by an unfamiliar peacefulness, being tuned in to what's happening to me at the moment, and an absence of the mobilization that is so familiar. For a workaholic, excessive work discharges emotional energy born of frustration and helplessness.

I do not know for a fact, but I suspect, that working does for me what smoking, excessive eating and, perhaps, sexual promiscuity does for others. And these seem to be on the same psychological continuum with the more dangerous alcoholism and drug addiction. None of these habits are purely escapes. Beyond simple avoidance of the unpleasant, I learned to associate my work with the pleasure of solving problems, of peering into unexplored mechanisms, of encountering the varieties of life forms and nature's ingenious strategies to help them survive. I learned to link my work with a sense of mastery and accomplishment, with recognition, and a good living. I continue this pattern because it rewards as well as protects. This is also conditioning, but somewhat different from the Pavlovian sort illustrated by the snail and rabbit. "Appropriate" work is instrumental in achieving successful outcomes. Instrumental conditioning links behavior to reward. The sensations that accompany the behavior become associated with the sensations of the reward.

Addictive behavior, in general, can be considered, at least initially, as instrumental conditioning. The addict learns to associate certain behaviors—smoking, drinking, eating, or taking drugs—with desired outcomes. The outcomes, as illustrated by my own experience, achieve the positive and avoid the negative. As the addiction progresses, the ratio of the positive to the negative usually decreases. Early, cocaine and heroin offer pleasant highs which provide respite from desperate lives. Later, withdrawal of the drug causes its own torture to be avoided at any cost. With chronic addiction, the new negative reinforcement, symptoms of withdrawal, plays a much more dominant role than the original painful stimulation to be avoided. Of course, the context and therefore probably the balance of critical environmental and constitutional factors varies for different individuals with the same addiction. An abused, abandoned, hungry street child will seek relief for his reasons, few of which may have anything to do with inborn tendencies of his cells to metabolize drugs. A soldier recovering from battle injuries may become addicted to morphine for other reasons. Teenagers experimenting with alcohol and drugs in middle-class suburbia may follow still other paths to addiction.

A classic animal model used to explore what happens in the nervous system to cause addiction is rat self-stimulation, originally introduced by James Olds, Sr., and Peter Milner. Fine stimulating electrodes are implanted permanently in a brain center responsible for giving the rat a sensation of pleasure. On command, electric current flows through the electrodes into the pleasure center, thereby generating a distinctly pleasant sensation. The current flow is triggered only when the rat presses a lever in its cage. In learning to link pressing the bar to pleasure, the rat has become instrumentally conditioned. There is no obvious reason why cellular mechanisms for learning this type of link should be very different from those for learning links between sensory stimuli during classical conditioning. The overall networks, the pathways that lead into and exit from the networks, and the integrative functions performed by the networks on information are probably quite different between classical and instrumental conditioning. But the fundamental network elements and the way they change during information storage could be quite similar. There is also no reason that the essentially conservative nature of associative learning should be different for instrumental and classical conditioning.

As suggested previously, new information that contradicts what is already stored in the memory banks can create conflict, uncertainty, and anxiety. Sufficient anxiety, as we all know, can be extremely painful. We are designed to reduce uncertainty and thus avoid anxiety. This is built into our nervous systems. It is this design that so effectively prevents us from changing self-destructive behavioral patterns learned in the past. Anxiety provides a painful incentive to be avoided at all costs even when attempting to withdraw from a debilitating addictive habit.

So called psychological dependence, then, undoubtedly has roots in the fundamental physiology of instrumental conditioning, whether for a rat or a human. Instead of psychological dependence, it might more accurately be called learned dependence. Obedience to learned behavioral patterns, the difficulty of unlearning, and the avoidance of anxiety can all contribute to learned or psychological dependence. The symptoms of withdrawal add to these to offer powerful incentives not to change. Even in the face of grievous losses of health, relationships, work, and self-esteem, the status quo is maintained. Looking down from the very edge of the precipice, many cannot stop themselves from sliding off. They don't jump, they just slide. I saw them collecting at death's door years ago when I briefly worked at Bellevue Hospital in New York City.

In those days, Bellevue served as the community hospital for those who could not afford private care. It had not been rebuilt since the middle of the nineteenth century. The great open hall housing rows of patients did not look like a hospital as we know it. One felt transported to the time of the Civil War when casualties waited in long lines of beds to receive emergency treatment and summary disposition. Then, there was often hardly time to decide who got morphine, who lost a limb, or who awaited burial. Despite the warlike footing of the medical staff, we did want to do something for these people. Yet, for murders, stabbings, and rapes we were little more than the cleanup detail. We had no illusions about stemming the daily flow of the victims into the emergency room. It was more difficult to understand our helplessness to deal with the ravages of chronic addictive behavior.

Between crises these patients were approachable. Some of them had families who cared about them. They would swear their determination to change. At first we felt we were working with people who had a chance. Homer, for example, an amiable seventy-year-old grocer, was wheeled into the emergency room in acute respiratory distress. Blue, panicked, drowning in his own secretions, he gasped for breath. Intravenous drugs, an artificial airway, fluids, and nasal oxygen had him pink and calm three hours later. Restored to life, he chatted casually with other patients in the amphitheater that served as his recovery room. Extending a hand missing several digits as a result of nicotine-induced circulatory failure, he couldn't stop thanking us. Twenty minutes later we found him in the men's room, pushing his intravenous bottle on a pole with one hand and holding his cigarette in the other. Then there was puffy-faced, red-eyed, big-bellied, and purple-nosed Sweeney. How many times had he been hauled to Bellevue bleeding from stomach ulcers or the bursting veins around his esophagus? Sweeney's gun was a beer can, which he emptied into himself many times daily in spite of the gradual loss of everything that defined his life—family, friends, work, consciousness. Mendoza's gun was a needle. The special pain of not pulling the trigger and ending the game in one shot came with their intermittent awakenings. Sober, Sweeney knew fully what he had become. His brain was not sufficiently wiped out by the alcohol to ablate the memories of what he had been.

Were these memories too searing or not searing enough? With self-destructive behavioral patterns, change often becomes possible only when the self-destruction is so great that a crisis is precipitated. Sliding is no longer an option. The choice becomes either to jump or step back from the cliff. The suffering and the anxiety produced by the addiction forces the individual into trying something different. Unfortunately, such crises offer the potential for ultimate demise as well as recovery. In her thirties, Michelle had become a chronic alcoholic. Close to death, she was hospitalized with alcoholic hepatitis or inflammation of the liver. It became very clear to her at this point in her life that she would not survive much longer with her addiction. In the midst of this crisis, she seemed to choose life. She swore off alcohol, joined Alcoholics Anonymous, and, at least for a brief period, sought counseling. Only a few months later, she experienced psychotic symptoms, which in all of her preceding years had never occurred. In her disequilibrium, with the certain knowledge that she could not continue her alcoholic dependence, she could not learn behavior that would allow her to cope with her past and thus her present.

Olds's rat experiment has and will continue to be useful in analyzing the cellular mechanisms within neuronal networks that produce instrumental conditioning and thus learned dependence. It can also be useful for tracking the cellular changes responsible for the other major component of addiction, metabolic dependence. Metabolic dependence has commonly been thought of as distinct from psychological dependence, although this may not be entirely the case. Among the characteristic features of metabolic dependence is the increased quantity of a drug necessary to achieve the same sensation. The longer the duration of a habit, the more tolerant an individual becomes to the effects of the drug, the less sensitive to its actions. Along with the tolerance comes an insatiable craving for the substance. When the substance is withheld, drastic physiological reactions result, most of them painful. These three features—tolerance, craving, and withdrawal—all seem to have an organic basis. Again, this is not to deny that learned dependence is also organically based. It only means that learned and metabolic dependence have distinct organic bases and that they involve distinct locations and distinct mechanisms in the brain.

There are some interesting new clues in addiction research concerning the quantities of particular synaptic transmitters, the derangement of their metabolism, and the distribution of their target sites on neuronal membranes. Little is known, however, of how these molecular changes participate in neuronal pathways within the brain. Are they specific to certain pathways but not others? Are they unique or just isolated examples of an entire constellation of changes that occurs during the addictive process? Are they more responsible for metabolic or learned dependence? Certainly animal models such as the self-stimulating rat should help us to start sorting out some of these issues.

For the present, therapeutic alternatives are limited and not at all tied to a fundamental understanding of cellular mechanisms. It is clear that different substances, when abused, will cause different foci of destruction and effect a different balance of metabolic consequences. But there are few, if any, pharmacological agents that act on particular substance targets. There is no medicine that will readily reverse tolerance or reduce learned dependence, although methadone does seem to ease heroin withdrawal. It seems likely that addiction, like memory storage, passes through stages of permanence and irreversibility. These stages may involve not only a long chain of molecular transformations within individual neurons, but also complicated sequences of transformations among neurons within networks and within brain pathways.

Brain changes responsible for learned dependence have to be distinguished from those causing metabolic dependence. And both types of changes have to be distinguished form the destructive consequences of the addiction. Pathological destruction of brain tissue can accompany addiction without in any way causing it. The pathology undoubtedly has its own symptomatic expression, such as the loss of coordination that accompanies alcoholic degeneration of the cerebellum, or the confusion, memory loss, and even coma that follow alcoholic destruction of a number of other brain regions. But these changes and their symptoms occur long after the addiction has become ingrained.

A similar dilemma confronts the investigator of Alzheimer's disease. By the time the diagnosis of Alzheimer's disease is made, the patient almost always has diffuse brain damage. Indeed, when the brains of Alzheimer's patients are examined after death, many areas show the characteristic "plaques." A proteinaceous substance, called amyloid, and a jungle of fibers, called neurofibrillary tangles, have replaced regions of precisely ordered neuronal networks. The cells, their synapses, their axons, and their insulating sheaths are all wiped out within the plaque region. Does this mean that the amyloid or tangles initiated the disease? Not at all. Does it mean that these pathological changes could cause some of the symptoms that characterize the disease? Absolutely.

Like alcoholic degeneration, Alzheimer's degeneration has symptomatic expression. But the pathological changes by which the diagnosis of Alzheimer's is finally confirmed may very well occur long after the onset of the disease. They may be only consequences of other metabolic changes, which cause the disease. Even the symptoms of Alzheimer's are probably not sufficiently understood to recognize the disease during its entire progression. We don't know, for example, that Alzheimer's disease is primarily a disorder of memory function in the brain, although memory loss is the disease's most universal expression. Only when we are able to diagnose Alzheimer's with reliable objective measures during its initial stages will we know whether the earliest pathology is specific to memory mechanisms.

Like other degenerative diseases of the nervous system, Alzheimer's appears fundamentally different from addiction in that it does not seem to depend on experience. Whatever genetic factors predispose an individual to drug dependence, addicts still must learn the habit and in rare cases learn to break that habit. Although environmental factors from toxic waste to infective organisms have not been excluded as causes of Alzheimer's, its origin seems to be independent of learning and memory. Early in the disease's progression symptoms may assume the guise of a loss of judgment. An individual might go to McDonald's for stuffed lobster or to Woolworth's for Wedgwood china. The memories required are only slightly off. McDonald's has been correctly linked with selling food, and Woolworth's with knick-knacks and household goods. The more precise associations of fast food with McDonald's and inexpensive items with Woolworth's have been forgotten.

A family often first senses a difference in the behavior of one of its members—but not always. In one case, an individual came to his doctor because he feared his wife had become unfaithful. He retained the judgment that the fear was absurd, yet he could not dispel the nagging thought of his wife's infidelity. More remarkably, he suspected that this might be a sign of incipient Alzheimer's disease, since he remembered that the same fear marked the onset of the disease in his father. Such symptoms are reminiscent of those originally reported in 1907 by Alois Alzheimer. He described a woman who had became uncharacteristically jealous of her husband. An autopsy four and a half years later revealed the now-famous plaques distributed throughout her brain.

As the disease progresses, the lacunae of memory become less subtle. Short-term lapses begin to appear. A patient may forget an appointment he made a few hours earlier. As is common with simple aging, some individuals compensate by writing down everything they want to remember. Insidiously, the disease begins to consume pieces of more permanent memory—the name of a grandchild is confused with that of a brother; a doctor's address is substituted for that of a priest. A watchmaker can still repair watches, but he doesn't know where he works or that this is the means of his livelihood. At home, he no longer pays the bills and ultimately forgets daily necessities such as when to take out the trash. Throughout the early deterioration of life, patients seem to sense the havoc the disease is wreaking. They seem to reach for what is missing and are often anxious in their helplessness. But it is the family members who feel the greatest anxiety and helplessness and on whom the burden of the patient's daily care usually falls. Finally, the results of diffuse brain destruction, no longer limited to memory loss, extend to the loss of sensations and emotion, impaired movement, and uncontrolled bodily functions.

To the student of memory, Alzheimer's disease presents a tempting target. But is it, in fact, truly a disease of memory, or is memory impairment a characteristic symptom simply because the disease affects so many brain regions? Yet, doesn't the course of Alzheimer's track the permanence of memory? At first patients forget what they learned a few weeks ago, then a few days ago, and finally only moments ago. They progressively lose the ability to consolidate and store a memory for any length of time. This is undoubtedly due to destruction of the hippocampus by plaques, as well as damage to other brain areas where plaques are found, but there is no one-to-one correspondence between plaque deposit and symptom occurrence. Furthermore, in older people plaques can appear without any Alzheimer's symptoms.

Pursuing the relation of Alzheimer's disease to memory loss further, we can ask if the disease, at its onset, affects molecular events unique to memory. Perhaps there is a subtle loss in sensory discrimination of particular odors, sound, or colors. Maybe there is a slight loss of coordination or loss of balance. Recent evidence suggests that a primary site for the disease could be protein kinase C, the enzyme that our laboratory has implicated in associative memory.[1] Saitoh and his colleagues reported a deficiency in this enzyme within cells taken from Alzheimer patients as compared to nonpatients of the same age.[2] Other workers have begun to observe hints of impairment in the biochemical steps required to generate the second messengers that activate protein kinase C. Still other investigators have shown that biochemical steps in the formation of beta-amyloid, a key molecule in plaque formation, involve protein kinase C activation. A genetic basis for Alzheimer's disease has also been linked to the beta-amyloid protein in a small percentage of cases.[3] There may be in every human a potential for any one of many molecular steps in our neurons to break down. With age, the probability for one or more of these steps to go awry may increase, accounting for the increasingly high incidence of Alzheimer's disease with age. An analogous biochemical vulnerability may explain the increasingly high incidence of cancer with age.[4]

Many research programs are now devoted to obtaining answers about chronic afflictions of the brain such as addiction and Alzheimer's disease.[5] These new frontiers require their own search strategies. Although useful animal models exist for research on addiction, such models are much more difficult to develop for many classic neurological diseases such as multiple sclerosis, Lou Gehrig's disease, and Alzheimer's disease. This is largely because, unlike the agents that induce addiction, those responsible for many neurological disorders are not well understood. For alcoholism, many of the recognizable stages in the progression of the human disease can be identified in rats as well. With the rat model, the symptoms can be directly related to what is happening inside the brain. Electrical recordings from cells in the rat's hippocampus and cerebellum can be made in the living animals as addiction takes hold. Slices from these brain regions can be analyzed for the biochemical and electrical changes responsible for stages of metabolic, as well as learned, dependence.

Should these experiments prove successful, what results could we hope for? For Alzheimer's disease, we would want to know the earliest possible molecular defect and its genetic locus—the flaws that are the primary cause of the disease. With precise knowledge, we might intervene to correct the flaw and predict its appearance in subsequent generations. In the case of addiction, the outcome of the dream is somewhat less clear. With all of the hoped for results in hand, we should be able to distinguish the neuronal network sites for learned dependence and metabolic dependence. Again, the critical molecular steps for each type of dependence would be identified and would be accessible to therapeutic manipulations. But would we really have discovered what addiction is? Learning and memory are phenomena that lend themselves to descriptions in general physical and mathematical terms. Information is acquired, stored, and accessed. Addiction, however, involves a need and eventually a craving for pleasure.

A rat, once addicted, will press a bar to stimulate its pleasure center to the extent of ignoring almost every other need. Starved, exhausted, it will continue to press and thereby stimulate groups of neurons in a circumscribed brain region. But what do these neurons do to give a sense of pleasure? Do they secrete chemicals such as endorphins to relieve pain and create pleasure? If they do, where do the chemicals act? Perhaps they act on neurons throughout the brain, but also on neurons and neuron fibers distributed all over the body, and maybe even on the body musculature. Are pleasure and pain expressed in the responses of much of the body as well as the nervous system? And if addiction is inextricably tied to chronic stimulation of neuronal groups responsible for creating pleasure, might not the potential for addiction be a feature intrinsic to animal brains? When children become "addicted" to television or comic books, do they also develop a metabolic dependence that is distinct from their learned dependence? Or is the potential for addiction a built-in consequence of their design as purposeful beings?

From our experience, we learn how events are related in time to maximize pleasure and avoid pain. These links, once permanently formed, help us create an equilibrium between our needs for pleasure and their gratification. Once achieved, the learned equilibrium is disrupted only when new relationships of events in time contradict the old relationships, creating conflict and possibly anxiety. Our natural tendency is to disbelieve, to reject the new relationships, to preserve the memory "establishment." We naturally wish to avoid the anxiety associated with conflict and disequilibrium. We cling to familiar, remembered ways of obtaining pleasure even at the price of discomfort or sometimes pain. This seems to be true of all learning, including addictive dependence. Perhaps addiction, then, is always lurking in the background, as a potential derangement of the learning process.

An accessible source of particularly intense pleasure monopolizes attention. Once found, it efficiently programs the brain with links to events by which it can be recognized and obtained again and again. Because the pleasure satisfies, because it dominates attention, it powerfully inhibits new learning, which might loosen its grip on behavior. The conservatism of the remembering, sometimes addicted, brain locks in a machinelike pattern and locks out our uniquely human options to choose. If the potential for addiction is, in fact, intrinsic to our brain systems, it is a powerful enemy indeed. For the enemy within would be the natural design of the brain itself.

MEN AND MACHINES

What makes us think our brain design is so unique? No one can deny its awesome complexity, its wondrous properties. Everything humans have created pales by comparison, and comparison instills a feeling of reverence. We regard the natural wonder of the brain itself as evidence of divinity in the universe. We hear God's voice in the crackling murmurs of the countless neurons that populate our brain world. Is there, nevertheless, a role for illusion in this as well?

Humans seem to have a need to believe in their own powers as much as in the powers of a divine being. Is this need also programmed into the brain? We seem to require a sense of control in our lives just as we proceed through life with an illusion of immortality. Let's get on with it! There's no time to be concerned that the plane might crash, that tomorrow a blood vessel might burst within my brain, or my heart might stop beating. Is there a hormone that circulates around the nervous system conveying a universal message of certainty and invulnerability? I imagine so. Could there also be a hormone that nullifies feelings of helplessness and makes us believe we have choices?

We proceed in life as if we are calling the shots. And relative to many of our contemporaries, maybe we are. Those who have great wealth or unusual talents are not mistaken about the many choices open to them and not to others. Compared to the have-nots, the haves are indeed free. There is no room in that perspective for a sense of machinelike programming. Rarely do we even consider the possibility that we are simply following a script etched in our genes and fleshed out by experience. We are not conscious of the behavioral patterns that we follow and complete over and over again. We are designed *not* to have such consciousness. What right does anyone have to go against the design? Yet the potential for a different level of consciousness can be searched for within all manner of internal and external laboratories. This potential is also part of our design. And when we are aware of machinelike aspects in our functioning, it is *we* who are aware. We accept the mechanistic banality of our bodies and in some sense transcend it at the same moment we achieve that self-conscious awareness.

Machines may someday rival, if not surpass, the brain at many tasks. They may be able to sense information we cannot, repetitively and massively process information we cannot, and go places we cannot. Rather than argue about when and if machines will supersede the brain in the processing and integration of information, let us assume that eventually in many important respects they will. Machines will still not be purposeful except for the purposes we intend. All of our learning and memory, all movement, all transformations undergone through stages of life are in the service of a reasonably few biological imperatives. Reproduction and survival of a species are commanded of its members. The commands are expressed by all-powerful overriding drives, which the networks of the brain exist to satisfy. Drives, just like stimulus events and patterns in the environment, must have representation within the brain. Early in life, their representation may be direct, closely related to satisfaction or frustration, pleasure or pain. Later, as layers of learned experience are stored and classified, representation of needs becomes more abstract. Experiences can be many times removed, connected by a long chain of learned links, from a primary need. Remembering events in our lives can stand in for the real thing. Symbolic satisfaction or deprivation can be gratifying or painful. However sophisticated our representations, however sublimated our gratification, the drives are still moving us about. They are what make us tick. We learn strategies on their behalf.

My search strategy is no exception. As much as anything else in my life, it defines who I am. Collecting information about how networks learn is itself pleasurable. It also has value for which others have exchanged the means for my physical survival and comfort. While I have so far succeeded only modestly in the search, the process has been in a sense completely successful. Essentially, I have had the chance to do my thing: to challenge my intellect, to commit my energies to a cause I value, and to be without hardship. So the duality of my strategy, with its abstract purposes as well as its roots within my own biology, is transparent. My strategy is socially acceptable. I learned it because it fit my needs as well as those of others. So, while I did my thing, I also more or less fulfilled the plans and expectations of parents, wife, children, and friends. This then is my version of a dimension of experience never found in intelligent machines, a dimension whose coordinates locate events in emotional space. Artificial intelligence has not been conceived of in the emotional context that is so characteristically human.

The movements of a robot can be programmed to perform a narrowly circumscribed set of functions. In this sense, the robot fulfills a function, serves a purpose. But the purpose is not to reduce one of a collection of drives with which it is endowed. Its acts are its purposes and its purposes are assigned. But so are ours. We don't decide to grow up, achieve a full sexual identity, raise children, and pass away. We don't decide what physical and mental endowments we will have to work with. We don't decide to whom we are born, what traits of personality, health, and disease they impart to us, or how they will treat us. We don't decide to be hungry, to crave love, to be tired, to be cold, or to be curious. These are our assignments. All of the information we learn and remember, all of the patterns we process, classify, abstract, and compare, are used to complete our assignments.

Robots don't have emotions because their designs are much less sophisticated. They do not have multiple purposes that have to be integrated. They don't develop elaborate strategies that may take years to complete and satisfy many needs at once. They don't have nerve centers that encode events as pleasurable or painful. They don't secrete hormones that fine-tune the intensity of painful and pleasurable signals. But, in principle, they could have. In principle, corners of their artificial networks could be devoted to classifying an environment as friendly or hostile, to sensing images as pleasing or repulsive. They could be programmed with drives that progressively build their need to be satisfied and once satisfied, within a time interval, build that need again and again. In principle is one thing; in practice, it might never be within our power to include all the necessary design features, the wiring, the working parts, to duplicate or simulate ourselves.

For humans, successful strategies to achieve regular emotional satisfaction often involve learning long sequences of behavioral patterns which introduce unavoidable delay between feeling or sensing an emotion and satisfying its underlying drive. Anger or aggression is often clothed in polite table talk and sly innuendos or secret ploys. "Naked" aggression is often less effective because it violates accepted patterns, which are learned in a society to delay and temper potentially destructive consequences. Sexual relationships may involve a prolonged courtship. Gradually familiarity is established, signals of mutual desire are exchanged, and defenses are relaxed. All of this can occur with varying amounts of symbolic banter and emotions that are sublimated rather than fulfilled before a decision to act is made. The effect of this complexity is to prolong the period between feeling a desire and acting on it. The longer the delay, the more information processing occurs before commanding and executing a behavior. The more information considered, the more calculation of predicted consequences. Immediate and far-off consequences can be pondered, consequences not only for the most relevant emotion but for many other needs.

This is our most human feature, the ability to act not for the moment, in response to impulse, but within an entire framework constructed from remembered experience. Unlike any other animal, we can mentally try out our behavioral scenarios, consider their possible outcomes, and with conscious awareness, make the choice of greatest advantage. It was this process of considered choice that became lost to Michelle.

Very early in her life impossible restrictions were placed on her. In fact, almost no choices were open to her. Life taught her that conscious awareness is of no use. Her human faculty to scan her possibilities had no impact on what befell her. As her illness worsened, her impulses became less under conscious control. Along with sensory deprivation and obsessive fantasies, she became more animal-like, even machine-like, in response to primal needs. What I wanted for her was the opportunity to rebuild the reflective part of her life, to reconnect signals from her emotions to signals that she sensed and to signals from her memory, so that she might once again imagine and plan for desired outcomes that had reasonable probabilities of being realized.

While reflecting, it is possible to put oneself in another person's shoes. What might he or she be feeling, intending, aiming for? It's like being temporarily programmed with someone else's emotions, sensations, and memories. This, too, seems to be an eternal human end point—the capacity to empathize with someone else. It does not involve a simple link of an image, perhaps a face, with an emotion, perhaps love, but a universe of links within an avalanche of images. That universe recreates an individual within the mind of another. Part of human love is the ability to get inside someone else's skin; to assemble in imagination a collection of feelings, characteristics, expressions, aspirations, and memories of the other. Despite our differences, I totally identified with Michelle. I felt her pain and her lack of fulfillment, and in a sense her battle became mine. The injustice of her deprivation, her dehumanization merged with and clarified my own. Michelle speaks with my voice.

Like the caricaturist, we need not fill in all the gaps. Enough crucial details create the essence of another being in our mind. Occasionally I call my daughter perfect. She knows that my use of the word is not full of expectations. There are no demands to be fulfilled. It is meant to describe who she is, not what she will become. This is how she sees her reflection in my eyes. This is what she transcribes inside her brain from my brain. Does she also know what I never talk of? Does she also transcribe my memories of Michelle? Is there something in my tone of voice, my intensity, my involvements, that gives clues to this unspoken side of me? The memories are always there. I can never call my daughter perfect without thinking of Michelle's desperate, driven desire to become perfect in her childhood years. The cruel irony of Michelle's God-given perfection being horribly transformed by what she saw in her father's eyes is never very far from my consciousness.

On the battlefield, men, I believe, sometimes give their lives out of love because they see themselves in their neighbors. A man who dies to save a comrade in a sense also survives. Complete identification includes shared beliefs and causes. It may be the abolition of slavery, the preservation of a union of states, the defense of inalienable rights. It may also be the persecution of a minority, the imposition of religious practice, the claimed superiority of a race. The uniquely human capacity for one individual to become another through remembered images provides the potential for uniquely human evil as well as love.

This is not to say that other animals are incapable of love or something akin to hatred, or that they are incapable of identification and empathy. Behavioral observations of wolves, apes, elephants, and other species strongly suggest that there are instinctive signals that promote identification or the opposite. There are also learned signals that bond members of animal groups together and help them to cooperate.

Instinctive as well as learned behavior forms the basis for one animal taking risks for another.

The human potential for identifying with, for knowing, for mentally recreating another human, however, expands the instinctive classification of friend or foe into another domain. This domain recognizes no temporal limits, is generated from years of remembered past experience, and projects into unlimited future experience. It is also a domain that knows no spatial limits, as it can be transferred from one human to another. The identification is a collection of information, of knowledge, which can be represented in a portrait or a novel and communicated to others. The essence of the individual is preserved in the painted or printed patterns of information, and in that sense his spirit lives on long after his bodily presence has ceased to exist.

Animals don't have the powers of classification, abstraction, and memory necessary to mentally represent and recreate themselves, let alone to communicate that recreation. They do to a small degree, but to compare that small degree with that of a human is to compare the vision of the snail *Hermissenda* to that of a cat. The snail's eye can discriminate the intensity of light, even, to a limited extent, its color. It can sense gradients of light, and it can turn away from a darkened shadow. It can even discriminate the direction in which a shadow is moving, so that it may avoid that shadow. The snail has no knowledge, however, about patterns of light intensity and color. It does not have the number of sensory neurons needed to represent such a pattern, let alone transmit that information to other neuronal layers for feature detection, classification, abstraction, and memory storage. The cat has those capabilities and is therefore privy to another level of knowing its visual world. Multiply the cat's capability to sense and represent an image a thousandfold. Not in the initial representation, but in the subsequent classification and the classification of classifications, the human capability leaps forward. Comparisons and classifications are made among images of taste, smell, hearing, touch, position, and emotions. Image comparisons are made not only within and among these modalities but in a stream of time. Each image is categorized by when it occurred with respect to other images that occur before and after, and reanalyzed and classified based on its position in time. This power to accumulate and reconcile vast quantities of information separates us from other animals.

Our primary emotions and drives are much less unique. Neural representation of emotions occurs in the structures known as the limbic system of the mammalian brain. The limbic template seems to be similar among many mammalian species. The breadth and depth of "knowing," however, can amplify and transform human emotional experience. Human cognition builds worlds on the limbic formation, worlds with a potential for the divine as well as the demonic. It is the contribution of intelligence that separates the human experience of emotions from that of animals. To understand the physiology of this contribution, however, we would have to understand the connections between emotional centers, integrative sensory and memory systems, and behavioral command networks. We would have to understand what is now close to incomprehensible—how all of this signaling and communication among neurons becomes an intelligent purposeful being. If we could model the human experience, might there still not be boundaries we could not cross?

What, for example, does it mean to experience pleasure? It is known that increased electrical signals of neurons within localized brain regions cause pleasure for an animal. The animal will overcome great obstacles to cause these electrical signals. It will learn behavioral strategies to stimulate that brain region. But does this mean that the pleasurable sensation derives from the firing of only those neurons in such brain regions? Or do those neurons signal many other neurons within the brain as well as in many parts of the animal's body. Is some of the pleasure generated also by the way these other distant neurons respond? Are there circulating chemicals, hormones such as the opiates, that coordinate responses in the remotest outposts into one deafening chorus? Are even the cells that sense stimuli from the outside world enlisted into the pleasure process? Does a "high" involve a large part of the entire brain and its peripheral sensory and motor minions?

How much of the totality of brain function would we need to know to understand what hunger is? It is known to involve neuronal electrical signals in brain regions such as the hypothalamus. Here, neuronal firing is sensitive to levels of glucose in the bloodstream, which in turn determine glucose levels in the cerebrospinal fluid bathing the brain. Hunger must involve levels of hormones secreted by other brain regions, such as the pituitary gland, and by organs outside the brain, such as the pancreas and the adrenal gland. The state of fullness of the stomach will generate another set of signals. Patterns of smell and taste are continually evaluated for their potential nutritional benefit. Some of those patterns fit criteria that are hard-wired into the brain to be pleasing and to induce interest in eating the substances associated with the patterns. Other patterns have been learned by being previously linked in time to pleasant experiences during and after consumption. In the absence of food, with the empty stomach and blood glucose low, hunger would be experienced as a gnawing sensation in the stomach and light-headedness. Now images from memory would begin to float into consciousness. Fantasies of past meals and future satisfaction would begin to preoccupy the mind and focus attention on behavioral strategies. So hunger is not only a flow of signals among neurons within a brain region or even among brain regions. It is also a dialogue between brain regions and structures outside the brain, all over the body. This is mass communication on a grand scale.

The electrical signals of any one neuron or neuronal array within the brain would be meaningless alone. The effect of hunger, as we know it, is an orchestration of this myriad of electrical signals. And the orchestration is forever being rewritten and compared to what was composed and transcribed into memory according to the frequency with which it occurred in the past. The voice of one neuron is distinguished by the number, frequency, and phrasing of its electrical signals. When that voice is joined by ten thousand others in a cerebral chorus, an entirely new sound emerges. No one neuronal voice can be heard. Is hunger, then, expressed with frequencies and phrases of collective signals in large groups of neurons? Are these phrases recognizable in different parts of the nervous system within a sequence, a sequence that itself may be repeated at certain characteristic frequencies? Primitive recordings from outside the brain and also outside particular brain regions are beginning to suggest these possibilities. Each feeling and variation of that feeling might have its own characteristic groupings of firing neuronal collections. Then, at any one time, complex mixtures of feelings might be represented by collections of the collections. What a person feels and is neurologically at a particular instant would be a blend of characteristic firing patterns of neuronal aggregates not only within the brain but throughout the rest of the body. But is this ultimately what the human experience is—the firing of neurons? Can our intelligence grasp this translation of what we know subjectively into the coded language of neuronal assemblies?

If pleasure is the firing of neurons in one region in dialogue with many others, what is pain? Is it too much firing? Does pain have only one locus in the brain? Or does it occur when the neurons that fire in response to touch fire excessively in response to great pressure? Does it occur when the neurons that fire in response to light go wild when the light is too bright, as taste neurons might when a food is too acid, or temperature-sensitive neurons when a stimulus is too hot? There are specialized neuronal receptors that are particularly sensitive to extremes of pressure. Perhaps other neurons are adapted to sense other extremes of stimulation. The translation of subjective experience into neuronal firing patterns is something most neuroscientists accept as true, but it is not easily demonstrated.

One instructive instance of such translation is provided by visual prostheses currently being developed. Individuals with degenerated or lesioned retinas can no longer sense patterns of light stimuli. Yet the nerve that carries information from the eye to the brain may still be intact. Electrical probes can be inserted into this nerve to deliver sequences of electrical stimuli. The individual actually experiences the sensation of light in response to such electrical stimulation of the nerve. The firing of neurons in the brain represents the electrical signals of the nerve in such a way that the subjective experience of illumination results. The sensory cells don't have to receive light for the brain to experience its presence. This is an elementary demonstration that events external to us are known to us only as the firing frequencies of neurons. In this case, the sensory cells of the retina, as well as other neurons within the retinal network have been circumvented. The electrical stimuli received by optic nerve axons from artificial light detectors only crudely resemble the stimuli normally received by the output neurons in the retina.

A primitive prosthesis functions when artificial light sensors receive illumination and generate electrical stimuli that are delivered to the axons of the optic nerve. At this stage of its development, the prosthetic device performs minimal information processing. It relays little or no information about the patterns of illumination it encounters. And if it could, there is at present no design that would allow it to transfer patterned information to the optic nerve so that it could be processed by neurons that receive signals from the optic nerve axons. But the potential is there. It is entirely conceivable that sensors could be configured as in a television camera to transform a pattern of illumination into a pattern of electrical signals. It is now only a dream, but still conceivable, that circuits will be designed to resemble neuronal networks, which then relay processed information to the brain. As long as our visual experience is reducible into electrical signals, then the apparatus responsible for that experience is potentially repairable or even, in parts, replaceable. The same is true for the human auditory apparatus, the touch networks, and motor networks such as those responsible for limb movement or bladder control.

Here the blurring of a distinction between artificial and natural networks works in our favor. It need not dehumanize. On the contrary, it may rehumanize. Restoring or replacing neural networks in the future need not be limited to artificial replacements. Neurons might be grown to form networks that could be added to defective regions of the nervous system. The neurons themselves might be added to the region and then stimulated to form networks. Or we might add only critical nutrients and factors that would stimulate neural elements and precursors already present in those regions to grow into new networks. And when the lesion does not involve defective neurons but defective experience, such as traumatic conditioning, perhaps one day we will be able to intervene physically to erase old memories and facilitate the formation of new ones.

Electroshock therapy was designed to do just this. But electroshock is probably even more crude in its effects on painful memories than electrical stimulation of the optic nerve is in its simulation of visual experience. Instead of selectively eliminating or blocking painful memories, it affects all memory. The hope is that the individual will be given a window of time in which to acquire new memories before familiar patterns return. Perhaps the goal will become more realistic when electrical and chemical interventions are based on molecular and biophysical understanding we are only now beginning to achieve. Then it may become clearer what intervention is appropriate.

Short-term memory is more likely to be susceptible to electrical disruption of the signal processing by neurons. Longer-term memory is more likely to involve irreversible biochemical and structural changes distributed throughout the dendritic trees of thousands if not millions of neurons. These long-term changes will probably remain as long as the neurons remain. It seems impossible, after a certain stage in life, to physically alter undesirable memories without altering desirable memories. The millions, if not billions, of acquired patterns that define an individual's personality, skills, and experience are not readily separable into good and evil, constructive and destructive. So the choice, even in a fantasy world where minds could be altered, would seem to be between acquiring new memories on top of the old, or simply starting over. Perhaps, chronically ill patients will someday be considered to require additional neurons to learn new patterns just as a Parkinson's patient might require neurons to make dopamine. Perhaps additional blank networks could be added to a patient's brain to provide the extra storage capacity required for a different outlook on life. The old structural and electrical patterns within the networks would remain, but might become subordinated, in time, to those added later. For any of these possibilities to come close to actuality, a new level of appreciation for the varieties of neuronal experience would be necessary—one that, for now, is in the realm of science fiction. It would require a vision of neuronal function that integrates genetic programming, growth and development, learning and memory, and age and degeneration. It would also require an ability to make moral judgments about when such steps should be taken, an ability mankind has by no means demonstrated up to now.

Such are the differences between men and machines. As we gain greater insight into our own biological machinery, the responsibilities and the choices become more complex and often more difficult. There is no difficulty in deciding that an ailing child should have a liver transplant, if that transplant restores the child to life. But what of an elderly patient who is tired of living? Must that patient be resuscitated when an arrhythmia causes his heart to stop beating? Who is to decide that another individual has reached a stage when hopelessness is intractable, when consciousness has been irreversibly impaired, when experience should be erased? Does understanding the distinctions between men and machines make such choices any less difficult? Are the choices clearer because we can think of human brain function as a chorus of a billion electrical voices?

Brain studies at cellular and molecular levels don't address the issues of intact brains. Demonstration that traumatic conditioning of a child by a parent is a causal factor in alcoholism or schizophrenia would be a breakthrough in telling us what has to be done to help prevent these diseases. But it doesn't provide the moral authority or legal means by which a parent is prevented from inflicting that trauma. We already know that child abuse is evil, that it increases the incidence of child abuse by those who were abused in their own childhood. Yet we are impotent to reduce that abuse significantly. How much damage is inflicted psychologically by parental neglect and abuse can be debated. It can be argued that the damage is short-lived in some but irreversible in others who are genetically so predisposed. But that it is damaging is not open to debate. Yet what can be done about it? I knew that Michelle was continually being traumatized, just as we know that citizens of other countries are regularly brutalized, even tortured by their governments. I was powerless to intervene just as a sovereign nation is powerless to intervene in its neighbor's internal affairs. Knowledge of how trauma is retained by the brain helps us to develop ways of treating the mental consequences, but not to prevent them.

Assume for a moment that we could bridge the gap between the microscopic and macroscopic, between the biology of neuronal networks, psychology, and sociology. Assume that every behavioral choice of an individual could be predicted by the neuronal signals we quantitatively track as a function of time and sensory experience. Assume that we could know ourselves entirely in the language of neuronal firing frequencies. We still would not know ourselves in the same way we each as individuals already know ourselves, with a knowledge both uniquely original to and limited by the total physical essence of our beings. The owl "sees" what the bat "hears." Each accurately locates objects in space. Yet their individual knowledge of these objects is not identical because their networks and the patterns of information they receive and process are not identical.

Our networks, stamped from a genetically prescribed template and then molded by experience, allow each of us to see in our uniquely human way, which will not be duplicated in a machine unless that machine is created human. What for now we cannot know is the possible existence of events in the universe that we will never see. The evolution of species left its traces behind for us to reconstruct. We infer that evolution occurred over periods of time that our brains do not directly perceive. Perhaps this will also be true of the evolution of the universe and of other natural phenomena in time and space zones that still elude our awareness. Perhaps there will always be traces whose trails we can follow to uncover still unknown worlds. Perhaps our own future evolution as organisms will lead us into such worlds. But I suspect there are aspects of natural phenomena we simply cannot know with the networks we now possess. Then, like machines, which cannot know their designer, we may be forever barred from penetrating certain hidden corners of the universe that hold the ultimate secrets of creation.

Perhaps we are blessed by an inability to solve certain intractable puzzles of existence. Like Babushka dolls in unending succession, each box of a puzzle may open only to reveal another. Still, we keep opening the boxes, not at all certain what we are searching for, whether we will recognize it if we do find it, and if we don't, whether in our hearts we would really want to.

AFTERWORD—LETTING GO

There was no way I could have anticipated what medical school would be like. I could not have imagined my shock at dissecting a cadaver, the sacrifices of my other interests, the assault on my brain by unorganized masses of undigested facts, or the steeliness of clinical mentors as they coped with the intractability and number of patients' ills. I could not imagine the intensity of the commitment I would have to make just to make it through. I could not have anticipated the way you cannot turn your head away from death and disease. You see it in the face of a leukemia-stricken child, sweet, expecting, still hopeful, but already tired and wise. You see it in the helplessness of a beautiful young woman, limbs limp, face wan, but still welcoming, though paralyzed by degenerating neurons. It's there in the confused struggle of an obsessive-compulsive, wanting to stop, but forced as if by invisible wires to repeat the same futile handwashing. In medical school, your twitching muscles signal Lou Gehrig's disease rather than your chronic fatigue. You feel as if it could be your sister who is wheeled into the emergency room with a drug overdose, or your mother who has fallen down the steps fracturing her hip, or your child who has been wheeled in on a stretcher, unconscious from the abusive beating of his stepfather. In extremes, there can be no denial. These are not tales of death and dying. This is the real thing. And these extremes define our lives, but in a way not possible to anticipate unless we experience them directly.

There was no way I could know what it would be like to have children. I could never anticipate the anxiety I felt—for my wife, about unknown genetic flaws in our children, about the vulnerability of their unformed but forming minds. Nor could I have really understood what it would be like to make discoveries. I did not know that at times it could feel like gardening with a green thumb. I didn't have sufficient consciousness to know that this was where my abilities, personality, and interests would lead me, that this would be the niche to best accommodate my pleasure in intellectual games, my sense of inadequacy before a disapproving father, and perhaps most of all, the aching sense of loss I felt for Michelle. Such is the complexity of the human brain that it issues the most profound and important direction for behavior as an orchestrated synthesis of so many sensations, memories, classifications, and emotions that they can't possibly all be brought into consciousness. Only a small fraction of their number ever attain logical arrangement and verbal expression.

There was no way, long ago, that I could have anticipated where my search would lead me or how, in the process, the proportions of loss, mission, curiosity, and fear would change. My relationship to science, as you may have learned from these pages, is defined by extremes, although they are rarely realized. At one extreme, I follow game plans with identified objectives. These are detective stories in which I play the detective, maybe solve a mystery. It's both a game and terribly serious at the same time. In reality, I struggle with nature's mysteries in a battle that I can never win and whose opening salvos were overwhelmingly one-sided in the enemy's favor. At this extreme, all my physical and mental energy pours into the pursuit. In pursuit of answers, I forget my fear.

But fear is my other extreme. In its grip, no longer pursuing but pursued, I am concerned with winning approval and recognition, justifying my existence, gaining social acceptance and easing loneliness. This is the extreme that inflates the need for achievement, success, and security, and which competes in excess. Fear disorients. It denies other needs for relaxation, pleasure, and sharing. A harsh taskmaster, it fuels resourcefulness and powers discipline. Yet, without the balance of curiosity and a sense of mission, efforts become misguided and unhinged. The train risks hurtling off the track.

In retrospect, detective stories sound like fun. There is romance, drama, perhaps even a touch of heroism. Fear is another matter. Aware of extremes in patterns of my behavior, I would not have chosen to live in fear. I cannot put a good face on harsh discipline and demanding tyranny. I don't console myself with the "silver lining" that "something good" came out of them. I would have chosen more freedom, less looking over my shoulder, less concern about how I'm doing than with such simple pleasures as vacations and getting paid. As life passes, as the distance from the primal relationships of childhood increases, parents are less imposing figures. Now the old reasons for doing science don't quite apply. The sense of mission, as well as the fear, assume more human dimensions. Although the patterns of my discipline remain, the mix of motives has changed. Yes, there is still devotion, a sense of inspiration in my way of practicing medicine. But the curiosity is less desperate, more pleasurable, and easier to share.

Just as I couldn't anticipate medical school, parenthood, or doing science, might this not still be the case as I look to the future? Who can with certainty fix value, positive or negative, to the current explosion of insights into biological and artificial brains? Who can predict what role brain science will ultimately play in the flow of history? Now, with memory intact, senses lively, body still quick, I cannot imagine a time when I won't relish asking the next question and pursuing the next answer. I cannot imagine being out of the activist, even arrogant, tradition of today, that science cures, invents, and charts the universe. While it is true that I occasionally find tedium in my work, it is also true that I am still startled and intrigued by what I haven't done, what I have never anticipated. I have not yet tired of the game.

Senses failing, muscles weak, and bones brittle, who knows what concessions I will be prepared and ultimately forced to make, reluctantly letting go of what has been so familiar for so long. For now, I know death and dying more intimately in my unconscious than in my conscious moments. But I am learning to live with how much I cannot anticipate. I am learning that there is also strength in more fully accepting how much I don't and may never understand, and that it is possible to admit helplessness without admitting defeat. There are even times for a necessary disengagement, as I learned in a moment of discovery years ago.

On vacation with my family off the west coast of Florida, I awoke at dawn with a deep aching pain in my chest. It wasn't anything like the gnawing, mild burning, or simple fullness familiar to me as indigestion. This was more like a severe toothache, but filling the volume of an orange planted under my sternum. It jolted me out of bed. Standing seemed to make it more bearable while I clenched my fist, tensing all of my muscles as if to direct the energy that impelled me to do something for relief or at least to scream. "It will pass," I thought. "If I can just bear with it a few more minutes I won't have to alarm my wife who is sleeping so peacefully."

I moved slowly, one arm braced against my abdomen, the other leaning on the wall for support. As the minutes passed, the pain worsened. Its grip seemed to pull me away from her, separating me from all that I loved and lived for. Out of this fear of separation, perhaps parting forever, I finally, gently, called to her. She answered through the haze that was beginning to cloud my consciousness, cooling my senses into a state of numbness. "I'll be all right," I mumbled as I groped my way into the adjacent bathroom.

I could not stop the separation. Now with both arms clinging to the bathroom wall, I felt myself slowly slipping down onto the floor. The towel rack was my last vision of the outside world before darkness enveloped me. In the darkness, I felt totally awake as time stopped and the memories of my life rushed before my eyes. I saw myself as a small boy, fresh, expectant, jubilant, curious, loving. I saw my mother, beautiful, nurturant, compassionate, suffering. I saw my brother and sisters, Michelle, my children, and Betty, my wife. I saw my father, stern, disciplined, curious, confused. I saw my work, my ambitions, the search I had pursued so long. And of all that I saw, I let go. In that instant eternity of darkness, a strange giddiness suffused my being. "You see," I thought, "there is nothing more you can do." Abandon all effort. No more hypotheses. No need for excuses. You are off the hook. I almost laughed with the relief, but for the sorrow of parting. But I had no fear. No mission, no fear, and no regrets. What was done and what was undone did not matter. There was in this rush of images from the past complete and unambiguous conviction that I was about to die, and with that recognition came a total acceptance of what had been my life.

As it turned out, there was still much more to learn, predict, and accept. With proper diet I could avoid another aspirin-induced gastric hemorrhage. This would be a trauma without a lasting grip. Ten years would pass before I perceived consciously what had struck me then with such clarity as I slipped into unconsciousness.

Puzzling over the meaning of semiconscious thoughts and dreams is like deciphering passages chiseled into ancient stone that time has worn away. The cryptologist keeps trying different letters and words to fill the gaps and reveal the meaning, thereby completing and creating in his own mind the pattern of thought in the mind of an ancient correspondent. The conscious self can look to the unconscious as its own mysterious and elusive correspondent. Late at night, in darkness, though fully awake, I am reminded of my seemingly fatal swoon. At the end of the day, with a need for sleep, I can begin to feel that it is time to abandon all effort. Nothing I do will make any difference. Now I must entrust myself and those I love to the unpredictability of the universe whose patterns I cannot anticipate. There, surrounded only by my thoughts, I no longer care, not hopeless but free, until I awake once more to begin another day.

NOTES

MEMORY'S DOMAIN

1. To track memory from behavior to molecules involves travel through different worlds of natural phenomena. At one extreme is the behavior of whole organisms and the functions of the organ systems of which they are made. The organs themselves consist of billions of cells. One organ system, the nervous system, coordinates the behavior. Within this system, electrical signaling is generated by the flow of electric charges across the membranes of individual neurons. Molecules within the neurons regulate the flow of these charges. Memory has behavioral expression, electrical coding, and a molecular basis. Memory is all of these and has to be describable at each different level of biological complexity. The language of description will be different for each level. Different rules will be followed. Yet somehow it must be possible to construct an interface between each level of complexity so that memory in the language of molecular phenomena can be translated into the language of electrical signaling and then into the language of behavior. The movements and gravitational interaction of heavenly bodies are described in the language of astrophysics. The movements and interaction of atomic particles are within the province of nuclear physics. At times it is totally inappropriate to mix such very different languages, but inevitably, macroscopic planetary behavior must be resolvable into the behavior of electrons, neutrons, and protons.

2. Today the word *marrano* means "pig" in Spanish. This is not so different from the connotation of "cursed one" acquired many centuries ago.

3. The Kol Nidre is chanted on the Jewish Day of Atonement, or Yom Kippur, the most sacred holiday of the year. It is thought to have originated in thirteenth-century Spain during the time of the Inquisition, when on each Yom Kippur the secret Jews, or *marranos*, asked forgiveness for either not observing their religious traditions at all or saving them for times of secrecy.

255

ROOTS

1. Stepping back from the developments of the seventeenth, eighteenth, and nine-teenth centuries, several clear patterns emerge. Mind, from the time of Descartes, was beginning to be regarded as part of the body, or at least its extension. Physics had uncovered and described phenomena—electrical signals—that expressed a fundamen-tal language of the mind's function, later identified as the language of the nervous sys-tem. And psychology was founded as a new science to study mental functions including sensations, memories, perception, behavior, and emotions. At the time of its emer-gence, psychology was considered a part of biology by some but by no means all mem-bers of the intellectual community. Over the past one hundred years, integration of physics, biology, and psychology has been partially accomplished in the discipline of neuroscience or neurobiology. To this day, however, no one can make the unequivocal claim that all aspects of mind and consciousness must be accounted for by physical and chemical events, although that is a popularly held belief. Nor are many psychological phenomena, particularly those involving higher mental functions such as pattern recognition, abstract thinking, and complex decision making, understood well enough to be explained as physical/chemical processes. Nevertheless, this integration of basic natural science with a new science of the mind was the direction in which human thinking was moving by the second half of the nineteenth century. And in spite of new subdisciplines, such as those of artificial networks, this trend has predominated until the present. Helmholtz's work on the electrical properties of nerve fibers, motivated by his interest in human perception, may represent the beginning of the integrated disci-pline of neuroscience. Yet Helmholtz did not begin his work in a vacuum.

2. In 1791 Luigi Galvani published his deduction that animal tissues generate electricity. He had come to this conclusion by causing frog legs to twitch from the elec-trical discharge of a Leyden jar. Then he found that strategic placement of two metal rods, one on the nerve to the leg, would elicit a twitch. Galvani had made the first bat-tery, in this case using living material. In 1800 Volta extended this discovery by making batteries out of layers of inorganic material. A contemporary and friend of Helmholtz, Du Bois-Reymond, introduced a whole new way of thinking about nerve conduction by constructing a biological framework for Galvani's and Volta's findings. Charged par-ticles of opposite charge were arrayed, he believed, in parallel along the lengths of nerves and muscles. Although much of this theory would be proven wrong, it was the immediate precursor to the definition of a nerve signal, later called an impulse, as a wave of moving charge along the outer wall or membrane of a nerve fiber. This theory, first developed by Bernstein in 1866 and later expressed in terms of physical chemistry by Ostwald, has survived today, although it has been transformed many times over by the detailed observations of investigators such as R. S. Lillie, Bernard Katz, Kenneth Cole, Alan Hodgkin, and Andrew Huxley.

3. Gustav Fritsch and Edouard Hitzig, contemporaries of Broca, introduced their own revolutionary approach. In effect, they combined anatomic localization with elec-trical stimulation. With fine electrodes made of platinum wire they introduced electric current to specific regions on one side of a dog's brain, thereby producing precise and reproducible movements on the opposite side of its body. Fritsch and Hitzig were doing for the brain what had already been accomplished for the nerves of the spinal cord. Their experiments offered a brilliant synthesis of what had been known until their time with what had been only guessed at. Electrical signaling of neurons in the brain could control the behavior of the body. Here was another fulfillment of Descartes's conceptual formulation through a direct, unequivocal demonstration. Still later in the nineteenth century and early part of the twentieth century, Karl Lashley in

America showed that memory of a learned task was progressively more impaired as the amount of cortical tissue destroyed in a rat's brain increased. Again, these experiments were greatly refined and reinterpreted over ensuing decades, but two important inferences are still considered valid today. Memory functions are located in the brain, and memory storage is accomplished in many regions distributed throughout the brain.

4. It may not be accidental that this breakthrough, like so many in the nineteenth century, came in Germany and continental Europe. No one can deny the important influence of English philosophers such as John Locke, George Berkeley, David Hume, and John Stuart Mill. Indeed, the English school focused on an "associationist" philosophy according to which all mental function was generated by elementary associations—not at all foreign to Leibnitz's "monads." Associationists had to derive their insights from introspection, as well as from the accumulated knowledge of their times. Yet few of them took their notions into the laboratory and attempted to reconcile their philosophical perspectives on mind with observable natural phenomena. In continental Europe, unlike England and America, this was the rule rather than the exception. Men like Leibnitz, Galvani, Helmholtz, Weber, Fechner, Bernstein, Golgi, and Cajal seemed to come out of one tradition, while the English came out of another. Presumably, the environment—intellectual, cultural, and social—inspired characteristic traditions of thought and experimentation. That environment in Germany and its immediate neighbors spawned the new discipline of neuroscience. But there were many exceptions. Charles Darwin, the preeminent English biologist, cannot be thought of as a psychologist, and he certainly did not concentrate his efforts on the brain and mental functions. He was, however, most definitely a behaviorist as well as a biologist. Darwin came to understand that natural selection sorts out which behaviors are adaptive for a species in its particular environment. And implicitly he realized that such behaviors were somehow genetically prescribed and that humans as well as other species were subject to the process of evolution. It would be logical, then, that human behavior was to a significant degree genetically determined (i.e., biologically based). Animals had long been considered to have no conscious experience or mental capacities qualitatively comparable to those of humans. But if the human brain evolved from those of other animal species, a biological basis for the human mind became much more plausible. This was one of the revolutionary implications of Darwin's work. The mind and the soul might be rooted in the concrete world of natural phenomena. These new insights had to have a profound impact on the founding of a science of the mind.

5. France had an early tradition of activism toward mental illness, beginning with the Viennese expatriot physician Franz Mesmer. Mesmer had only vague ideas of how he was affecting his patients, but an impression of hypnosis emerges from descriptions of his sessions held in the late eighteenth century. This tradition, relying heavily on hypnotic therapy, was continued and developed in France throughout the nineteenth century by such physicians as A. A. Liebeault, Hippolyte Bernheim, Jean-Martin Charcot, and Pierre Janet. Early in his career, Freud trained with Charcot, who was particularly interested in hysteria. He also visited and attended clinical demonstrations by Janet and Bernheim. Later, Freud hoped to substitute the technique of free association for hypnosis to uncover deep-seated memories of past trauma.

THE AGE OF TECHNOLOGY

1. Sherrington demonstrated that a sensory stimulus such as touch, pain, or heat, when administered to the limb of a dog, elicits reflexive movement such as limb withdrawal. He eventually proved that the stimulus elicited signals that traveled along one nerve leading to the spinal cord, followed by signals that traveled from the spinal cord

to the muscles to cause movement. Sherrington began by electrically stimulating the nerves exiting from the spinal cord and traveling to the muscles. He mapped out the distribution of these motor nerves, showing they were controlling movement in an orderly and reproducible manner. He then demonstrated an entire set of sensory nerves, which receive signals from the body's limbs. The sensory nerves also had an orderly and reproducible distribution. He showed further that electrically stimulating a sensory nerve caused signals in the motor nerves to elicit muscular contraction and movement.

2. Even Du Bois-Reymond suggested the possibility that a message might be carried across a synapse from one neuron to another by a chemical rather than an electric current. Claude Bernard provided some intriguing initial evidence for this not yet clearly formulated hypothesis. With a chemical called curare, Bernard was able to block the effect of a nerve's electrical signal to the muscle to produce contraction. Curare did not prevent the muscle from contracting in response to direct electrical stimulation. Nor did it block the electrical signal's travel down the nerve. From these observations, Bernard's colleague Edmond Vulpian inferred that the drug must work at the synapse itself. It wasn't until the early twentieth century, however, that a hypothesis favoring chemical signaling at the synapse was clearly formulated.

3. This was the first chemical messenger shown to deliver a synaptic message. Dale proposed that no single neuron could synthesize and release more than one chemical messenger at a synaptic junction. Dale's Law, as it came to be known, has largely stood the test of time, although occasional exceptions have since been encountered.

4. Eccles was able to link chemical messengers with both inhibitory and excitatory events and with the flow of the particular ions responsible for those events. It is somewhat ironic that once Eccles and his colleagues had unequivocally established a chemical basis for synaptic transmission, exceptions began to emerge that were consistent with his original position. For example, Edwin Furschpan and David Potter found a case, admittedly rare, where electrical messages were transmitted across a synapse. Later, other exceptions would be found.

5. Katz, together with colleagues such as Fatt, DelCastillo, and Miledi, took the analysis of chemical synaptic transmission to an even more fundamental level. In his ultrasensitive recordings of synaptic events in muscle cells, he found that what at first appeared to be noise was really a number of microsynaptic events. He was able to show that electrical signals in the presynaptic knobs increased the frequency of the events recorded from the postsynaptic muscle target. Furthermore, larger synaptic events were generated from the summation of the micro or "quantal" events. Through these studies Katz conceived of the quantal theory of synaptic transmission.

6. Helmholtz's measurement of the speed with which an electrical signal moves along a nerve fiber gave a surprising result. The conduction time of 20–30 meters per second was much slower than might be expected for an electrical signal traveling along a good conducting path such as an insulated copper wire. In 1856, only a few years after Helmholtz's measurement, Baron Kelvin set forth his principles for the transmission of electrical signals along cables. These principles were thought by many to apply to nerve signals, but there were enough differences between the biological and industrial cables to make application of cable transmission principles inappropriate for any significant portion of nerve. For one, the internal contents of the nerve, its "core conductor," consisted mainly of a solution of salts. This solution was a poor conductor of electricity, offering great resistance to current flow. By contrast, a metal such as copper was chosen as a conductor for industrial cable because of its unusually low resistance to current flow. Another difference concerned insulation. A transmitting copper wire can be well insulated with nonconducting material such as rubber so that almost no current leaks out and all of the current must travel forward along the copper. Biological insulation is not nearly so successful in preventing current leakage from a nerve fiber. One

other unknown factor that complicated Helmholtz's measurement was the delay introduced by the release of a chemical messenger across a synapse. Helmholtz's measurement depended on the fiber signal activating a synapse onto a muscle and was therefore even slower than would be anticipated from the poor transmission conditions of the nerve fiber. In any case, the mystery of nerve transmission had become apparent.

7. The term *membrane* had acquired its own special meaning to chemists. Membranes could be porous to some molecules and not others. Charged ions might ordinarily be contained within a cell's membrane but let out under special conditions. Electrical potentials could be created across a membrane that were due to differences in the numbers of charged particles on the inside and outside of the membrane. Bernstein brilliantly joined what was known in his time about membranes with what was known about nerve conduction. His synthesis, the membrane theory of nervous conduction, proposed in 1902, contained principles that have stood the test of time. Many aspects were later shown to be invalid or insufficiently detailed, but the essence was amazingly accurate. Bernstein reasoned that potassium ions were ordinarily kept within the nerve fiber by its wall or membrane, but during the instant in which an electrical signal is transmitted across a local patch of membrane, the patch opens to let the positively charged potassium ions flow out of the fiber.

8. Carlo Matteucci, in Italy, had already obtained evidence for Bernstein's later formulation by recording the flow of current from an injured portion of a nerve or muscle to an adjacent intact portion. He inferred that the broken membrane allowed ions to flow out of the fiber core that normally flowed only during the transmission of an electrical signal. At almost the same time that Bernstein proposed his formal theory, E. Overton demonstrated that conduction of a nerve impulse (i.e., its electrical signal) failed when sodium ions were removed from the fluid in which it was immersed, suggesting that sodium, as well as potassium, was flowing across the membrane during the impulse.

9. Cole and Curtis made additional observations which also confirmed Bernstein's view that separation of potassium ions across the membrane was responsible for this potential difference across a membrane at rest (i.e., in the absence of a nerve impulse).

10. Within the mathematical formulas were imbedded key theoretical elements that are still being tested and, in many cases, validated today. According to this new theory, the ions move through pores, or channels, in the membrane. These pores open in a precise sequence in response to potential differences across the nerve membrane, and this sequence underlies the progressive movement of the impulse down the axon. There are of course, other pieces to the puzzle. An electrical impulse is also "pushed" down the axon with the help of other mechanisms such as biochemical "pumps," which help keep the balance of ions distributed across the axon membrane. The channels themselves can only stay open a certain length of time and at limited frequencies. Ultimately, new techniques would bring a new reality to ion flow across membranes. Richard Keynes, in England, exploited recently developed techniques of tagging molecules by making them radioactive. With their radioactive tags, ions could then be followed as they flowed into and out of an axon during an impulse. Such radioactivity measurements confirmed the measurements made with Cole's voltage-clamp technique.

11. During the early 1980s, Erwin Neher and Bert Sakmann developed a new technique called the patch-clamp, which allowed measurements of an extremely small number of ions flowing through what could only be interpreted as single channels within the membrane.

OPEN FRONTIERS

1. Sensory cells receive signals from limb muscles to monitor stretch, position, and pain. The sensory cells in one region of the spinal cord send out branches that

make synaptic connections on an entirely different group of neurons. This group, located in its own identifiable region of the spinal cord, sends long axons back to the muscle groups from which the sensory signals were received. The sensory cells in the spinal cord also relay their signals along a chain of neurons that extends right into the brain. The brain, in turn, has groups of cells that relay information back down the spinal cord to the sensory and motor cells. Many of the stations along these chains are now well known. The chains in essence provide pathways for signals to and from the brain. Centers inside the brain have been identified for the experience of touch, pain, position, vision, hearing, and smell.

2. Vernon Mountcastle showed that there were cylinderlike chunks or "columns," of neurons that responded to common touch stimuli. Within the columns, composed of characteristic layers, neurons were connected in characteristic ways to direct the output of information to other brain regions. David Hubel and Torsten Wiesel found similar organizations in areas of cortex responsive to visual stimuli. Other investigators such as Roger Sperry concentrated on asymmetries between representations on the right and left sides of the brain.

3. The American physiologist Horace Magoun and the Italian Giuseppe Moruzzi, working at Northwestern University, stimulated another area called the reticular activating system, which controls states of arousal and alertness.

4. Earlier in the twentieth century, Edgar Adrian had recorded the signals of individual nerve fibers of sensory and motor nerves of the spinal cord, demonstrating that the signals called nerve impulses encoded information by changing their frequency. H. Keffer Hartline, working at the Marine Biological Laboratory some years later, demonstrated that the signals elicited by light in optic nerve fibers of the horseshoe crab had a comparable language. Steven Kuffler recorded the signal frequencies of the output cells in the frog retina. Light received by sensory cells within a limited area, or "field," increased the signals of the output cell. Light received by sensory cells surrounding the field decreased the signals of the output cell. Hartline demonstrated a similar "center-surround" organization in the responses of output cells for the eye of the horseshoe crab. He further showed that inhibitory synapses between output neurons enhanced the perceived difference of light intensity at a light-dark border, such as that created by a shadow. These inhibitory synaptic connections increased the contrast detected by the crab eye at the shadow's edge. Hartline, Kuffler, and others were revealing that neurons acted according to their spatial location within the layer. This organization creates connections that enable the neurons to send signals to one another.

Jerome Lettvin delved further into the subtleties of retinal signaling. He and his collaborators found that objects the size of a fly or a moth elicited no signals from many of the frog's retinal cells unless the object was moving. Sensory cells received the light patterns, but many cells within the layers receiving signals from the sensory cells did not respond unless the object moved. The frog's eye was telling its brain when an object moved and, therefore, that there was food to be flicked into the frog's mouth by a darting tongue. This is a clear instance of feature detection by the neuronal system of the frog's retina. Other features such as the edge of an object are also enhanced as the signals of neurons pass from layer to layer. Within signals transmitting the image, differences of color, light intensity, or movement are exaggerated. Neurons deep within the brain respond only to lines oriented at certain angles, groups of lines, or ultimately to well-defined forms and objects. These observations demonstrated that progress of image-elicited signals through neuronal layers helps us to see more clearly what's actually out there. Exaggeration of differences in light intensity, color, movement, and angle of orientation makes them more obvious to us, very similar to the way increasing contrast on a television set can make the televised image clearer.

5. Mach was not proceeding on inference alone, however. He did not directly measure properties of neural networks, but he did measure properties of human responses to objective visual stimuli. By carefully collecting the reports of his subjects, he could distinguish between actual and perceived changes of light intensity. He believed, correctly as it was established decades later, that his human response measurements (i.e., the psychophysical measurements), indirectly reflected the properties of neuronal networks in the retina. From his psychophysical measurements, and his inferences about the retina, Mach formulated mathematical equations. These equations were, in fact, a mathematical model, one of the first, to explain the function of biological neural networks. The equations described the operations of the retinal network without assumptions about its mechanisms. Any one of a host of hypothetical groups of neurons, their synaptic connections, and their responses could be fit to the model. But Mach predicted features of the network's synaptic organizations with remarkable accuracy.

EVOLUTION'S COMPROMISE

1. Ceratae are appendages that sense touch and increase the animal's surface area for respiratory and digestive function.

2. Since their invention by Ralph Gerard and Gilbert Ling, such microelectrodes have revolutionized the investigation of neural networks. They are made by shaping hollow glass cylinders on a very small forge into a long narrow needle whose tip cannot be seen with the naked eye. The tip is many times smaller than the neuron, so it can be inserted into the neuron with the aid of a microscope. Signals can be reliably recorded for many hours at a time while the nervous system is completely healthy and functional.

3. Turbulence causes the snail to reflexly contract its muscular undersurface, called a foot, to produce a suction-cuplike effect, which stabilizes the animal in the swirling water. This clinging response reduces stimulation of the animal's vestibular organ, the statocyst, by the buffeting waters.

4. During the snail's training, a light turns on about half a second before a 2-second period of rotation begins. These light-rotation pairs occur about 50 times over the next 90 minutes before the animal is returned to its aquarial home. Typically, 90 minutes of training is given to the animal on three successive days. Terence Crow, Izja Lederhendler, Louis Matzel, and Bernard Schreurs all made important contributions to the training and testing of the snails.

5. Turbulence could eventually be adequately simulated by rotating the snails on a turntable, which resembled a large record player. This stimulus offered the advantage of being precisely directed with respect to the snail's body axis and thus could be shown to have quantifiable effects on individual hair cells of the snail's vestibular organ, or statocyst.

6. Before training, and hours and days after training is completed, just the light is presented. After training, the animal no longer reacts to light as if it were a neutral or novel stimulus. Now, the snail responds to the light as if it were rotation. As a result of training, the snail contracts its foot and clings whenever the light appears. The meaning of light has now become connected to the meaning of rotation within the animal's brain. An entirely new behavioral response to light, one that never occurred before training, demonstrates that there is a remembered link between light and rotation. If, during training, light and rotation occur randomly, the link is not learned. If either light or rotation occur frequently in the absence of each other, even when they are more intense or more frequent, there is also no learning. This means that it is the precise relationship in time between these two stimuli that is learned.

UNEARTHING THE RECORD

1. Forgetting is another identifying feature of Pavlovian conditioning and associative learning in general. With a limited number of light-rotation presentations, forgetting in the snail will occur spontaneously. Type B cell responses decline spontaneously in close parallel to such forgetting behavior. Forgetting becomes more rapid (i.e., it extinguishes) when light stimuli occur in the absence of rotation, and the decline of the type B cell's responses parallels the extinction behavior.

2. The B cell is itself a small network of compartments, which communicate with each other. Light is first received in one of these compartments, which contains the same visual pigment molecule present in our own eyes: rhodopsin. Rhodopsin, activated by light, opens channels for a positively charged particle called a sodium ion to flow in through the wall of the light-receiving compartment. Positive charge then spreads from the light-receiving compartment to the main body of the type B cell and then continues to spread to the signal-generating zone on the axon, where electrical signals arise from explosive increases in the positive charge across the membrane. These signals result from sodium ions rushing through additional channels into the cell. Because these sodium channels are distributed along the entire axon, the signal, once triggered, spreads quickly and efficiently down the axon to the terminal endings to release chemical messages onto the branches of receiving neurons.

3. Other sensory neurons, known as type A cells, showed evidence of changes that did persist after isolation. Observations in our laboratory, as well as that of Joseph Farley, suggest that decreased excitability of the type A cell complements increased excitability of the type B cell to record the memory of light associated with rotation. Such complementary changes could introduce a bias in the network, which may be important for memory storage.

4. By inserting two or more microelectrodes into the same B cell, my collaborators and I measured the flow of different ions across the type B cell membrane. The sodium ion flow directly activated by light was the same for all cells, regardless of their training history. We did, however, find that fewer potassium ions flowed from the inside of the cell to the outside within the major compartment called its body, which contains the cell nucleus. Only type B cells that had been isolated from animals trained to associate light with rotation showed a reduction of potassium ion flow. Paradoxically, reduced potassium ion flow makes a cell more excitable in response to stimuli such as light. Learning made the B cell more excitable because specific channels, with particular molecular structure and ability to regulate the movement of potassium ions through them, were altered during memory storage.

Light and rotation occurring randomly with respect to one other caused no change of potassium channels in the type B membrane. Rotation preceding light caused no change of potassium channels. Only light followed by rotation caused the learned behavioral changes.

The channels first had to be altered in the snail by training effects on the intact visual-vestibular network. The channels remained altered, however, after the type B cell had been isolated from the rest of the nervous system and even, as shown by Dr. René Etcheberrigaray in our laboratory, within an isolated patch of the cell wall that had been removed from the type B cell. Once altered, the channels did not have to remain together with the network. Enough of the molecular apparatus could be isolated, even within a small patch of membrane with its channels, to preserve the memory record.

5. The molecule DAG interacts with other molecules such as arachidonic acid

(AA) and calcium to potently activate the enzyme protein kinase C, or PKC. This enzyme was most thoroughly characterized in the pioneering work of Yazutomi Nishizuka, who showed that protein kinase C becomes activated by moving close to or into cell membranes.

6. Drug-induced activation of the enzyme PKC causes exactly the same prolonged changes of potassium ion flow found after training. Furthermore, a chemical marker that labels cells in which the enzyme has been activated picked out exactly those neurons that show potassium flow changes and increased excitability after conditioning. Another enzyme, called calcium-calmodulin type II Kinase, like PKC, is activated by calcium inside the B cell. We found some years ago that injection of either enzyme closely mimics learning's effects on potassium channels when calcium rises inside the cell.

7. This protein belongs to a class of proteins, G-proteins, first described by Alfred Gilman, that have the general function of transmitting signals across and within cell membranes. G-proteins are usually activated when synaptic and hormonal messengers combine with receiving molecules, or receptors, in a target cell membrane.

8. The parchment was signed by Katsama Dan, then director of the station. Professor Dan, an outstanding developmental biologist, continued a collaborative relationship with M.B.L. for decades later and lives today into his tenth decade.

9. The scenario is built around a dialogue between a neuron's body, where the machinery for protein assembly resides, and the neuron's branches, where synaptic interactions mediate incoming messages from other cells within a network. It is a dialogue that could continue during successive phases of memory storage. According to this scenario, training stimuli are first translated into electrical and then chemical events on a restricted portion of a neuronal branch.

THE KINGDOM OF REAL BRAINS

1. One of the most specific of such correlations was reported by Larry Squire and his colleagues. A patient had suffered a brief interlude of compromised circulation in his brain. This interlude, called a transient ischemic attack, had left the patient without recent memory. When the patient passed away and his brain was examined, apparently only one layer of neurons in the hippocampus had been destroyed. This layer was composed of neurons called the CA1 pyramidal cells.

2. We also wanted to look at a brain region more directly implicated in the rabbit's learning to associate a tone with a corneal air puff. Recent experiments directed our attention to a particular region of the cerebellum. In our laboratory Bernard Schreurs and Juan V. Sánchez-Andrés were eventually able to insert microelectrodes into the dendrites of the cerebellar neurons. They then recorded memory-specific changes of the dendrites themselves in the identical cerebellar region implicated by lesion experiments. Once more this was evidence for the memory record—prolonged or permanent alteration of ion flow through membrane channels of neurons.

3. Recently, Tom Nelson showed that learning alters a protein in the hippocampus that is very similar to or identical with the conditioning protein of the snail.

4. We do know that to learn that the air puff follows the tone after a long delay—for example, 2 seconds—a rabbit needs its hippocampus. The hippocampus is also necessary for a rat to learn how to solve a maze or for a monkey to learn how to match similar objects. For some learning, the hippocampus is not only necessary for acquiring, but also for retrieving a memory. The requirement that a structure such as the hippocampus be present for retrieval suggests, but does not prove, that the memory is

being stored there. As already discussed, information may have to flow through this structure to access the memory elsewhere in the brain. Alternatively, a structure such as the hippocampus may be crucial for directing the flow of information only during the learning process but not later in the final storage and retrieval. Finally, it is also likely that memory of a task or experience is stored in multiple structures within the brain. Loss of any one of the structures may not necessarily mean the loss of the memory entirely, because it may be found in many other storage sites. The studies of Hiroshi Asanuma and Charles Woody, for example, implicate the motor cortex as a site for storing memory of movement sequences. Storage of these movements seems also to occur in other regions of the brain. Once the remembered movements become sufficiently automatic, however, lesions of these other regions have less effect on the animal's ability to execute the behavior. Again, the memory is probably represented in multiple sites, but lesions of these sites may alter the behavior only at certain stages of the learning process.

A STORY NOT YET TOLD

1. For instance, all attempts at demonstrating LTP-triggered channel changes similar to those we found after learning have failed. Instead, the pyramid cell apparently responds more sensitively to chemical messages released at the synapses. Observations of Timothy Bliss, Aryeh Routtenberg, and others suggested that increased release of chemical messages from the axons onto the pyramid cells produces LTP. The observations of other investigators, such as Gary Lynch and Per Andersen, have indicated that pyramidal cells that receive the chemical messages during LTP play an important role in changes. It was Lynch, for example, who first showed LTP's requirement for high calcium within pyramidal cells, just as we found in the snail neurons during Pavlovian conditioning. What has emerged is a complicated mix of LTP mechanisms that may vary with the region of the hippocampus involved, the stimulation conditions, and the duration of the LTP induced.

LINKS IN TIME

1. Increased synaptic weight causes the signal of the sending or presynaptic cell to trigger a much larger synaptic message in the receiving or postsynaptic cell.

2. So in our artificial network we would program fixed-weight pathways for stimuli to trigger reflexive responses, and adjustable-weight pathways for stimuli to acquire reflexive value and new responses through links in time to the reflexive stimuli. Training our artificial network with linked images should transfer the value of one image to the other, just as conditioning a dog transfers the value of meat's smell to the bell's sound.

3. Before learning occurs, synaptic connections that join the snail's visual and vestibular networks at strategic locations make no major contribution to the real time responses of the visual and vestibular pathways. The vestibular sensory cell's synaptic messages to the visual sensory cell, for example, do not alter the snail's reflexive clinging response to rotation or its turning toward a light. Such synapses, part of a memory network, correspond to the apparatus for recording what the video camera monitors. With training, these synapses record that light precedes rotation and thereby transform the animal's response to light from turning to clinging.

To review briefly, there are two independent sensory networks, the visual and vestibular, which sense and respond to separate stimuli, light and rotation. These are real time networks. There is, in addition, another network, a shadow of the other two, which joins the two independent networks at strategic locations. This shadow network makes records of the temporal relationships of light and rotation and thereby generates remembered time.

The entire collection of neurons with their synapses acts as a unit to sense and record any one of four possible relationships between light and rotation. Light and rotation occur together, light occurs in the absence of rotation, rotation occurs in the absence of light, or both light and rotation are absent. These four possibilities fully define the potential relationships in time for the light and rotational stimuli. The network between the visual and vestibular pathways, as a unit, will respond differently to each of these four possibilities.

BRAIN BUILDING

1. While no networks have been designed to fully accomplish such preprocessing, there is general agreement that successful designs would have to incorporate some of the functions known to be performed by the human brain. One function is to focus attention. The human eye moves so as to focus attention and allow visual networks to extract certain features of a pattern such as the eyes of a face, the corners of the mouth, the spacing of the nostrils, the angles between lines in letters, or the orientation of the lines with respect to vertical and horizontal axes. Human vision also involves continuation of lines across gaps when they appear and completion of boundaries to form enclosures within regions of a visual field. Much of this preprocessing seems to occur before entire images are reconstructed by the brain for storage, later recognizedz, and perhaps associated with other images. Additional insights into the brain networks that accomplish such functions should also inform the design of artificial networks.

2. Patent granted 1992.

NEURONS GONE AWRY

1. We have shown that the frequent association of stimulus events in an animal's environment leads to the association of messengers that activate this enzyme, protein kinase C, with neurons.

2. Since these cells, called fibroblasts, are not even from the brain, their kinase deficiency may reflect a general metabolic derangement, perhaps under genetic control. Thus there might be a genetic predisposition to protein kinase C malfunction, which becomes expressed in brain function after a certain age.

3. A site in chromosome 21 has been linked to the occurrence of the disease in families, as well as the occurrence of mongolism (or Down's syndrome), in which Alzheimer's also develops. Another site on the same chromosome, but not close to the first site, has been linked to the beta-amyloid protein. The two sites, therefore, are near each other on the genetic map, suggesting some common genetic control. Furthermore, those individuals whose bodies are less able to break down the beta-amyloid protein reliably develop plaques and Alzheimer's disease. There are additional examples of familiar Alzheimer's cases linked to defective gene loci. In no case, however, is the linkage so strong that we can conclude that a defect of an identifiable chromosomal site is unequivocally responsible for the disease except for the site involving the beta-amyloid protein. Furthermore, all of these cases together compose only a small proportion of the total for which no genetic basis has been implicated. We are therefore not in a situation remotely similar to that of cystic fibrosis, in which a specific genetic locus, responsible for the impaired flow of chloride ion through channels within cell membranes, is always responsible for the disease.

4. Support for this way of thinking comes from recent comparison of molecular events observed during memory storage with those linked to cell derangement. Our conditioning protein called cp20, for instance, produces the same electrical and structural changes in neurons that occur with memory storage. Carlos Collin found that the physiological signature of this memory protein is in many respects identical to that of the cancer-causing protein called v-ras. Cp20 and v-ras have precisely the same effects on each neuronal channel and the electrical properties it controls. This remarkable parallelism suggests that a cell can undergo drastic transformations once the right molecular targets are hit. Some of the targets could be the same for learning, cancer, or development, but the array of signals and messengers required to trigger such diverse processes could be radically different.

Similarly, some of the targets for memory storage, but not the conditions for striking the targets, might be common to old age, Alzheimer's disease, and even stroke. A number of investigators have begun to implicate prolonged elevation of the intracellular calcium ion and activation of the enzyme protein kinase C in the destructive consequences of strokes within the human brain. These might result from, among other causes, abnormally active channels in membranes, which let too much calcium into the neurons. Normally, these channels would never be so active. Under conditions of circulatory failure and anoxia, which only occur as a cataclysmic event, calcium begins to rush into massive numbers of neurons within the brain region to cause damage and symptoms of lost movement, sensation, and memory. By contrast, during learning, calcium elevation and protein kinase C activation occur only locally, in extremely restricted compartments of neuronal branches where the resulting transformations would store precise information, which later will only be accessed by precisely appropriate sensory patterns.

5. Imaging of cerebral blood flow or of labeled glucose molecules is already revealing areas of pathology, although the spatial resolution of such techniques is quite limited. Alternatively, imaging techniques based on molecular steps of memory storage might be developed. Nontoxic labels, similar to the radioactive label of membrane-associated protein kinase C, for example, might reveal early disruption of neuronal function during the acquisition, storage, and/or recall of memories distributed throughout the brain. If the illness is localized not only in regions tied to symptoms but in hosts of other neurons and even non-neuronal tissue, other looks inside could be attempted. Olfactory epithelium, for example, can be painlessly sampled from humans. The neuronal membranes and metabolism of neuronal receptor cells in the epithelium might show abnormalities that are widespread throughout the brain, particularly if some genetic flaw were expressed as some such generalized neuronal dysfunction. Brain tissue analyzed at autopsy would be more meaningfully interpreted by referring retrospectively to the patient's history of symptoms and earlier performance on measures of neurological function. Other cellular measures would be less directly related to brain function, but could be helpful. These include a number of immunologically active molecules, known as antibodies, that might be synthesized by blood cells known as lymphocytes. Alzheimer's disease might be accompanied by changes in the amounts of certain proteins. The body might respond to such proteins as if they were foreign bodies or infective organisms and therefore manufacture antibodies to combat them.

BIBLIOGRAPHY

MEMORY'S DOMAIN

Baddeley, A. D., and Hilgard, E. R. 1981. *Theories of Learning*. 5th ed. New Jersey: Prentice-Hall.

Baddeley, A. D. 1986. *Working Memory*. Oxford: Oxford Univ. Press.

Boakes, R. 1984. *From Darwin to Behaviorism*. Psychology and the minds of animals. Cambridge, England: Cambridge Univ. Press.

Bower, G. H., and Hilgard, E. R. 1981. *Theories of Learning*. 5th ed. New Jersey: Prentice-Hall.

Glass, A. L., and Holyoak, K. J. 1986. *Cognition*. 2nd ed. New York: Random House.

Klatzky, R. L. 1980. *Human Memory: Structure and Processes*. 2nd ed. San Francisco: Freeman.

Lorenz, K. 1970. *Studies in Animal and Human Behavior*. Translated by R. Martin. Cambridge, Massachusetts: Harvard Univ. Press.

Mackintosh, N. J. 1983. *Conditioning and Associative Learning*. Oxford, England: Oxford Univ. Press.

Pinker, S., ed. 1985. *Visual Cognition*. Cambridge, Massachusetts: MIT Press.

Squire, L. R. 1987. *Memory and Brain*. New York: Oxford Univ. Press.

Stillings, N. A., Feinstein, M. H., Garfield, J. L., Rissland, E. L., Rosenbaum, D. A., Weisler, S. E., and Baker-Ward, L. 1987. *Cognitive Science: An Introduction*. Cambridge, Massachusetts: MIT Press.

ROOTS

Adrian, E. D. 1928. *The Basis of Sensation: The Action of the Sense Organ*. London, Christophers.

267

Bernard, C. 1878. *Lecons sur les Phénomènes de la Vie Communs aux Animaux et aux Végétaux.* Paris: Bailliere.

Bernstein, J. 1902. *Investigations on the thermodynamics of bioelectric currents.* Translated from *Pflugers Arch.*, 92:521–562. In G. R. Kepner, ed., 1979. Cell Membrane Permeability and Transport. Stroudsburg, Pennsylvania: Dowden Hutchinson and Ross.

Boring, E. G. 1942. *Sensation and Perception in the History of Experimental Psychology.* New York: Appleton-Century.

Boring, E. G. 1957. *A History of Experimental Psychology.* 2nd ed. New York: Appleton-Century-Crofts.

Brazier, M.A.B. 1988. *A History of Neurophysiology in the 19th Century.* New York: Raven Press.

Brazier, M.A.B. 1984. *A History of Neurophysiology in the 17th and 18th Century.* New York: Raven Press.

Broca, P. 1865. "Sur le Siège de la Faculté du Langage Articule." *Bull. Soc. Anthropol.*, 6:377–93.

Broca, P. 1878. "Anatomie comparée des circonvolutions cerebrales. Le grand, lobe limbique et la scissure limbique dans la serie des mammifieres." *Rev. Anthrop.*, 1: 385–498.

Cajal, S. R. 1906. "The structure and connections of neurons." *Nobel Lectures: Physiology or Medicine, 1901–1921.* Amsterdam: Elsevier, 1967, pp. 220–53.

Cajal, S. R. 1911. *Histologie du Systeme Nerveux de l'Homme et des Vertebres.* Paris: Malonie.

Cajal, S. R. 1937. *Recollections of My Life.* E. Horne Craigie (trans.). Edited in 2 vols. as *Memoirs of the American Philosophical Society*, Philadelphia.

Darwin, C. 1860. *On the Origin of Species by Means of Natural Selection.* New York: Appleton.

Darwin, C. 1872. *The expression of the emotions in man and animals.* Revised and abridged by C. M. Beadnell. 1934. London: Watts.

Descartes, R. 1985. *The philosophical writings of Descartes*, V. 1. Cambridge: Cambridge Univ. Press.

Du Bois-Reymond. E. 1848–1849. *Untersuchungen über Thierische Elektricität*, vols. 1,2. Berlin: Reimer.

Fechner, G. T. 1860. *Elemente der Psychophysik*, 2 vols. Leipzig: Breitkopf and Härtel.

Flourens, J. C. 1824. *Recherches Experimentales sur les Proprietés et les Fonctions du Système Nerveux dans les Animaux Vertèbres.* Paris: Crevot.

Freud, S. 1900–1901. *The Interpretation of Dreams.* Vols. 4 and 5. J. Strachey (trans.) 1953. London: Hogarth Press and the Institute of Psycho-Analysis.

Freud, S. 1917. "Mourning and Melancholia." *The Collected Papers*, Vol 4. New York: Basic Books, 1959, pp. 152–170.

Freud, S. 1940. *An Outline of Psychoanalysis.* J. Strachey (trans). New York: Norton, 1949.

Fritsch, G., and Hitzig, E. 1870. "Über die elektrische Erregbarkeit des Grosshirns." *Arch. Anat. Physiol. Wiss. Med.*, pp. 300–332. G. von Bonin (trans). *Some Papers on the Cerebral Cortex.* Springfield, Illinois: Thomas, 1960, pp. 73–96.

Gall, F. J. and Spurzheim, G. 1810. *Anatomie et Physiologie du Systeme Nerveux en General, et du Cerveau en Particulier, avec des Observations sur la Possibilite de Reconnoitre Plusieurs Dispositions Intellectuelles et Morales de l' Homme et des Animaux, par la Configuration de leurs Têtes.* Paris: Schoel.

Galvani, L. 1791. *Commentary on the Effect of Electricity on Muscular Motion.* R. M. Green (trans.) Cambridge, Massachusetts: Licht, 1953.

Golgi, C. 1906. "The Neuron Doctrine—Theory and Facts." *Nobel Lectures: Physiology or Medicine, 1901–1921.* Amsterdam: Elsevier, 1967, pp. 189–217.

Helmholtz, H. von. 1850. "On the rate of transmission of nerve impulse." *Monatsber. Preuss. Akad. Wiss. Berl.*, pp. 14–15. Trans. in W. Dennis (ed.), *Readings in the History of Psychology.* New York: Appleton-Century-Crofts, 1948, pp. 197–198.

Helmholtz, H.L.F. von. 1877. *On the Sensations of Tone* (2nd English ed.) New York: Dover, 1954.

Helmholtz, H. von 1911. *Helmholtz's Treatise on Physiological Optics,* V. 2, Washington D.C.: Optical Society of America, 1924. Translated from the 3rd German edition.

Leibnitz, G. W. 1985. *The Monadology and Other Philosophical Writings.* Sleigh, R. C., ed. New York: Garland Publishing, Inc.

Muller, J. 1834–40. *Handbuch der Physiologie des Menschen.* 2 Vols. Coblenz: J. Holscher.

Pavlov, I. P. 1927. *Conditioned Reflexes: An Investigation of the Physiological Activity of the Cerebral Cortex.* London: Oxford University Press, Oxford, England.

Stevens, L. A. 1971. *Explorers of the Brain.* New York: Alfred A. Knopf.

Watson, R. I. 1963. *The Great Psychologists: From Aristotle to Freud.* Philadelphia and New York: J. B. Lippincott Co.

Weber, E. H. 1846. "Der Tastsinn und das Gemeingefühl." In R. Wagner (ed.), *Handwörterbuch der Physiologie,* V.3, Abt. 2. Braunschweig: Vieweg, pp. 481–588.

THE AGE OF TECHNOLOGY

Bacq, Z. M. 1975. *Chemical transmission of nerve impulses.* New York: Pergamon Press.

Catteral, W. A. 1984. "The Molecular Bases of Neuronal Excitability." *Science,* 223:653–661.

Dale, H. 1935. "Pharmacology and Nerve-Endings." *Proc. R. Soc. Med.,* 28: 319–332.

Dale, H. H. 1953. *Adventures in Physiology.* London: Pergamon Press.

del Castillo, J. and Katz, B. 1954. "Quantal components of the end-plate potential." *J. Physiol.,* 124:560–73.

Eccles, J. C. 1964. *The Physiology of Synapses.* Berlin: Springer.

Hille, B. 1984. *Ionic Channels of Excitable Membranes.* Sunderland, Massachusetts: Sinauer.

Hodgkin, A. L. 1964. *The Conduction of the Nervous Impulse.* Springfield, Illinois: Thomas.

Hodgkin, A. L. 1977. "Chance and Design in Electrophysiology: An Informal Account of Certain Experiments on Nerve Carried out between 1934 and 1952. *The Pursuit of Nature: Informal Essays on the History of Physiology,* pp. 1–21, Cambridge, England: Cambridge Univ. Press.

Katz, B. 1966. *Nerve, Muscle, and Synapse.* New York: McGraw Hill.

Kuffler, S. W., Nicholls, J. G., and Martin, A. R. 1984. *From Neuron to Brain* (2nd ed.). Sunderland, Massachusetts: Sinauer.

Sackmann, B., and Neher, E. (eds.) 1983. *Single-Channel Recording.* New York: Plenum Press.

Sherrington, C. S. 1906. *The Integrative Action of the Nervous System.* Reprinted by Yale University Press, New Haven, 1977.

OPEN FRONTIERS

Bekesy, G. von. 1959. "Similarities between Hearing and Skin Sensations." *Psychol. Rev.*, 66:1–22.

Bekesy, G. von. 1960. "Neural Inhibitory Units of the Eye and Skin: Quantitative Description of Contrast Phenomena." *J. Opt. Soc. Am.*, 50:1060–70.

Bekesy, G. von. 1960. *Experiments in Hearing.* New York: McGraw-Hill.

Einstein, A. 1916. "Ernst Mach." *Physik. Z.*, 17:101–4, Leipzig: S. Hirzel Verlag.

Hartline, H. K. 1949. "Inhibition of activity of visual receptors by illuminating nearby retinal elements in the Limulus eye." *Fed. Proc.*, 8:69.

Kuffler, S. W. 1953. "Discharge patterns and functional organization of mammalian retina." *J. Neurophysiol.*, 16:37–68.

Mach, E. 1866. "Uebr den Physiologischen Effect Raumlich Vertheilter Lichtreize," 2. *Sitzber. Akad. Wiss. Wien* (Math—nat. Kl.), Abt. 2, 54:131–44.

Mach, E. 1914. The analysis of sensation and the relation of the physical to the psychical. C. M. Williams, trans., revised by Sidney Waterlow. Chicago and London: The Open Court Publishing Co.

Mach, E. 1942. *The Science of Mechanics.* T. J. McCormack, transl. La Salle, Illinois, & London: The Open Court Publishing Co. 5th edition.

Ratliff, F. 1965. *Mach Bands: Quantitative Studies on Neural Networks in the Retina.* San Francisco: Holden-Day.

Von Bekesy, G. 1960. *Experiments in Hearing.* New York: McGraw-Hill.

THE BRAIN'S PHOTOGRAPH

Fuster, J. M. and Jervey, J. P. 1981. "Inferotemporal Neurons Distinguish and Retain Behaviorally Relevant Features of Visual Stimuli." *Science*, 212:952–55.

Gross, C. G., Bender, D. B., and Rocha-Miranda, C. E. 1969. "Visual receptive fields of neurons in inferotemporal cortex of the monkey." *Science*, 166:1303–6.

Hubel, D. H. (ed.) 1979. *Scientific American* Issue on the Brain, 241 (3) September, 1979. Reprinted as *The Brain, A Scientific American Book*, W. H. Freeman, New York, 1979.

Hubel, D. H. 1982. "Exploration of the Primary Visual Cortex, 1955–78" (Nobel Lecture). *Nature*, 299:515–524.

Hubel, D. H. 1988. *Eye, Brain, and Vision.* New York: W. H. Freeman and Co.

Konishi, M. 1986. "Centrally Synthesized Maps of Sensory Space." *Trends in Neuroscience*, 9:163–68.

Mishkin, M., Ungerleider, L., and Macko, K. 1983. "Object Vision and Spatial Vision: Two Cortical Pathways." *Trends in Neuroscience*, 6(10): 414–17.

Mishkin, M., and Appenzeller, T. 1987. "The anatomy of memory." *Scientific American*, 256 (6):62–71.

Mountcastle, V. B. 1976. "The World Around Us: Neural Command Functions for Selective Attention." *Neurosci. Res. Program Bull* (Suppl.), 14.

Nauta, W. J. H., and Feirtag, M. 1986. *Fundamental Neuroanatomy.* New York: W. H. Freeman.

Perrett, D. I., Mistlin, A. J., and Chitty, A. J. 1987. "Visual Neurons Responsive to Faces." *Trends in Neuroscience*, 10:358–64.

Wiesel, T. N. 1982. "Postnatal Development of the Visual Cortex and the Influence of Environment" (Nobel Lecture). *Nature*, 299:583–91.

EVOLUTION'S COMPROMISE

Alkon, D. L., and Fuortes, M.G.F. 1972. "Responses of Photoreceptors in Hermissenda." *J. Gen. Physiol.*, 60:631–649.

Alkon, D. L. 1973. "Neural Organization of a Molluscan Visual System." *J. Gen. Physiol.*, 61:444–461.

Alkon, D. L. 1973. "Intersensory Interactions in Hermissenda." *J. Gen. Physiol.*, 62:185–202.

Alkon, D. L. 1974. "Associative Training of Hermissenda." *J. Gen. Physiol.*, 64:70–84.

Crow, T. J., and Alkon, D. L. 1978. "Retention of an Associative Behavioral Change in Hermissenda." *Science*, 201:1239–1241.

Alkon, D. L. 1983. "Learning in a Marine Snail." *Scientific American*, 249:70–84.

Alkon, D. L. 1987. *Memory Traces in the Brain*. Cambridge, Massachusetts: Cambridge Univ. Press.

UNEARTHING THE RECORD

Alkon, D. L. 1975. "Neural Correlates of Associative Training in Hermissenda." *J. Gen. Physiol.*, 65:46–56.

Alkon, D. L. 1976. "Neural modification by paired sensory stimuli." *J. Gen. Physiol.*, 68:341–58.

Alkon, D. L. 1980. "Membrane depolarization accumulates during acquisition of an associative behavioral change." *Science*, 210:1373–75.

Alkon, D. L., Lederhendler, I. I., and Shoukimas, J. J. 1982. "Primary Changes of Membrane Currents during Retention of Associative Learning." *Science*, 215:693–5.

Alkon, D. L. 1984. "Calcium-Mediated Reduction of Ionic Currents: A Biophysical Memory Trace." *Science*, 226:1037–45.

Alkon, D. L. and Rasmussen, H. 1988. "A Spatio-temporal Model of Cell Activation." *Science*, 239:998–1005.

Alkon, D. L. 1989. "Memory Storage and Neural Systems." *Scientific American*, 260:42–50.

Farley, J., and Alkon, D. L. 1980. "Neural organization predicts stimulus specificity for a retained associative behavioral change." *Science*, 210:1373–75.

Neary, J. T., Crow, T., and Alkon, D. L. 1981. "Change in a Specific Phosphoprotein Band following Associative Learning in Hermissenda." *Nature*, 293:658–60.

Nelson, T., Collin, C., and Alkon, D. L. 1990. "Isolation of a G Protein that is Modified by Learning and Reduces Potassium Currents in Hermissenda." *Science*, 247:1479–83.

Nestler, E. J., and Greengard, P. 1988. *Protein phosphorylation in the nervous system*. New York: Wiley.

Nishizuka, Y. 1988. "The Molecular Heterogeneity of Protein Kinase C and its Implication for Cellular Regulation." *Nature*, 334:661–65.

THE KINGDOM OF REAL BRAINS

Bank, B., De Weer, A., Kuzirian, A. M., Rasmussen, H., and Alkon, D. L. 1988. "Classical Conditioning Induces Long-Term Translocation of Protein Kinase C in Rabbit Hippocampal CA1 Cells." *Proc. Natl.Acad. Sciences*, U.S.A. v. 85. pp. 1988–92.

Cohen, N. J., and Squire, L. R. 1980. "Preserved Learning and Retention of Pattern-Analyzing Skill in Amnesia: Dissociation of Knowing How and Knowing That." *Science*, 210:207–9.

Coulter, D. A., Lo Turco, J., Kubota, M., Disterhoft, J. F., Moore, J. W., and Alkon, D. L. 1989. "Classical Conditioning Alters the Amplitude and Time Course of the Calcium-dependent After Hyperpolarization in Rabbit Hippocampal Pyramidal Cells." *J. Neurophysiol.*, 61:171–81.

Disterhoft, J. F., Coulter, D. A., and Alkon, D. L. 1986. "Conditioning Causes Intrinsic Membrane Changes of Rabbit Hippocampal Neurons in Vitro." *Proc. Natl. Acad. Sciences*, U.S.A. v. 83. pp. 2733–37.

Damasio, A. R. and Geschwind, N. 1984. "The Neural Bases of Language." *Ann. Rev. Neurosci.*, 7:127–47.

Goldman-Rakic, P. S. 1988. "Topography of Cognition: Parallel Distributed Networks in Primate Association Cortex." *Ann. Rev. Neurosci.*, 11:137–56.

Olds, J. L., Anderson, M., McPhie, D., Staten, L., and Alkon, D. L. 1989. "Imaging Memory-Specific Changes in the Distribution of Protein Kinase C within the Hippocampus." *Science*, 245:866–69.

Penfield, W., and Milner, B. 1958. "Memory Deficit Produced by Bilateral Lesions in the Hippocampal Zone." *Arch. Neurol. Psychiat.*, 79:475–97.

Penfield, W., and Rasmussen, T. 1950. *The Cerebral Cortex of Man: A Clinical Study of Localization of Function.* New York: Macmillan.

Reivich, M., Kuhl, D., Wolf, A., Greenberg, J., Phelps, M., Ido, T., Casella, V., Fowler, J., Hoffman, E., Alavi, A., Som, P., and Sokoloff, L. 1977. *Circulation Research*, 44(1):127–37.

A STORY NOT YET TOLD

Changeux, J. P. 1985. *Neuronal Man.* New York: Pantheon.

Collingridge, G. L. 1985. "Long-Term Potentiation in the Hippocampus: Mechanisms and Modulation by Neurotransmitters." *Trends in Pharmacol. Sci.*, 6:407–11.

Collingridge, G. L. and Bliss, T.V.P. 1987. "NMDA receptors—their role in long-term potentiation." *Trends in Neurosci.*, 10:288–93.

Dudai, Y. *The Neurobiology of Memory.* 1989. Oxford: Oxford Univ. Press.

Edelman, G. M. 1987. *Neural Darwinism: The Theory of Neuronal Group Selection.* New York: Basic Books.

Greenough, W. T. 1984. "Structural Correlates of Information Storage in the Mammalian Brain: A Review and Hypothesis." *Trends in Neurosci.*, 7:229–33.

Hebb, D. O. 1949. *The Organization of Behavior: A Neuropsychological Theory.* New York: Wiley.

Horn, G. 1985. *Memory, Imprinting, and the Brain.* Oxford: Oxford Univ. Press.

Ito, M. 1987. "Characterization of Synaptic Plasticity in the Cerebellar and Cerebral Neocortex." *The Neuronal and Molecular Bases of Learning* (ed. J. P. Changeux and M. Konishi, pp. 263–80). New York: Wiley.

Lomo, T. 1966. "Frequency Potentiation of Excitatory Synaptic Activity in the Dentate area of the Hippocampal Formation." *Acta Physiol. Scand.* 68, suppl. 277, 128.

Lynch, G., and Baudry, M. 1984. "The Biochemistry of Memory: A New Specific Hypothesis." *Science*, 224:1057–63.

Lovinger, D. M., Wong, K. L., Murakami, K., and Routtenberg, A. 1987. "Protein Kinase C Inhibitors Eliminate Hippocampal Long-Term Potentiation." *Brain Res.*, 436:177–83.

Menzel, R., and Erber, J. 1978. "Learning and Memory in Bees." *Scientific American*, 239(7):80–87.

Shashoua, V. E. 1985. "The Role of Extracellular Proteins in Learning and Memory." *Am. Sci.*, 73:364–70.

Thompson, R. F. 1986. "The Neurobiology of Learning and Memory." *Science*, 233:941–47.

Woody, C. D. 1982. *Memory, Learning, and Higher Function.* New York: Springer-Verlag.

VARIETIES OF NEURONAL EXPERIENCE

Fantz, R. L. 1964. "Visual Experience in Infants: Decreased Attention to Familiar Patterns Relative to Novel Ones." *Science*, 146:668–70.

Harlow, H. F. 1959. "Love in Infant Monkeys." *Scientific American*, 200 (6): 68–74.

Knudsen, E. I. 1985. "Experience Alters the Spatial Tuning of Auditory Units in the Optic Tectum During a Sensitive Period in the Barn Owl." *J. Neurosci.*, 5: 3094–109.

Purves, D., and Lichtman, J. W. 1985. *Principles of Neural Development.* Sunderland, Mass: Sinauer.

Purves, D. 1988. *Body and Brain.* Cambridge, Mass: Harvard Univ. Press.

Rakic, P. 1977. "Prenatal Development of the Visual System in Rhesus Monkey." *Philos. Trans. R. Soc. Lond.* (Biol. Sci.), 278:245–60.

Spitz, R. A. 1945. Hospitalism: "An Inquiry into the Genesis of Psychiatric Conditions in Early Childhood." *Psychoanal. Study Child*, 1:53–74.

Wiesel, T. N., and Hubel, D. H. 1963. "Single-Cell Responses in Striate Cortex of Kittens Deprived of Vision in One Eye." *J. Neurophysiol.*, 26:1003–17.

BRAIN CHILDREN

Albus, J. S. 1971. "A Theory of Cerebellar Function." *Math. Biosci.*, 10:25–61.

Alkon, D. L., Blackwell, K. T., Barbour, G. S., Rigler, A. K., and Vogl, T. P. 1990. "Pattern-Recognition by an Artificial Network Derived from Biologic Neuronal Systems." *Biol. Cybern.*, 62:363–76.

Amari, S. 1977. "Neural Theory of Association and Concept Formation." *Biol. Cybernetics*, 26:175–85.

Anderson, J. A. 1972. "A Simple Neural Network Generating an Associative Memory." *Mathematical Biosciences.* 14:197–220.

Anderson, J. A., and Rosenfeld, E. (eds.) 1988. *Neurocomputing: Foundations of Research.* Cambridge, Massachusetts: MIT Press.

Chomsky, N. 1959. "Review of Verbal Behaviour by B. F. Skinner." *Language*, 35: 26–58.

Fukushima, K. 1987. "Neural Network Model for Selective Attention in Visual Pattern Recognition and Associative Recall." *Applied Optics.* vol. 26. No. 23, 4985–92.

Grossberg, S. 1976. "Adaptive Pattern Classification and Universal Recoding: Parallel Development and Coding of Neural Feature Detectors." *Biol. Cybernetics*, 23: 187–202.

Grossberg, S. 1982. *Studies of Mind and Brain.* Boston, Massachusetts: Reided.

Hebb, D. O. 1949. *The Organization of Behavior.* New York: Wiley.

Hinton, G. E. and Anderson, J. A. (eds.) 1981. *Parallel Models of Associative Memory.* New Jersey: Erlbaum.

Hopfield, J. J. 1982. "Neural Networks and Physical Systems with Emergent Collective Computational Abilities." *Proc. Nat. Acad. Sci.*, 79:2554–8.

Koch, C. 1989. *Methods in Neuronal Modeling: From Synapses to Networks*. Cambridge, Massachusetts: MIT Press.

Kohonen, T. 1988. *Self-Organization and Associative Memory*, 2nd ed. New York: Springer-Verlag.

Marr, D. 1969. *A Theory of Cerebellar Cortex*. N.P.

Minsky, M. L., and Papert, S. 1969. *Perceptrons: An Introduction to Computational Geometry*. Cambridge, Massachusetts: MIT Press.

Rosenblatt, F. 1962. *Principles of Neurodynamics*. New York: Spartan Books.

Rumelhart, D. E., and McClelland, J. L. (eds.) 1986. *Parallel Distributed Processing*, vol. 1, Cambridge, Massachusetts: MIT Press.

Von der Malsburg, C. 1973. "Self-Organization of Orientation Sensitive Cells in Striata Cortex." *Kybaernetik*, 14:85–100.

NEURONS GONE AWRY

Butters, N. 1984. "Alcoholic Korsakoff's Syndrome: An Update." *Semin. Neurol.*, 4:226–44.

Bick, K., Amaducci, L., and Pepeu, G. (eds.) 1987. *The Early Story of Alzheimer's Disease*. Liviana Press distributed by Raven Press, New York.

Collin, C., Papageorge, A. G., Lowy, D. R., and Alkon, D. L. 1990. "Early Enhancement of Calcium Currents by Ha-ras Oncoproteins Injected into Hermissenda Neurons." *Science*, 250:1743–45.

Cutler, N. R., Haxby, J. V., Duara, R., Grady, Parisi, J. E., White, J., Heston, L., Margolin, and Rapoport, S. 1985. "Brain Metabolism as Measured with Positron Emission Tomography: Serial Assessment in a Patient with Familial Alzheimer's Disease." *Neurology*, 35:1556–61.

Davis, J. M., and Mass, J. W. (eds.). 1983. *The Affective Disorders*. Washington, D.C.: American Psychiatric Press.

Katzman, R. (ed.) 1983. "Biological Aspects of Alzheimer's Disease." Cold Spring Harbor, New York: Cold Spring Harbor Laboratories, *Banbury Reports*, V. 15.

Kety, S. S. 1979. "Disorders of the human brain." *Scientific American*, 241 (3):202–14.

Kosik, K. 1991. "Alzheimer's Plaques and Tangles: Advances on Both Fronts." *Trends in Neuroscience*, 14:218–20.

Masliah, E., Cole, G., Shimohama, S., Hansen, L., De Teresa, R., Terry, R., and Saitoh, T. 1990. "Differential Involvement of Protein Kinase C Isozymes in Alzheimer's Disease." *J. Neuroscience*, 10 (7):2113–24.

Olds, J. 1976. *Drives and Reinforcement*. New York: Viking Press.

Snyder, S. H. 1982. "Neurotransmitters and CNS Disease." *Schizophrenia*, Lancet 2:970–4.

Synex, F. M., and Merril, C. R. (eds.) 1982. *Alzheimer's Disease, Down's Syndrome, and Aging*. New York: The New York Academy of Sciences.

MEN AND MACHINES

LeDoux, J. E. 1987. "Emotion." In *Handbook of Physiology, Section 1: The nervous system, V. 5: Higher functions of the brain, Part 1* (ed. F. Plum), pp. 419–59. Bethesda, Maryland: American Physiological Society.

McGaugh, J. L. 1983. "Hormonal Influences on Memory." *Ann. Rev. Psychol.*, 34: 297–323.

INDEX

Italics indicates illustrations.

275